Urban Encounters

Urban Encounters

Affirmative Action and Black Identities in Brazil

André Cicalo

URBAN ENCOUNTERS
Copyright © André Cicalo, 2012.
Softcover reprint of the hardcover 1st edition 2012 978-0-230-33852-4
All rights reserved.

First published in 2012 by
PALGRAVE MACMILLAN®
in the United States—a division of St. Martin's Press LLC,
175 Fifth Avenue, New York, NY 10010.

Where this book is distributed in the UK, Europe and the rest of the world, this is by Palgrave Macmillan, a division of Macmillan Publishers Limited, registered in England, company number 785998, of Houndmills, Basingstoke, Hampshire RG21 6XS.

Palgrave Macmillan is the global academic imprint of the above companies and has companies and representatives throughout the world.

Palgrave® and Macmillan® are registered trademarks in the United States, the United Kingdom, Europe and other countries.

ISBN 978-1-349-34151-1   ISBN 978-1-137-09601-2 (eBook)
DOI 10.1057/9781137096012

Library of Congress Cataloging-in-Publication Data

Cicalo, André, 1973–
  Urban encounters : affirmative action and black identities in
  Brazil / André Cicalo.
     p. cm.
     1. Affirmative action programs in education—Brazil.
   2. Blacks—Education (Higher)—Brazil.
   3. Blacks—Race identity—Brazil. I. Title.
LC213.53.B6C43 2012
379.2'60981—dc23   2012013462

A catalogue record of the book is available from the British Library.

This book is printed on paper suitable for recycling and made from fully managed and sustained forest sources. Logging, pulping and manufacturing processes are expected to conform to the environmental regulations of the country of origin.

Design by Newgen Imaging Systems (P) Ltd., Chennai, India.

First edition: October 2012

10 9 8 7 6 5 4 3 2 1

*To Flávia
and the crowd of the seventh floor...*

Contents

List of Figures, Maps, and Tables		ix
Acknowledgments		xi
1	Toward an Ethnographic Study of Racial Quotas for "Black" Students in the University of the State of Rio de Janeiro	1
2	Dreams and Hard Places: Main Settings and Socioeconomic Profile of Quota Students	21
3	Race between the Class Rows: Urban Encounters and Dis-encounters in the Changing University Space	55
4	From Race *or* Color to Race *and* Color? Ethnography beyond Official Discourses	91
5	Narrowing Political Gaps: Black Awareness and University Education as Ways to Be "Central"	127
	Toward a Conclusion	167
Notes		187
References		209
Index		221

Figures, Maps, and Tables

Figures

2.1	The UERJ seen from the footbridges just outside the tube station on Avenida Castelo Branco	22
2.2	Several interior shots of the UERJ	22
2.3	View of wealthy areas in Zona Sul: the encounter between three neighborhoods—Lagoa, Ipanema, and Leblon	27
2.4	View of the favela of Mangueira from the UERJ	28
2.5	Partial views of the Esqueleto area, before and after its removal	29
2.6	Borders between favelas and suburban neighborhoods are often very blurred, especially away from Zona Sul	33
3.1	A group of informants at the UERJ	59
4.1	My visualization of the possible relationship between blackness and mestiçagem/brownness as described by Eliane	115
4.2	Relationship between blackness and mestiçagem/brownness as proposed by the Black movement	115
4.3	A virtual classification system that would reflect my findings at the UERJ	122

Maps

2.1	Metropolitan area of Rio de Janeiro divided by Zones (Centro, Sul, Norte, Oeste)	24

2.2 Closer view of Zona Sul, Centro, and Zona Norte, highlighting the tube 1 and 2 lines and the railway — 25

Tables

2.1 Socioeconomic data about classified candidates in vestibular 2008 — 37

2.2 Socioeconomic data about some of the neighborhoods (and municipalities) of provenance of *cotistas* (inclughting other municipalities) and about some of the neighborhoods of provenance of non-*cotistas* in the first year of law in 2007–2008 — 40

2.3 Socioeconomic data about classified candidates in vestibular 2008 — 42

Acknowledgments

This book is rooted in PhD fieldwork carried out in Rio de Janeiro (2007–2008) during my doctoral studies in Social Anthropology at the University of Manchester (UK). I am especially grateful to Peter Wade who provided precious orientation during my PhD and represented an inspiring interlocutor with whom to develop my ideas. I also deeply thank John Gledhill and David Lehmann, who provided vital comments to my PhD work, allowing me to improve this book. More in general, I thank the University of Manchester and the UK Economic and Social Research Council (ESRC) that funded my doctoral research, and the desiguALdades network at Freie Universität in Berlin, where I am currently enrolled as a postdoctoral researcher and where this book has taken his final and crucial shape.

In Rio de Janeiro, I deeply thank my friends Patrícia Ferreira and André Gumarães, who opened several spaces for my fieldwork and made my view of Brazilian race relations much richer. André, in particular, introduced me to the black organization Educafro and to the University of the State of Rio de Janeiro (UERJ), both crucial context for my ethnography of affirmative action. I am also grateful to Peter Fry and Yvonne Maggie, who represented my first local connection to the reality of racial quotas in public universities in Rio de Janeiro.

At UERJ, my research would have not been possible without the support of the direction and administration staff, the Undergraduate Admission Department (Vestibular Office) and the Proiniciar Office, which provides scholarships for affirmative action beneficiaries. In the Vestibular Office, I am particularly grateful to Stella Amadei, who disclosed crucial statistical data about the socioeconomic questionnaire filled in by undergraduate applicants at UERJ between 2007 and 2008; these data informed a relevant section of my discussion in this book. I should also mention the Rede Syrius, which provided me with photographic and bibliographic documents concerning UERJ's history.

More crucially, I express my gratitude to the UERJ staff and students who agreed to spend time with me within and without the university. Among them, special mention goes to some first-year law students who were kind enough to open their lives and friendship to a foreign researcher: Daniel, Dandara, Bruna, Cláudio Fernando, Denise, Fernanda, Amanda, Tamires, Murillo, Fábio, Evelyn, and Rafael. Without the help of these students (and many others), this work would have been less engaging and meaningful. I should also mention Renato Ferreira, who was a PPCOR (Políticas da Cor) coordinator at UERJ in 2008 and released precious interviews for my research. Fragments of those interviews are extensively reported in this book.

I feel very obliged to Palgrave Macmillan for offering me the opportunity to publish my first monograph, as well as to the anonymous reviewers at Palgrave who received my work with enthusiasm. My appreciation also goes to the anonymous reviewers of an article that is presently under evaluation at the *Journal of Latin American Studies* (JLAS). The advice of these reviewers positively influenced the restructuring of some sections in this book.

Finally, I thank my mother Delia, who provided me with patient and lovely support during these years.

1

Toward an Ethnographic Study of Racial Quotas for "Black" Students in the University of the State of Rio de Janeiro

Racial Affirmative Action in Brazil: A Complex Object of Study

National censuses divide Brazil's population into three main phenotypic categories: *branco* (white), *pardo* (brown-skinned and/or mixed), and *preto* (black-skinned). These categories, which altogether make up about 98 percent of the country's population,[1] represent a rough simplification of what several authors have described as an extremely complex and ambiguous system of everyday identifications in Brazil (Sheriff, 2001; Fry, 2005; Petruccelli, 2007). The *pardo* category is generally understood as that which best reflects ambiguity: Brazil is in fact internationally famous for its mixed-race (*mestiço*) and culturally syncretic identity, due to consistent miscegenation (*mestiçagem*) between people of European, African, and Amerindian descent. Early scholars such as Gilberto Freyre (1956 and 1961) particularly celebrated this mixture as an explanation for the lack of racial friction in Brazil, which he also explained by the "kinder" attitude of the Portuguese to slavery in comparison to the English and French colonial powers.[2] While racial mixture is considered crucial for Brazilian national identity, as well as the reason for low racism in the country, social inequalities have traditionally been explained in terms of class in Brazil.[3]

The official pride in the miracles of racial mixture in Brazil has survived almost intact until these days, even though a number of social scientists had already claimed the impact of race on Brazilian social inequalities at least from the 1950s.[4] Only in 2001 did this pride start taking the blow quite seriously, as the law of the State of Rio de Janeiro introduced a system of quotas for "black" and other disadvantaged social categories of students in state public universities. This system was finally implemented for first time in 2003 by the University of the State of Rio de Janeiro (UERJ); it was then repeatedly revised through legislation and specified according to university administrative autonomy (*autonomia administrativa*), provoking a chain reaction for the adoption of similar measures in other Brazilian states.[5] The implementation of racial quotas for black people has raised a heated debate in Brazil for different reasons. According to some critics, the quota logic racializes a country whose national pride is still largely founded on racial mixture, risking the fomenting of racial resentment without really redressing structural inequalities in Brazilian society. Competing arguments in this debate represent the general framework for this book, where I deal with these matters in an ethnographic way through an analysis of quota implementation at the UERJ and the experiences of its users.

At present, Rio de Janeiro's law foresees that 20 percent of openings in any course should be reserved for students self-identified as *negros* (black) who choose to apply by this channel. A further 20 percent is reserved for students coming from public schools, while a remaining overall 5 percent addresses indigenous ethnic minorities, physically challenged people (*deficientes físicos*), and other residual categories.[6] As an additional parameter, the UERJ requires that quota applicants prove themselves to be *carentes* (needy), often revising the levels of household income that define such neediness. Quota candidates have to do the same entrance examination as the rest of the applicants. At the UERJ, the quota applicants classified with the highest score go on to fill the quota percentages until completion, assuming that they do not fail the examination and that they score at least in the "A" (top) to "D" (lowest admitted) range. In case there are no classified quota applicants, these openings are filled by nonquota candidates.

Quota measures in public universities can be specifically understood as a way of redressing a paradox in the education sector in Brazil, where lower-class people (most of them black and brown) have been traditionally excluded from free higher education, which is still quite prestigious in this Latin American country (Rosemberg, 2004). Lower-class students usually attend poorly resourced public (and private) schools and are not sufficiently academically competitive to pass the tough selection process (vestibular) for public higher education.[7] Most higher education openings in the public sector in Brazil, therefore, are occupied by middle- and upper-class students who come from competitive private high schools and are predominantly light skinned or white. Paixão and Carvano (2008) show that, despite a general growth in education for white and nonwhite people (whose category can be conceived as the sum of *pardos* and *pretos*), the gaps between the two groups have persisted substantially unaltered over the period since the beginning of the last century, both in terms of literacy rates and years of study.[8] Although the differences seem smaller in relation to the *ensino fundamental* (schooling of people aged between 7 and 14), white people over 15 years of age in 2006 studied for an average of 8.0 years, whereas their nonwhite counterparts (brown- and black-skinned people) studied for just 6.2 years (Paixão and Carvano, 2008: 70, 76). In addition, according to figures published by the Brazilian Institute for Geography and Statistics (IBGE), the percentage of nonwhites with a university degree in Brazil was just 2.2 percent in 1997, compared to 9.6 percent of whites.[9] Such distribution does not proportionally reflect national demographic data, where nonwhite people represent 50 percent of the Brazilian population.[10] In 2007, these figures had increased slightly for the different racial and color groups (13.4 percent for whites and 4.0 percent for *pardos* and *pretos* altogether), but the gap between whites and nonwhites had actually increased in absolute terms.[11] On a similar note, as Carvalho (2005) notes, the percentage of nonwhite (*pardos* and *pretos*) university teachers in Brazil is still less than 1 percent.

The quota system fits into the wider sphere of affirmative action policies. These measures, the theory of which largely developed in the United States, grant differential rights to sectors of the population that are marginalized in the process of redistribution, such as women, racial and ethnic groups, religious minorities, and physically challenged people, just to offer some examples. The concept of affirmative action relies on a revised version of the universalistic principle of equality by envisaging that the state should recognize the differences and redress the vulnerabilities of socially identifiable groups through special corrective measures that are nonspecifically class based. This idea somehow recalls the theory of "Justice as Fairness" proposed by John Rawls (2001) and occupies an important place in theories of "equality through difference" that are quite popular in liberal multiculturalism (Taylor, 1994; Kymlicka and Norman, 2000). It is not by chance that the introduction of racial quotas in Brazil coincided with a process of proliferation of cultural politics in Latin America, where territorial and ethnic rights are being largely granted to indigenous and black rural communities, especially in Colombia (Wade, 1999; Restrepo, 2004) and Brazil (Arruti, 1997; French, 2002). This trend is taking place in the context of the general growth of identity politics, which Escobar and Alvarez (1992) label as the new social movements, in contrast to merely class-based ones (see also Alvarez, Dagnino, and Escobar, 1998). Quotas fit into this framework of differential cultural politics because, in addition to relying on the identification of groups supposedly different or separate for reasons other than class, they aim to provide these disadvantaged groups with differential rights with regard to access to public services and resources.

According to Mala Htun (2004), the debate around racism and antiracism has developed in Brazil since the 1980s as a consequence of two important events. The first was the presidency of Cardoso, a sociologist whose main research dealt with the socioeconomic marginality of Afro-Brazilians. The second was the Conference on Racism and Discrimination held in Durban in 2001. At a historical moment when Brazil was trying to prove its political and financial reliability to the world, and international pressure was being exerted on countries to take a stance against racism, "the debate about races, equality and democracy found receptive ears."[12] In addition to these explanations, Brazil began experiencing a phase of democratic opening (*abertura democrática*) and increasing liberalism during the 1980s, opening a fertile space for the social movements described by Escobar and Alvarez. These movements and their transnational connections have served as important lobbying actors for the implementation of affirmative action policies in Brazil.[13]

By May 2008, 69 of the federal, state, and municipal higher education institutions in Brazil had already established racially based affirmative actions of some sort, in addition to or as an alternative to other socially inclusive measures.[14] The methods of selecting black-quota candidates, however, differ substantially across Brazil. A particularly discussed case is that of the University of Brasília (UnB), whose selection methods have been widely condemned for including the assessment of photos and interviews aimed to prove the blackness of candidates.[15] However, the system implemented in Brasília is rather atypical; most universities, including the UERJ, select black-quota candidates by the students' own self-declarations.

Affirmative action in higher education also reached the private sector in 2004, through the federal program University for Everybody (Prouni), which funds fees and offers small scholarships to black and needy students enrolling in undergraduate programs at private universities.[16] Other kinds of racially and socially based affirmative action policies that are implemented in Brazil do not utilize the quota logic. One example of this is the bonus, which, in spite of not reserving openings for certain categories of people, adds an additional score to black and other disadvantaged groups of applicants in the vestibular at some Brazilian universities such as Unicamp in São Paulo.[17] Further examples of black affirmative measures that escape the quota logic are the 10639 law, which has made the teaching of Afro-Brazilian culture and history compulsory in public and private schools, as well as the recognition of land rights for black rural communities populated by descendants of runaway slaves (*quilombos*) in Brazil.[18] Although the state is a central actor in establishing affirmative action by law, religious organizations and NGOs also play an increasing role in this arena.[19] Some of these groups coordinate preparation courses to train black and needy applicants (*negros* and *carentes*) for the vestibular[20]; other organizations promote aspects such as black culture and black entrepreneurialism.[21]

Although affirmative action in principle has the purpose of shifting social inequalities, its redistributive validity is deeply questioned. Affirmative action measures often appear to be more problematic when they are implemented through public policies, and especially through quotas, as these threaten to undermine the rhetoric of state impartiality toward equal citizens, one of the crucial pillars for democracies. However, not all affirmative action in favor of certain social categories generally accepted as vulnerable have raised a huge debate. Example of this are the federal law 8112/90, which reserved 20 percent openings to physically challenged people in the public service, and the law 9504/97, which introduced 30 percent of openings for candidate women in political parties, all measures inspired by the Brazilian Constitution of 1988. In Brazil, only the introduction of quotas in favor of black people, specifically, has raised much contestation due to the fact that they treat certain groups differently and could be considered as discriminating in this sense.

Most contemporary scholars agree that depictions of Brazil as a racial democracy in the early twentieth century were seriously overstated, while a number of studies show clearly that social gaps in Brazil have their colors and cannot be solely explained through class.[22] A frequent question, however, is whether a country like Brazil really needs to rely on "foreign" measures such as racial affirmative action as an alternative to class policies, or whether, in addition to the thorny problem of how it is possible to define people racially, this racializing process will increase the racism and inequality that it actually aims to redress. A common prediction, for example, is that mixed-race (brown) people might feel incentives to self-identify as black in order to enjoy policy advantages. In this sense, racial affirmative action poses questions not only about national identities but also about the relevance of color/racial categories as they are officially imagined in Brazilian demographic surveys. In fact, racial affirmative action in Brazil coincides with a trend that, in the social sciences and at the institutional level, increasingly considers the Brazilian population as divided into white and black (*brancos* and *negros*), with this last term including both brown- and black-skinned people (*pardos* and *pretos*, respectively). Quotas are seen as an effect of this trend but also as a possible fostering factor of a biracializing process. It is not random that, although different kinds of quotas exist in Brazilian universities, racial quotas are the ones that have often monopolized the debate.

A crucial point raised by skeptics of racial quotas against these measures is that science has widely refuted the scientific validity of the idea of race. The implementation of racial affirmative action therefore represents both a stab to the mixed-race pride of the nation, where racial identifications are so complex, and a contradiction to modern scientific knowledge. A racialist approach, it is often said, would also endorse the discrimination against entire groups that took place under Nazism, Jim Crow, and apartheid. Brazilian critics particularly claim that affirmative action makes it necessary to identify separate racial groups, implementing logics of categorization that would be more typical of the racial logics present in the United States.[23] This debate has spread not just in mass media and public opinion but also in the social sciences, where a number of intellectuals are working passionately to support or undermine the philosophical foundations of these measures.

Some more general questions about quotas relate to the infringement on fairness and merit and the risk of producing a less competitive social collective by rewarding less skillful people. Other questions concern whether racial affirmative action is really redistributive and transformative, or whether it represents a superficial panacea for the liberal state, thereby reducing its responsibilities for more structural and universalistic or class-based approaches to inequality. This account clarifies why the public questioning of racial quotas has been so prominent in Brazilian society that terms such as quotas and affirmative action in Brazil have broadly become synonyms for racial quotas and black affirmative action. This has occurred even if the quotas applied at public universities, as well as their beneficiaries, vary significantly according to the legislation of each Brazilian state, while rules of implementation also depend upon the administrative autonomy of each academic setting. Anxieties about the divisive spirit of quotas in Brazil have been particularly well expressed in the Manifesto "113 anti-racist citizens against racist laws"[24] signed by intellectuals, civil society organizations, and private citizens, and sent to the Supreme Federal Court (STF) in May 2008.[25] The spirit of these actions against the establishment of black affirmative action, at the time of my fieldwork, was also influenced by discussions about the possible introduction of a statute of racial equality (*Estatuto da Igualdade Racial*) in Brazil, with the aim of setting differential rights for black Brazilians in a number of social spheres such as education, health, media, and politics.[26]

In contrast to these critiques, some social scientists and the Brazilian Black movement insist that racially based affirmative action is an important tool to redress historical inequalities, or at least to start talking about them. The Black movement, in particular, sees the logic of quotas as something that will positively reinforce black consciousness. According to activists, a biracializing logic will also contribute to raising the numbers of the black population politically in Brazil by incorporating the brown- (*pardo*) and black-skinned (*preto*) color categories of official censuses into a single "black" racial group (*negro*). As several American scholars agree, the presence of the mixed (*pardo*) category in Brazilian social censuses has been an aggravating factor for hampering black identity.[27] Most Afro-Brazilians, in fact, might consider it less demeaning to self-identify as brown or mixed, something that, at a superficial glance, is much appreciated in national imagery. However, this mixed category also hides and silences much of Brazilian racism, at the same time as it negotiates racial oppositions between black and white poles in an apparently democratic and nonracial way.[28]

The presence of these strong competing arguments about quotas in academia is well reflected in the ambiguous ways in which public opinion has reacted to the topic of quotas. According to the data found in Folha online (2008a),[29] 62 percent of the Brazilian population believe that racial quotas are fundamental in expanding access to education. At the same time, 53 percent of Brazilians believe that quotas are humiliating for their users, and 62 percent believe that these measures might encourage racism.[30]

Purpose and Structure of This Book

When I first approached the study of quotas, before my fieldwork in 2007, I realized that most of the debate about racial affirmative action in Brazil limited its focus to the philosophical reasons and speculations about the possible risks or usefulness of these measures.

Conversely, I noticed less attention given to empirical research in the academic settings where these measures are being implemented. Although the introduction of quotas was still recent at that time, and objections to their implementation were well supported by theory, I believed that ethnography and some statistical evidence about the performance of the quota students might be useful in enriching the generally abstract debate on this matter.[31]

For this reason, I chose as the main locale for my research a university, the UERJ, which was also the first public academic institution that implemented quotas in Brazil. The immediate goal of my research was not to establish whether racial or other kinds of quotas might be good or harmful, as most of the quota debate has tried to demonstrate. Without denying the importance of the intellectual quarrel mentioned earlier, it was my intention to go further. More precisely, I planned to observe the different experiences and understandings of quotas among the people who gravitate toward the UERJ and especially the quota beneficiaries. As a broader goal, the objective of my work is an ethnographic exploration of how race and its interconnections with class, gender, and space operate in a particular setting, a state university that implements quotas by requirement of law.

As with many other settings, a university is a space that reflects certain racial, class, and gender equations within the city. Parts of these equations have been naturalized and historically constructed, and quotas may hold the symbolic power to challenge them. I suggest that the impact of quotas extends beyond the university and the city, by entailing more general considerations about citizenship and nation. In this sense, I explore quotas as a symbolic vehicle to question relations between center and periphery in the city, and more indirectly in the state, which also function as abstract idealized locales for power and subalternity, respectively.[32]

Most of the literature about race in Rio de Janeiro has not dealt much with "space," although some more direct reference is present in Goldstein (2003) and Alvito (2001). In some cases, literature about race and space has focused on places that are typically imagined as racially segregated in the urban context, such as the favelas and the generally lower-class carioca suburbs (Oliveira, 2001 and 2000; Vargas, 2006), the kinds of settings that ethnographic studies about race in Rio de Janeiro have also traditionally privileged (Burdick, 1998; Sheriff, 2001; Goldstein, 2003). I was instead more interested in settings that apparently are not divided along racial lines, exploring the possible hierarchies that are both reproduced and challenged by the interaction of race, class, and gender in these locales. Since quotas allow a higher number of lower-class and black young people to achieve free university education, these students are apparently equal to their wealthier peers. This fact implicitly questions traditional servant-employer patterns that also significantly reflect the geographical divides that are historically crystallized in Brazilian metropolises. However, there are several questions to this apparent equality that state policies are artificially producing. If people from different backgrounds can now use the academic space as equals, in which ways do they distribute themselves within that space and relate to others? Do racially based affirmative action programs produce equality *tout court* and in a straightforward manner, or do they emphasize differences? Do they promote encounters or dis-encounters, racism or antiracism? These are questions that this book intends to explore but not to resolve completely, mainly due to the complexity of the subject and the relative novelty of the institution of quotas.

This book is also significantly about identities. In a country where *mestiçagem* would be threatened by the racialist foreign models of race relations that affirmative action might embody, it is worth asking whether quotas actually have the power to create "black" identities as separate from the rest of the social collective. In fact, it is not clear to what extent blackness would replace national *mestiçagem* and how irreconcilable these concepts could be. It is not even clear whether and how emerging blackness may represent an element of division for Brazilian society, affecting the traditional peculiarity of its relatively harmonious system of race relations. University is an important setting in which to explore these questions, not only because it is the place of implementation of affirmative action in favor of black students, but also because it represents more generally a fertile terrain for the identity growth of young people. In addition, university is the place where some non-Black-politicized students come into contact for the first time with the ideas of the Black movement through their interaction with politicized peers, and this process might, at least in theory, encourage the shaping of racial identities. However, this is not to assume that black identities are well-bounded and fixed, or that they develop separately from other processes of social identification that are believed to be less typically racial or more clearly class based.

Even more generally, this book is about transformation. However, transformation should not be interpreted in terms of striking and immediate shifts in wider society. On the one hand, it should be understood in the short term as observable changes in the lives of both the beneficiaries and the academic setting. On the other, it relates to possible transformations in the future of black students and the possible impact of affirmative action in society at large, by revising dominant collective readings of national identity.

In the rest of the introduction, I provide some information about the methodology and reasons for choosing certain informants in a specific Brazilian city, Rio de Janeiro. In chapter two, I define the settings and the profile of my main informants, locating the UERJ physically and historically in the city web and especially in relation to the lower-class carioca[33] suburbs, where most of my informants live. I explore the topic of social mobility in relation to class, family structure, gender, and religion, all aspects that play the simultaneous roles of incentives and constraints to informants' projects and their academic success. Race will remain an underdeveloped subject in chapter two for a very specific reason: race and color were not immediately emphasized by my main informants when disclosing their social background and their experience of social inequalities. The topic of race will instead be gradually untangled in the rest of the book. In chapter three, I analyze how discourses of race, class, and space are translated and concealed at university, sometimes intertwining and reproducing quite faithfully the contradictions of the ideology of "racial democracy" and the divides typical of the Brazilian urban space. In this sense, I also look at whether dynamics of race, class, and space typical of the urban milieu are to some extent reflected in the geographies of the classroom and in the socializing process that quotas now favor between the groups. This is useful in exploring the new and the old elements that the implementation of quotas suggests about Brazilian race relations and their possible future under the influence of affirmative action. In chapter four, I explore more directly the topic of race, especially among quota students. For example, I will discuss whether racial quotas have the power to foster black identities by relying on a "black" administrative category. I will also look at how students' identifications, in practice, fit the biracial model proposed by the Black movement or the traditional multipolar model of race relations, which is widely appreciated as a reflection of relative racial harmony and ambiguity in Brazil. Chapter four will also be the space to discuss deeply the literature favorable and critical of racial quotas, relating directly this literature to my ethnography. In chapter five, I debate whether the university experience as a whole reinforces the black identity of some non-Black-politicized students through their inevitable academic contact with student activists and certain academic subjects. A question is how this contact happens and whether this process occurs at the expense of other less typically racialized identities.

In the same chapter, before drawing the conclusions of this book, I also reexamine aspects of urban space, class, and racial mixture as they emerge in relation to quotas and social mobility, especially among female students. I show how, along with the new opportunities that affirmative action opens up to these students, there are some paradoxes and hazy areas, which should not be overlooked in the assessment of affirmative action.

Methodology

My ethnographic fieldwork at the UERJ started in August 2007, after receiving formal permission for my research from the Direction of the university. During my work, I followed the university activities of undergraduate students and ended up focusing more closely and systematically on first-year law students or freshmen (*calouros*). "If you want to study the impact of racial quotas," I was strongly advised, "you should go to the Law Department." According to general understanding, law was one of the departments that had changed the most after the introduction of quotas, having traditionally been an elite course, often described as typically white and middle-class by teachers, students, and ex-students at the UERJ. Courses such as the social sciences, mathematics, education, and social work, on the other hand, had had a less elite pool of students even before 2003, by the fact of being less appealing to local elites. I was frequently told that these courses had a history of keeping people in typically underpaid jobs, for example, as public school teachers, which did not really offer chances for social mobility. For this reason, quota openings remained often unfilled in less-demanded courses at the UERJ, as the availability of openings made quotas less determinant for students' admission in these undergraduate courses. The Law Department, as I said, was one of those where the social profile of students had changed the most since 2003. The change, according to informants, could be easily assessed in visual terms. As several members of the staff and ex-students at the UERJ mentioned, law was suddenly counting with a good number of dark-skinned students, something that had been significantly less common in prequota times. At the same time, the law course at the UERJ was largely considered the most prestigious in Rio de Janeiro, making it rather attractive for the elites. What surely increased my interest in this department was the fact that law at the UERJ was still frequented by the elite even though it had a diverse population in terms of users' class and phenotype as a consequence of the quotas. In fact, my original plan was not simply researching black quota users at the UERJ, but studying them in relation to white and wealthier people in the academic setting. Observing social mixture at the UERJ represented a first way to say something about the inclusive potential of affirmative action in Rio by focusing on a relatively small place.[34]

There was another reason for making the Law Department my main research focus. This department seemed less touched by Black activism, especially among students in the early stages of their academic careers. My choice might sound inappropriate, considering that the Black movement should be a crucial space in which to study a highly politicized topic like racial affirmative action. However, I was already relatively familiar with the political stands of the Black movement through literature and fieldwork in the city, while a sweeping assumption is that less Black-politicized people would have little to say about race relations, simply because they do not speak through a solidly articulated Black discourse (Burdick, 1998). Such considerations shaped my personal curiosity and this curiosity eventually added to my interest in the Law Department, where no single freshman seemed to be interested in Black politics at the time of my fieldwork. This does not mean that my research overlooked Black-politicized students. In the first stage of my fieldwork, well before my arrival at the UERJ, I had become quite familiar with organizations of the Black social movement in Rio and assiduously frequented some of the prevestibular community courses that the organization Educafro offers in the suburbs in order to prepare black and needy students (*negros e carentes*) for the university entrance examination. Many of the students from community prevestibular courses were studying subjects such as social sciences, history, social work, and education at the UERJ, and some of them participated in the activities of the UERJ's main Black-activist student organization, Denegrir.[35] The clustering of these less Black-politicized students in less prestigious undergraduate courses was not random; it was significantly due to the fact that the Black movement's community pre-vestibulares are not high quality enough to make applicants achieve openings in competitive courses such as law, journalism, and medicine. I also stress that, due to my involvement with Educafro, some militant students in the humanities had represented my first contact at the university and remained an important point of reference during my research.

Finally, I confess that, after moving between several departments at the beginning of my fieldwork, I established an immediate and productive connection with people from law. The law freshmen I met in 2007 seemed generally very enthusiastic, curious about my research, and keen on disclosing some social and personal information. Some of them very soon invited me to attend their favorite classes and to meet for lunch in the local canteens. This fact made my work much easier and pleasurable.

At the same time that I focused more intensively on people in the Law Department, keeping some research in less competitive programs allowed me to grasp important differences in terms of social mobility expectations and identity formation between people studying different disciplines. In my everyday fieldwork life, I interviewed and socialized with hundreds of quota and nonquota students of any color and class in several departments at the UERJ, including numerous administrative and teaching staff members. This process let me compare research findings on a wider scale than a strict focus on the Law Department would have allowed. On the other hand, I cannot deny that focusing more intensively on law students had an impact on the general texture of this book, emphasizing the reality of a specific group of people. Broadly speaking, I noticed that quota students in elite undergraduate courses (*cursos de elite*) were less politicized and less committed to their communities, as they had prevalently studied in private and expensive pre-exam courses (pre-vestibulares) with little community and political approach. These informants in prestigious courses generally were more enthusiastic about their chances to change their future and that of their families, in a close match with the overall spirit of affirmative action. If my research had focused more systematically on students attending less demanded courses, on the other hand, their reality would have inevitably provided this book with different shades. Many of these students, in fact, had tried the vestibular exam in law and other elite courses on several occasions without being successful, and they felt much less confident about the social mobility that university could grant them. At the same time, these students still appreciated the personal growth they were experiencing through university education, linking undergraduate studies to their commitment to the neighborhoods of origin and their annexed social problems. Keeping an eye open on these less prestigious departments in my research is also crucial for another reason: it shows, somehow, that certain dynamics of social and racial segregation do not simply operate *within* undergraduate courses at the UERJ but also *between* them.

Although I carried out research with law students further along in their studies, I ended up focusing more intensively on first-year students in order to explore the transition of these students into university and to research what this process might represent for them.

The time of my research, on the other hand, did not allow me to research the access of quota students to the job market, as the first ranks of quota students were just about completing their courses and my main informants are presently approaching graduation. The advantage of studying freshmen was that classes remained quite compact during the first years, and the same group of students attended classes together everyday. Students in later years tend instead to spread across different courses and spend much time practicing in their legal internships, thus hampering my regular interaction with an established group. In terms of methodology, I was particularly interested in getting closer to the life of a group, giving priority to the quality of my relation with informants more than to the amount of interviews with the highest-possible number of informants. This aspect was crucial to carry out deep participant observation of informants' academic experience, as well as of their socializing process and life. I complemented these methods with the analysis of quantitative data, some of them first-hand, to which I had exclusive access through the Vestibular Office and DINFO, the UERJ Informatics Section.

Insisting on a smaller group, one might contest, sets problems in terms of the representativeness of my sample. I tried to play down these risks by my continuous reference to statistics and literature concerning broader samples. Without diminishing the relevance of other social methods, my priority was collecting data put into context instead of limiting myself to sporadic and formal interviews with informants with whom I had never socialized. In this way, I had the opportunity to explore the same matters with the same people a number of times, individually or in groups, across a full academic year. I was then able to observe possible contradictions and variations in answering due to context, but also changes of opinion and clarifications of previous statements across the year. There were also several opportunities for socializing with students outside the university. I had the chance to visit the homes of some of them on a number of occasions, while it became quite common to celebrate birthdays in the city center and to join in with students' cultural activities (free visits to museums and exhibitions, cheap theater and cinema events), all of which occurred in the city center of Rio de Janeiro. I believe that the assiduousness with which I spent time with my main informants represents an interesting methodological point of my research.

In a class of about 70–80 students, I socialized with most quota and nonquota students, but even more closely with a group of 20 *cotistas* (quota students) of different colors who were in the process of establishing a relatively solid friendship. All these students self-identified as lower-class and lived in the lower-class areas spread across Zona Norte, Zona Oeste, and the Baixada Fluminense, commonly identified as suburbs in Rio de Janeiro's context. A number of informants surprisingly disclosed their quota status quite easily once I had explained my research interests on affirmative action. In addition to this information, I relied on the list of admitted candidates published by the journal *Folha Dirigida*, where the student admission list appears by course, specifying the name of candidates, their shift of studying at university (morning/evening), the kind of opening (quota/nonquota and type of quota), their rank within each opening group and their score in the admission examination. About half of my main informants self-identified as *negros* in one way or another, and I give particular space to some of them within my ethnography. This is an important point because, despite the fact that I often had a personal and biased guess of which students might self-identify as *negros*, my predictions were not always correct. In this book I refer to students as *negros* only if they actually used this term for themselves. Another important aspect is that, by socializing with students on a systematic basis, I seldom had to ask my informants directly about their racial/color identification. In most cases this information was revealed spontaneously and indirectly during student socializing and conversations about the quota system. In some specific cases I did ask the question, but this was usually framed in relation to the use of quotas.

Even though this matter deserves attention, it is difficult for me to precisely estimate how much my racial and gender role as a white, European male played interference within my research. This role was for sure more problematic in my interactions with Black activists, who often saw my interest in race relations as something bizarre and/or suspicious. In this sense, I did not perceive clear limitations with my non-Black-politicized informants, students of different skin colors who gave great importance to *mestiçagem* and racial conviviality, both in terms of national ideals and their own family histories. I believe that my intense socializing process with students managed, at least partially, to balance the potential disadvantages implied in my social background; this idea is proved by the fact that the opening of my informants to intimate racial aspects of their lives was gradual during my fieldwork and grew once our social interaction started producing some confidence and trust. I add that a considerable amount of the ethnography about race and color presented in this book did not emerge from face-to-face interviews but during situations of normal socializing between students and everyday academic life, where I sometimes was a pure spectator or a secondary participant. On other occasions, I managed to play with my supposed lack of knowledge of the local context to raise impertinent questions about race relations that a white middle-class Brazilian person might feel more constrained to ask. In this way, I made the most of my in-theory disadvantageous background, while I could also provoke discussions within the group of students and follow as a listener.

My study turned out to have some gender bias in favor of female students. These represented the majority of people who self-identified as black in their everyday lives among law freshmen, or at least those who were more willing to talk about racial topics with me. Among first-year law students, there are some characters who appear more often in my account. In this choice, I was influenced by Donna Goldstein's ethnography of race in Rio de Janeiro, which is engaging and theoretically rich while focusing on a reduced number of characters. Goldstein reaches her aims not only by complementing her study with statistics, historic information, and other people's ethnography; she is also very successful because the apparently individual stories of her characters speak a much broader picture of race, class, and gender in Rio de Janeiro and in Brazil.

During fieldwork I never hid the objectives of my research from informants; however, I did not constantly emphasize my role, as I hoped to gain easier access to informal spaces to research students' life. Consequently, it was not always completely clear to informants (and, perhaps, not even to me) where/when my research role was more actively deployed. Boundaries were obviously clearer to informants when I had a tape recorder in my hand and when I took notes; however, this by no means was the systematic way by which I collected fieldwork data. Normal hanging out with informants was also an integral and crucial part of my research, providing me with crucial ethnographic information.

A different set of considerations about methodology relates to limiting a research of affirmative action and race relation to the UERJ and Rio de Janeiro. In fact, different systems of racial and social quotas or affirmative action are used throughout Brazilian universities, as well as the racial terminology used at the administrative level for quotas. In addition, patterns of race relations, use of racial/color terminology, and urban racial distribution in other Brazilian states may differ from those in Rio de Janeiro, also depending on whether a urban or a rural context is considered. Therefore, this study should be read by acknowledging its many specificities and limitations, even though it is also representative of affirmative action and race relations in Brazil described in other literature. Because of this general

Brazilian context on which I draw from, the book's title refers to affirmative action and black identities *in Brazil*, even if I am aware of the generalizations that this fact implies.

Why Rio de Janeiro?

There were several reasons to choose Rio de Janeiro as the location for my research. The State of Rio de Janeiro has been the first to introduce a law for racial quotas in state universities, opening the way to similar legislation in other states. The UERJ has been the first state university to implement this system by legal requirement in Brazil, receiving extensive coverage in the media from 2003 to the present. As some Black activists pointed out, Rio de Janeiro is a powerful symbol for quotas at the national level; in fact, as many activists told me: "if quotas disappear in Rio, they will disappear everywhere else in Brazil."

Rio de Janeiro is very central to Brazilian life and was for long time the imperial and national capital, a place where the destiny of an entire country was decided. The city is certainly one of the first things that foreigners think of when hearing the word "Brazil," also due to Rio's constant representation in the media and to its tourist commercialization. Indeed, tourism makes Rio a very strong symbol for Brazil. Carnival, the samba and the *mulatas*, the Maracanã football stadium, *caipirinha* drinks, the Cristo Redentor and the Sugar Loaf, the *feijoada* stew, Copacabana and Ipanema beach, *bossa nova* music, without forgetting the favelas (hill shantytowns) and the related popular *funk* rhythm are all emblematic of Rio before being understood and appropriated as part of national imagery. In addition, by virtue of its particular geography, Rio de Janeiro is said to be one of the Brazilian metropolises with less segregation, both in class and in racial terms, due to the presence of a number of shantytowns even within wealthy areas. This may generally be favored by the many mountains and hills (*morros*) that have been gradually occupied by lower-class people and shaped into favelas, largely present in the heart of the wealthy Zona Sul neighborhoods.[36] I believed that a less typically segregated location might be interesting for a study that constantly refers to the idea/ideology of racial democracy. Equally important, the proportional racial/color division of the population of Rio de Janeiro is relatively close to the overall Brazilian figures, making the place quite representative of the national scenario. In Rio de Janeiro, in fact, the percentage of white, brown, and black people is 55.8, 32.6, and 11.1, respectively; for Brazil, the percentages are 48.2, 44.2, and 6.9, respectively (PNAD 2009).[37]

Furthermore, Rio de Janeiro held a sad importance in the nineteenth century for the slave trade, a fact of the past that might have a great significance today for the implementation of quotas, although processes of urban transformation have made this history quite cryptic to view in the urban landscape.[38] A number of researchers have pointed out the process of peripherization and dispersal of poverty and blackness from their original urban locales in the city center of Rio de Janeiro to the suburbs, as envisaged by city planners from the beginning of the twentieth century (Abreu, 1988; Campos, 2006; Conde, 2007). This process, implying the demolition of large portions of the carioca city center, responded to multiple aims: on the one hand, governors planned to convert Rio de Janeiro into a beautiful, modern, and sanitized city according to Haussmanian[39] models; on the other, there was some inclination to delete the traces of the shameful colonial past. This tension between visible and invisible stories is something that increased my interest in Rio de Janeiro, especially in considering the importance of affirmative action in conferring public visibility to issues that are traditionally downplayed and silenced in the name of national solidarity in Brazil.

Clarifications of Terminology

Some basic terminological clarifications will help in the reading of this book. When referring to the Black social movement, I have opted to use the word "movement" in lower case because the Black movement is not a coherent and centralized organization in Brazil. On the other hand, the word "Black" in uppercase is intended to stress the politico-identity character of this movement. Following this logic, the same word is often used lowercased since it does not always and necessarily stress a politico-identity nuance but, for example, merely "color identity" or, more simply and generally, "color" and "phenotype." I also use lowercase whenever I am not completely sure how to operate this conceptual distinction. This might provoke the question of how I am making the decision to switch between one style and the other. I am aware of the limits of my choice. However, I also feel that some distinction is important in this book, even in those cases where I fail to ensure clear coherence in my use of these ideas.

When I write "*negro*" and other terms in italics, I use these terms in Portuguese and in the ways that they are widely used in Brazilian culture. These terms have different usages at regional level in Brazil, but the way I employ them is intended to mainly reflect their use in Rio de Janeiro. I avoid offering here an overview of the complex race/color terminology implemented in Brazil, a discussion of which will be a more extensive later part of this book. The inverted commas present in some cases around these terms are used in some contexts to catch attention, or to highlight a problematic use of the word; in this sense, this use might sometimes appear inconsistent. Some clarification should be provided for the word "*cotista*," which extensively replaces "quota student" in the text. *Cotista* is an emic term used by most people in Rio de Janeiro and strongly appropriated by beneficiaries in order to define quota users. I also widely used it in this sense in this book.

Some additional terminological clarification concerns the difference between "black quota students," which stresses the racial/color self-identification of some quota students (or *cotistas*), and "black-quota students," which refers to students who make use of quotas set aside for "black" students, and who do not necessarily have dark skin, as I will show more clearly in chapter four. I provide a similar clarification about my use of the adjective "Black-politicized," a term I created to describe students politicized through Black politics, rather than those just generally interested or involved in politics in broad terms.

Other clarifications are necessary about the way I refer to city areas like Zona Sul as "wealthy" areas and Baixada Fluminense, Zona Norte, and Zona Oeste as "poor" areas and "suburbs." This definition is far from being perfect due to the presence of favelas in Zona Sul and relatively wealthy neighborhoods in some areas generally understood as poor (e.g., Barra da Tijuca in Zona Oeste). My generalizing use of these terms intends to reflect the way they are widely used in Rio de Janeiro as symbols of wealth and poverty.

Finally, I need to call attention to my use of the concept of middle class, the understanding of which could be very different in Brazil from European and North American contexts. In Rio de Janeiro, lower-class people often use this concept (*a classe média*) as a way to generally mean "wealthy" people and the elite. Only in more specific questioning on this subject did lower-class and other informants distinguish the "middle class" from the very rich or very upper class, which, as some informants said, are "those who send their kids to study in prestigious universities in the United States or Europe." Contextually, distinctions were eventually also made by informants between high-middle class (*classe média alta*), middle class going to middle-high (*classe média para média alta*), very middle class (*classe média média*), and low-middle class (*classe média-baixa*). However, in common everyday language, *classe média* is widely understood as reasonably wealthy and this is how I generally use this term in this book.

2

Dreams and Hard Places

Main Settings and Socioeconomic Profile of Quota Students

A University in the City: A Place for Whom?

I visited the UERJ for first time in late August 2007, about three months after starting my fieldwork in Rio de Janeiro. The university had been on strike for some time and activities had been postponed due to the Pan-American Olympic Games held in the nearby Maracanã football stadium. Considering this situation, my first access to the key setting of my research coincided with the beginning of the academic semester; this moment, for many of my informants, represented the beginning of their undergraduate programs.

The UERJ is a concrete twelve-story block built in a modernist/brutalist style (figure 2.1), which struck me on my first visit due to its unpleasant aesthetics. At first glance, it reminded me of a huge hospital or one of the massive blocks of flats that stood in my imagination of the Soviet era. The style, severe and repetitive in its architectural elements, seems to conciliate the functionality typical of transnational modernism with the authoritarian and formally egalitarian ideology of the military period (1964–1985) when the university was built. The structure of the building is composed of six equally high and partially prefabricated buildings, which are linked by footbridge systems. Floors, which usually host a few departments, are also interconnected by a complex interweaving of stairways (*a escada*) and ramps (*a rampa*), in addition to the elevator system (figure 2.2).

It took me some time to get used to the building, to orient myself within its labyrinthine interconnections and appreciate the thriving vitality of its academic life, hence balancing my depressing first impressions. The UERJ is in fact a lively microcosm with cafeterias, bookstores, and banks; it also contains many social organizations

Figure 2.1 The UERJ seen from the footbridges just outside the tube station on Avenida Castelo Branco. This is the side of the building façade opposite to the favela of Mangueira.

(a)

Figure 2.2 (a) Several interior shots of the UERJ. Ramps and staircases are visible in (b), the lift system in (c).

(b)

(c)

Figure 2.2 Continued

and cultural events. Classrooms, staff offices, and cafés lie, therefore, in a concentrated space, favoring encounters between users (Somosur, 1994).

One of the first aspects that caught my attention was the location of the university in the city. Finished in 1976, the building represented a very unusual model of an academic establishment. At that time, modern universities were mainly conceived in terms of city-garden campuses (*Cidade Jardim*) with relatively low, scattered buildings interposed with pleasant green areas and, more importantly, carefully isolated from the rest of the urban space (Rodrigues, 2001: 52, 173). In stark contrast, the UERJ is fully integrated into the city landscape in many ways. Its location on the urban map is intermediate between the center and the suburbs. Placed at the margin of a middle-class area (*parte nobre*) in Zona Norte[1] but away from wealthy Zona Sul, the university looks relatively close to the business and administrative areas of the city center (*Centro*) and is projected toward the lower-class *subúrbios*, mostly located in the rest of Zona Norte, in the Baixada Fluminense, and Zona Oeste. This fortunate location is enhanced by the proximity of the university to a twofold rail transport system, which adds to the several bus lines. The railway connects Zona Norte, the Baixada Fluminense, and Zona Oeste to

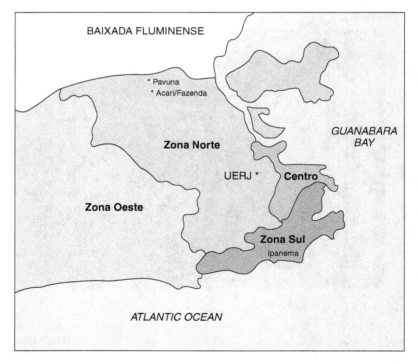

Map 2.1 Metropolitan area of Rio de Janeiro divided by Zones (Centro, Sul, Norte, Oeste). The white area corresponds to a portion of Baixada Fluminense, a number of municipalities that form the "Greater Rio de Janeiro" area.

Central do Brasil,[2] a crucial exchange point for thousands of lower-class suburban workers traveling every day to their jobs in wealthy Zona Sul. The underground (*o metro*), which actually runs on the surface in proximity to the UERJ, connects Zona Sul more directly—via Centro—with most of Zona Norte and with Pavuna, the gateway to typically working-class Baixada Fluminense (maps 2.1 and 2.2). This important transport hub faces the UERJ and separates it from the favela hill (*morro*) of Mangueira. The train and tube stations are connected to the university by a complex system of footbridges that bypass the Avenida Castelo Branco (parallel to the railways) and also lead to the famous Maracanã football stadium. As an example of its integration in the city landscape, the ground floor of the university is crossed by hundreds of pedestrians every day as a normal and safe communication link between the railway/tube hub and the

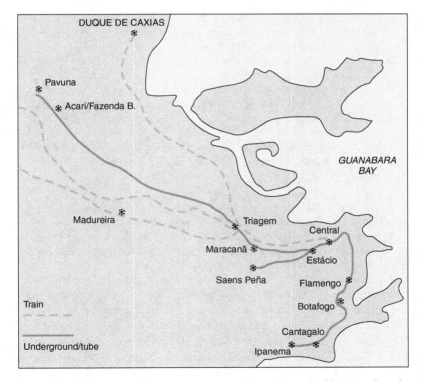

Map 2.2 Closer view of Zona Sul, Centro, and Zona Norte, highlighting the tube 1 and 2 lines and the railway (as they looked in 2008). The area above and left of Maracanã can be generally understood as suburbs.

nearby residential neighborhood of Vila Isabel. I had the general first impression that the UERJ was democratically located in the city and easily reachable by a diverse pool of people. I imagined the architectural plan as a sort of metaphorical dialogue with poverty (the suburbs, the favela), oriented to encourage the presence of the lower classes in the academic setting. By thinking in this way, I was also assuming that the main façade of the UERJ was that in front of the favela and the railways. My interpretation was reinforced by the fact that this side of the building is the one more frequently represented in the institutional pictures of the university. However, when I shared my intuitions with a group of lower-class students, they reacted with hilarity, laughing at my supposed lack of knowledge of the local context.

> Look, if you are suggesting that the university was planned here to include the poor, you are quite wrong. If they [governors] really wanted to build a university for us, why didn't they put good courses in the suburbs? Or even in the city center, which is easier and cheaper to reach from everywhere by using less transport? I have to pay for at least two buses to come here every day! . . . In the suburbs they [governors] put just undergraduate courses such as education, math . . . courses for the poor to stay poor (*pra o pobre ficar pobre*) . . . why they don't put law or engineering or medicine over there? (Daisy, first-year law quota student)

Comments also related to the proximity of transport to the suburbs, which in my view aimed to facilitate the use of the university by different social classes.

> The fact that the railway passes nearby is a mere coincidence; it was already there from colonial times to bring sugar and coffee to the port (*pra os navios*) . . . The tube, instead, was built probably in the 1980s to connect the Maracanã football stadium with the rest of the city. (Gabriel, first-year law lower-class student)

The presence of the tube, then, was not to facilitate access to the university for potential users of any social background. In the way my lower-class informants saw it, it was instead meant to transfer waves of supporters to the Maracanã football stadium, one of the main icons of carioca identity. This reading would basically suggest that there are popular sectors of local life, of which football is a crucial example, where lower- and upper-class people are allowed to participate equally in the construction of local identity.[3] The same interclass conviviality, however, would not in principle be envisaged for the sharing of educational resources.

To stress the questionable social philosophy of the university project, my informants made me notice that the proper main façade of the UERJ was not the one I had imagined it to be, but the one on the other side (*a de atrás*) on Francisco Xavier Street. This side of the building leads directly and even abruptly onto the middle-class neighborhood of Vila Isabel and represents the official address of the university. Subverting my subjective interpretation of the building's architectural philosophy, the students pictured the UERJ as a place built for the upper social classes and one that substantially turned its back on lower-class areas. This interpretation was confirmed by most of the staff I interviewed in the institution. They described the original beneficiary of the university to be *the* middle class (meaning, generally, wealthy people), although this seemed to be less clearly the "elite" in the view of the teachers than the students had suggested. A teacher who grew up in Vila Isabel remembered that the courses and cultural facilities offered by the UERJ mostly benefited his neighborhood, as well as the nearby middle-class areas of Tijuca, Grajaú, and Maracanã. Most of those interviewed described these neighborhoods as properly middle class, differentiating them from Zona Sul, where a more prosperous kind of middle class (middle-upper) and the rich would generally live. Elite courses such as law and medicine, however, have traditionally and also typically served Zona Sul people (figure 2.3).

Figure 2.3 View of wealthy areas in Zona Sul: the encounter between three neighborhoods—Lagoa, Ipanema, and Leblon.

Referring back to the construction of the university, it is possible to conclude that the building, at least in origin, followed the same pattern of relative segregation of the Brazilian city space, even though Rio de Janeiro is considered less segregating than other Brazilian metropolises from an urbanistic point of view. This segregating model is also reflected in the geography of many carioca blocks of flats (*condomínios*), where special entrances and sectors of the houses have been traditionally imagined as spaces for servants (Holston, 1989: 178–179). It may not be by chance that the service areas at the UERJ look to be more clearly projected to the suburbs. In this sense, I eventually noticed that the nearby favela of Mangueira—whether intentionally or not—is isolated from the UERJ not just by the physical presence of the railways, but also by the lack of footbridges in its direction (figure 2.4). This is an example of how apparently neutral urban infrastructures such as railways and big roads may function as ways to segregate the urban space, as some literature shows for the United States (Goldberg, 1993), or for specific cities such as Kansas City (Gotham, 2002) and, in Brazil, for São Paulo (Caldeira, 2000).[4]

I gradually gathered more detailed information about the planning of the UERJ through research carried out in the university archives, and also thanks to the UERJ's published book "*Acervo de*

Figure 2.4 View of the favela of Mangueira from the UERJ (with the train line and Avenida Castelo Branco barely visible in between).

Memórias: exposição comemorativa do cinqüentenário da UERJ[5] (Rede Sirius, 2001). The building was finished in 1976, under the Lacerda government, and following a very long negotiation process, which had started in the early 1960s. This process implied the painful and costly demolition of a well-known carioca favela, Esqueleto (literally, "skeleton"). The favela-dwellers were mostly resettled in remote areas of the periphery and suburbs, especially in the Baixada (Perlman, 2010). In the official documents of the university, the close presence of the railway had actually been seen as an obstacle for the academic establishment, forcing the construction of a very concentrated multistory building in a noisy environment (Cunha, 1988: 37). I also found out that, at the time of planning, several plots had been considered for a more convenient establishment of the university in wealthy Zona Sul (36). The final location was eventually preferred according to a cost/benefit reasoning. In building the UERJ in that area, carioca governors saw two practical advantages. First, they had an excuse to remove the "damned" (*maldita*) favela (41),[6] addressing the complaints of the middle-class citizens of Vila Isabel and Tijuca, which were important electoral districts, according to informants. Second, the plot was located on the periphery of Rio de Janeiro, this making its price appealing enough despite the necessity of the costly removal of Esqueleto (figure 2.5). From this angle, the construction of the UERJ matched a pattern of urban planning implemented in Rio de Janeiro throughout the last century (Alvito, 2001: 272). This model followed a modern-city ideal that could be achieved through the building of extensive infrastructure, as well as through the simultaneous removal of the poor from the city and their confinement to

Figure 2.5 Partial views of the Esqueleto area, before and after its removal. Photos kindly provided and scanned by Syrius—Acervo de Memórias UERJ, originally from the Public archives Acervo AGCRJ/Arquivo Geral da Cidade do Rio de Janeiro and Acervo DEMOP-UEG/Universidade do Estado da Guanabara.

the margins of the urban space (Abreu, 1988; Campos, 2006). This new view of a sanitized city followed Haussmanian and more rational divisions of the city space (Goldstein, 2003), but also a developist imagination in which the poor represent a physical and social impediment for urban modernization (Abreu, 1988).

Discourses of urban segregation and exclusion in Brazil strongly interlace with race, both in the private and the public city landscape. This works not only for middle-class households, whose *empregadas* (housemaids) are commonly imagined as black women (Burdick, 1998: 47), but also for the common stereotype of Zona Sul as a white living space, and the favela and the suburbs as black ones (Oliveira, 2000; Alvito, 2001; Vargas, 2006; Campos, 2006). The construction of social and spatial hierarchies has consistently intertwined with phenotypes from the time of slavery, with equations that have never really been subverted since abolition. It is not by chance that Black militant students often referred to quotas as a way to occupy a "space of power" (*espaço de poder*), an expression that I heard several times during my fieldwork. This would be a space that is both geographical and symbolic. It is within this framework that a Black militant student instrumentally read the removal of Esqueleto in the following way:

> And who do you think the dwellers in Esqueleto were? Black fellows (*a negrada*), my friend . . . What's the meaning of this place (UERJ)? For whom was this place? Where does slavery (*escravidão*) fit into all this? . . . So, look at quotas! They are a way for the descendants of these people to come back here and finally benefit from the construction of UERJ. (André, History student at the UERJ and Educafro coordinator in Rio)

Escaping the Trap

During my stay in Rio de Janeiro I had the opportunity to visit the houses of law quota students on a number of occasions. Most of these places were located in lower-class areas between Zona Norte, Zona Oeste, and the Baixada Fluminense, in general quite distant both from the university and the city center. Students who live in the Baixada, in São Gonçalo,[7] and in low-income areas of Zona Norte and Zona Oeste (mainly faraway Campo Grande and Santa Cruz) spend at least an hour to an hour and a half reaching the UERJ. For many of them, this means getting up between 4.30 and 5 A.M. during the week in order to start classes at 7 A.M. The way back home is usually more time-consuming because it coincides with rush hour and heavy road traffic (*engarrafamentos*), which starts around 4 P.M. until approximately 8.30 P.M. Many quota students mentioned that, depending on traffic conditions, they spent at least two to two and a half hours on local transport to get home.

Among the *cotistas*, Flávia is one of the luckiest in terms of transportation to and from university. Although she lives in Fazenda Botafogo, a section of Acarí, a poor neighborhood in Zona Norte, the distance to the UERJ can be covered in about 30 minutes' journey by tube. The station Acarí/Fazenda Botafogo (see upper left corner in map 2.2) was inaugurated in 1998 with the extension of Zona Norte's surface tube line to Pavuna (at the limit of the Baixada Fluminense). Flávia was able to pay for this journey with a pass she got with her part-time job as surveillance staff in the Vila Olímpica of Fazenda Botafogo, a sports complex for lower-class children, where she worked at weekends. This spares her from train and bus transportation, which would be cheaper than the tube if not for the free pass, but also more uncomfortable and time-consuming. Even though Flávia's home is relatively close to the city center, about a 40-minute tube journey, its distance from the heart of Zona Sul is about one hour, reflecting, to some extent, the segregation of the metropolitan space.

I managed to visit Fazenda Botafogo a number of times. My last visit was in February 2008, during the summer break, when Flávia invited me for lunch. I waited for her on the footbridges outside the tube station Acarí/Fazenda Botafogo on a terribly hot and sunny day. In front of me was the typical spectacle of the metropolitan suburbs: a relatively urbanized lower-class neighborhood surrounded by several *morros* (hillside favelas). On the Wikipedia web source, Fazenda Botafogo is described as a nonofficial neighborhood of Rio de Janeiro or a sub-bairro (subneighborhood) of Acarí,[8] which, in spite of having achieved the status of neighborhood, is still commonly mentioned as a big shantytown (Alvito, 2001: 22). Fazenda Botafogo is named after an old sugar plantation in the area, which is presently divided by Avenida Automóvil Clube and Avenida Brasil in the industrial area of Rio de Janeiro. According to the municipal database of Rio de Janeiro, the Acarí neighborhood is the one with the lowest life expectancy, lowest per capita income, and lowest general human development index in the city (2000). It also belongs to the district with the highest murder rate (102 every 100.000 inhabitants) in Rio de Janeiro (Bastos and Cavallieri 2002: 7). This information contrasted with my impressions, as the area looked more or less urbanized and quiet during my visits.

When Flávia arrived at the tube station and we walked into the neighborhood, I could make better sense of the surrounding space.

The streets, roughly asphalted, were delimited by simple one- and two-story houses contrasting with wealthy areas' tall buildings, while some dreary grocery premises replaced the better-equipped shops of Zona Sul. The previous time I had visited Fazenda Botafogo was on Christmas Day. On that occasion, the atmosphere had seemed livelier, with families sitting outside their houses and children playing in the street. On a normal weekday, the place looked as ghostly and empty as any other dormitory neighborhood in a Brazilian metropolis.

Flávia shares a flat with her mother, in a five-story council houses block (*conjunto*), one of many built in the area by the government in the 1970s, as a modern alternative to favelas (Perlman, 2010; 1979: 228–230). They are in fact faithful copies of those created in Cidade de Deus, in Zona Oeste. As Perlman (2010: 291, 294) notes, the structural and social conditions of the *conjuntos* do not differ too much from those of the favelas and people who lives there are equally stigmatized.

Flávia's flat is very small, probably about 40 square meters, composed of a microscopic living room, two modest rooms, and services. Her bedroom is tiny but perfectly equipped, with shelves full of Portuguese and law books. A number of memo sheets hung on the bedroom's walls, reminding Flávia of various goals and academic skills to achieve in order to become a good student. I have to say that Flávia was the only one among my informants who actually lived in a flat. Many *cotistas*' households that I had the opportunity to observe in Baixada Fluminense and poor sectors of Zona Norte were houses with several interconnected units where other nuclei of the extended family live.[9]

It is always difficult, in these areas, to understand where the neighborhood ends and the favela starts. Favela houses are often imagined with their characteristic unpainted redbrick façades, usually leaning up against the hills (*morros*) and the bush (*mato*) due to the lack of building space in flatter areas. My informants, however, usually lived downhill, or on lower hills, in more or less urbanized spaces. Although the boundaries with the favelas look quite blurred (figure 2.6), and many of these neighborhoods are often referred to as favelas by middle-class people, my quota informants always made the distinction very clear in an attempt at status differentiation: "[T]he *favela* people (*favelados*) live over there, uphill!" These distinctions seemed particularly important to suburban students and appeared even more striking when some of them suggested that I should interview some university students from the favelas. In most cases, these students strongly denied being from the favela, which was sometimes described

Figure 2.6 Borders between favelas and suburban neighborhoods are often very blurred, especially away from Zona Sul. Here, a shot from Fazenda Botafogo, with flat blocks exactly like the one where Flávia lives in the foreground.

as starting from the next corner, or the next group of houses, a bit further uphill (Perlman, 2010: 232).

My visits to the suburbs and to some favelas were also important in scaling down obvious preconceptions of these areas as typically "black" spaces. I realized that lower-class areas in Rio de Janeiro were phenotypically very diverse, with a high percentage of whites and light-skinned *mestiços* from the Brazilian Northeast (*nordestinos*), massive amounts of whom have migrated to southeastern metropolises since the beginning of the last century. This perception of phenotypic diversity was confirmed by looking at the users of community prevestibular courses for needy students, which I often attended in the suburbs and which were set up by the organization Educafro.

Before I caught the tube back to Zona Sul from Fazenda Botafogo, and after the other lunch guests left, Flávia insisted on buying me a drink in a local *barzinho*, one of the many improvised and open-air bars that spread at night all over the metropolitan area. The day had been pleasant, but Flávia suddenly did not look very happy.

> You know, I'm stuck here (*me sinto presa aqui*) . . . I want to leave this place [Fazenda Botafogo], help my mother, pay for her medical insurance, give her a better life . . . It seems that everything has worked to

prevent me from getting something better in life. It's the structure of this place that doesn't help at all . . .

Initially I could not understand Flávia's sadness, as she had had to struggle in order to achieve an opening in law and this could represent her gateway to a better future. However, financial constraints and crucial doubts about her academic abilities were threatening her dreams. Also, contact with students from better educational and economic backgrounds made her more aware of the magnitude of the gap she was trying to fill and that, in the end, she might have to scale down her dreams.

> I spend all the time studying but my results are not as good as I expected . . . I'm already 25 and I feel I've lost so much time in life and there are all those [better off] younger students who already speak several languages fluently and master academic subjects so easily . . . I didn't get a good education because public schools are bad quality (*ruim*) . . . After finishing high school, I spent several years fixing printers. This was the future that was assigned to me (*feito pra mim*) and that I didn't accept . . . However, I wonder if I will be really able to finish my course and to survive financially during it (*me sustentar*) . . .

COTISTAS' PROFILE IN THE LAW DEPARTMENT: FIGHTING FOR FINANCIAL SUSTAINABILITY

> I'd say that we belong to that group which is poor (*que é pobre sim*) but still has hope, aspiration and some conditions to move up socially. People who are extremely poor don't even come out from high school. For them it is even more difficult to be here. (Glória, first-year law quota student)

Law, along with medicine, dentistry, journalism, nutrition, and industrial design, is considered an elite and highly popular course (*um curso muito disputado*) in public universities. Consequently, this course is not only difficult to get into but appealing in terms of professional opportunities. Not by chance, these courses were particularly described to me as traditionally white and middle-class. As some students argued, "[B]efore the quotas were introduced, blacks and the poor did not get into law" (*no Direito, antes das cotas, pobre e negro não entravam*). For this reason, if they score a good mark in the first phase of the vestibular, students usually avoid applying for subjects such as math and education. This second group of courses was described as less rewarding in terms of jobs, and, unless students are able to carry on to MA and PhD studies, almost necessarily leading to underpaid professions such as public-school teachers. It is worth saying that things do not always work as students would wish. Due to low performance in the first phase of the admission test, a number of applicants have to fall back on less prestigious courses, where competition is usually less fierce. Nonetheless, if students are still quite young or have some financial support to try more prestigious courses in the future, the less popular programs are accepted as a possibly temporary stage or waiting room. Some students actually graduate from less prestigious courses such as education, history, infirmary, and social sciences hoping to switch to law, medicine, or journalism afterward, or choosing them as a second degree.

There is usually some difficulty with defining *cotistas* (quota students) in terms of class. In some critical approaches to quotas, these students are often idealized as middle-class, in order to stress their distance from extremely poor people ("Manifesto Contra as Cotas," May 2008).[10] A common idea, in fact, is that very poor people do not even manage to finish high school. This stance highlights problems in relation to the fluidity and the relativity of the concepts of class and poverty, and about which segments of the population quotas seem to favor the most. These doubts find some justification in the fact that UERJ has gradually increased its per capita income limit for quota applicants' households since 2003. The amount established in 2004 (300 *reais*)[11] significantly reduced the numbers of potential candidates and was subsequently slowly increased until it reached 960 *reais* in 2009. At the time of my fieldwork, the value was 630 *reais* (Almeida, 2007: 10). Having said this, most quota informants in the Law Department insistently declared themselves to be poor and were seen as such by classmates. Of course, the concept of poverty can be very relative. Depending on the terms of comparison, my main law informants could be considered nonpoor in relation to more deprived people. Despite living in depressed neighborhoods or municipalities of the metropolitan area, most quota students, for example, occupied a family property, had decent clothes and guaranteed meals at home. In addition to this, almost all of them had a mobile phone (usually just used for receiving calls), a sometimes-working landline, and, in some cases, a PC and Internet dial-access from home. If my informants were neither properly middle-class nor completely impoverished, a question remains about how they could be described in terms of class. In general, I would say that the universe of quota and nonquota students is very heterogeneous but, overall, the gap between these two groups of students is quite visible.

Distinguishing between courses may be relatively important if it is assumed that there is some correlation between class and the ability to pass a tough admission examination. For example, I suspected that the *cotistas* who manage to enter the Law Department might generally have a higher social profile than those who get into courses like education. In this regard, analyzing individual cases might not be very indicative, whereas looking at statistics might be more useful. There are actually socioeconomic data that the university collects at the time of the vestibular exam, and these include 40 questions that disclose much of the reality of students' households. I did notice some differences in patterns between elite and nonelite courses, although the socioeconomic criteria to select *cotistas* are the same for all courses.[12] On the other hand, socioeconomic questions also show that differences are always more consistent between quota students and non-*cotistas* in different courses. I looked at some statistical evidence drawn from the vestibular database concerning students admitted in 2008, the first vestibular database in which statistical information was shown by course.[13] I considered two courses, law and education, although, as the asterisk suggests, data about black-quota students who started studying education in 2008 was very limited (11 students) and therefore not particularly significant in statistical terms. In general, it can be seen that the profile of non-*cotistas* in less competitive courses such as education is relatively similar to that of *cotistas* in law.

For table 2.1, I calculated percentages over a total amount of respondents to each question by category; this amount is shown within parentheses as "NR." The variation of total respondents for different questions suggests that some students did not answer all the questions or that some data are missing from the university database.

The socioeconomic information here is, in my view, very important because it is information that students provide separately from the quota selection process. In the quota application form, students might feel encouraged to adjust[14] their per capita family income so that it does not exceed the established amount for quotas. Quite differently, the socioeconomic questionnaire collects social background information in a more indirect way, and students might feel less immediate pressure to manipulate their real social situations.

Other interesting and perhaps more crucial data relate to the exemption to the admission examination fee. For the vestibular 2007[15] this fee was 35 *reais* (less than 15 Euros at the time of my fieldwork), an amount that might be relatively accessible even for

Table 2.1 Socioeconomic data about classified candidates in vestibular 2008 (NR: total number of respondents to each question by category and course)

	Nonquota	(NR)	Pub. sch. quota	(NR)	Black quota	(NR)
% students in whose households there are no cars or motorbikes						
Law	11%	(142)	64%	(69)	71%	(58)
Education	51%	(304)	84%	(25)	100%	(11)
% students who have a PC at home						
Law	99%	(143)	70%	(67)	67%	(58)
Education	80%	(300)	44%	(25)	27%	(11)
% students who have never worked						
Law	87%	(158)	57%	(68)	52%	(58)
Education	52%	(306)	32%	(25)	36%	(11)
% students who contribute to family income						
Law	8%	(142)	21%	(68)	24%	(58)
Education	32%	(305)	35%	(25)	64%	(11)
% students whose mothers did not study further than high school						
Law	20%	(143)	81%	(68)	81%	(58)
Education	68%	(301)	92%	(25)	100%	(11)
% students whose fathers did not study further than high school						
Law	20%	(143)	78%	(69)	69%	(58)
Education	69%	(300)	75%	(25)	100%	(11)
% students who managed to be fee-exempt for the admission exam*						
Law	0%	(167)	40%	(78)	40%	(64)
Education	16%	(297)	71%	(42)	72%	(18)

* These data are from the UERJ's complete database for the 2007 vestibular. This information cannot be seen online but through the Excel file kindly provided for me by the Vestibular Office. This is much more detailed than the information published online on the university website.

lower-class people in Brazil. In order to get an exemption, students had to prove that the general gross income in their family was less than 630 *reais* per month (about 250 Euros) through a very long and arduous bureaucratic process. This suggests that students who applied for exemption were genuinely needy. Table 2.1 shows that there are substantial differences depending both on the kind of opening and the course.

Despite the general relatively higher socioeconomic profile of law *cotistas* in comparison to those on other courses, this suggests that a significant proportion of these students are quite needy. Jamerson mentioned that some of his classmates were thinking of dropping out because they could not gather the money for fundamental needs such as transport, as was also confirmed by some teachers. "Some people," Jamerson said, "even have problems with having meals at university." He, as I found out, skipped lunch every day, while other students had a cheap lunch in the Community Canteen (*Restaurante Popular*) of Maracanã, a place that was frequented by massive numbers of lower-class workers and homeless people. Jamerson and some other students had their only meal in the evening when they returned home after spending all afternoon studying in the library. As this shows, the kinds of problems *cotistas* have to face at university are very basic. At the time of my fieldwork, the university granted quota students a scholarship (190 *reais* per month, approximately 80 Euros) only during their first two semesters. This barely sufficed to cover students' travel expenses.[16] To guarantee their own sustainability, lower-class students mostly look for the possibility of finding a well-paid internship in the legal sector once they are further ahead in their studies. Until then, they will need to deploy alternative strategies to pay their expenses.

Part-time jobs were an obvious way for lower-class students to survive. However, the amount of time that my informants spent working was usually inversely proportional to their academic performance. Jamerson, realizing this, decided to live on savings gathered by working for several years as a shop assistant at Lojas Americanas, a popular multistore chain. Although he knew that his financial autonomy would last for only two semesters, he resolved to quit his job and improve his performance, which he successfully achieved. Many other students, however, tried to keep part-time, low-paid jobs in order to contribute to the family income. To make her academic dream possible, Glória had to work as a telemarketer for NET, a broadband provider, from 2.30 P.M. until 9.30 P.M. except on weekends. She usually arrived at home, on the periphery of Caxias (Baixada Fluminense), at 11 P.M., had something to eat and studied until 1 A.M. In the morning she had to get up at 4.30 A.M. to be at university at 7 A.M. Flávia, as I mentioned earlier, enjoyed a better situation. She worked only at weekends in a community sports center, the Vila Olímpica of Fazenda Botafogo. However, her situation was not completely reassuring as she constantly questioned her chances of financial survival during the course, and her mother's employment was precarious.

I do not deny that some quota informants displayed better resource situations, which usually coincided with the fact that both parents contributed to the household income, as I noticed in the cases of Daisy and Eliane. Another first-year law quota informant, Thalita, whose mother works as a maid for a middle-class family in Volta Redonda,[17] had her studies sponsored by her mother's employer. This family was in fact covering most of Thalita's costs relating to university, including her stay in local student accommodation (*república*) in nearby Maracanã. This is a form of *apadrinhamento* (sponsorship) that often links lower-class workers (most commonly female cleaners) with their employer's household (Goldstein, 2003: 83, 89). Having said this, the social context from which these luckier students came was always relatively vulnerable.

In general, many similarities can be seen between the social profile of quota students in the Law Department and the concept of *batalhadores* (class fighters) coined by Jessé Souza (2010) to describe a new kind of Brazilian working class, which strives for social mobility through hard work and perseverance. Souza distinguishes this group not only from the proper middle class but also from the *ralé* (rabble), the very marginal sectors of the social ladder. What differentiates the *batalhadores* from the most depressed social strata is not clearly financial capital but, more crucially, their hope for social change accompanied by perseverant lifestyle strategies, a solid networking, and a set of moral habits that help these people to achieve their dreams. Because of such motivation and entrepreneurialism, the *batalhadores* would be the groups that better make the most of policies of social promotion and redistribution. Unlike the middle class, on the other hand, *batalhadores* are still steeped in social uncertainty; this is due to financial scarcity and precarious cultural capital, something that would easily undermine lower-class people's motivation, convincing them about the actual impossibility of escaping marginality. The typical profile of the *batalhadores*, as Souza defends, is that of people who often study at night and accept facing underpaid and extenuating job shifts in order to save money, which they will reinvest in strategies of social mobility. If middle-class families quite simply tend to expect their kids to finish undergraduate studies, while also spending significant portions of their time for leisure, the social expectations that surround young lower-class people are normally of a very different kind. Lower-class youngsters are encouraged to enter very early exploiting sectors of the job market, in order to contribute to the family income or leave the household; their involvement in education is often considered by the family to be a waste of subsistence resources that will not bring anything good to the group. A similar description fits well the majority of my informants, even though it is not always clear when these lower-class people that strive for social mobility can be clearly separated from the *ralé*, which sometimes characterizes family and neighborhood patterns of *batalhadores* students. These *batalhadores* of a *ralé* background have to overcome additional obstacles in comparisons to those from families where spirit and strategies of social mobility are already relatively diffused and where there is a more encouraging environment for the life projects of members.

While, by following Souza, the peculiarity of *batalhadores* relies more on an analysis of social habits and cultural environment than on income, the quantitative socioeconomic gaps between quota and wealthier nonquota students at the UERJ can be broadly imagined by looking at the social indexes related to the neighborhoods/municipalities where these groups are largely from (table 2.2).

Table 2.2 Socioeconomic data about some of the neighborhoods (and municipalities) of provenance of *cotistas* (including other municipalities) and about some of the neighborhoods of provenance of non-*cotistas* in the first year of law in 2007–2008

Typical neighborhoods of provenance of law *cotistas*	Life expectancy at birth (years)	Adult literacy rate (%)	School attending rate (%)*	Per capita income in 2000 (*reais*)	Human Development Index (IDH)
Acarí	63.93	91.68	79.44	174.12	0.720
Guadalupe	70.11	97.27	85.58	336.58	0.810
Santa Cruz	65.52	93.19	79.82	206.23	0.742
Campo Grande	69.80	95.98	87.42	351.11	0.810
Bangú	68.78	95.45	82.95	296.55	0.794
Compl. Alemão	64.79	89.07	72.04	177.31	0.711
Inhaúma	70.64	96.39	86.56	324.30	0.810
Pavuna	69.27	95.96	85.51	286.38	0.790
Jacarepaguá	67.51	90.18	77.14	331.44	0.769
Cosmos	67.51	94.86	82.17	205.90	0.759
Other municipalities[†] of provenance of law *cotistas*					
Nova Iguaçú	–	–	–	–	0.762
Nilópolis	–	–	–	–	0.788
Seropédica	–	–	–	–	0.759
São Gonçalo	–	–	–	–	0.782
Belfor Roxo	–	–	–	–	0.742

(*Continued*)

Table 2.2 Continued

Typical neighborhoods of provenance of law cotistas	Life expectancy at birth (years)	Adult literacy rate (%)	School attending rate (%)*	Per capita income in 2000 (reais)	Human Development Index (IDH)
Typical neighborhoods of provenance of law wealthier students					
Ipanema	78.68	98.92	107.98	2465.45	0.962§
Leblón	79.47	99.01	105.18	2441.28	0.967
Gávea	80.45	98.08	118.13	2139.56	0.970
Copacabana	77.78	98.48	107.54	1623.42	0.956
Botafogo	78.25	98.46	113.01	1376.47	0.952
Flamengo	77.91	99.28	119.08	1781.71	0.959
Laranjeiras	77.84	98.74	115.98	1679.22	0.957
Jardím Botánico	77.84	98.71	104.89	1952.77	0.957
Barra da Tijuca	77.84	99.38	110.09	2488.47	0.959
Vila Isabel	73.46	97.16	100.89	931.25	0.901
Tijuca	75.04	98.02	107.38	1204.61	0.926
Maracanã	77.91	98.91	113.97	1206.73	0.944

* Reference value used 100 percent.
† Data PNUD (2000). http://pt.wikipedia.org/wiki/Anexo:Lista_de_bairros_do_Rio_de_Janeiro_por_IDH .
§ For a comparative view of IDH: Iceland (0.969), Canada (0.966), Switzerland (0.960), United States (0.956), Gabon (0.729), Sri Lanka (0.743), Algeria (0.748), and Iran (0.771). Data PNUD (2000).
Source: IBGE. Tabela 1172—Índice de Desenvolvimento Humano Municipal (IDH), por ordem de IDH, segundo os bairros ou grupo de bairros—2000. http://pt.wikipedia.org/wiki/Anexo:Lista_de_IDH_dos_bairros_do_munic%C3%ADpio_do_Rio_de_Janeiro.

Dreams and Surviving at University: The Influence of Family Networks and Gender

Flávia mentioned that one of her main goals was to provide her mother, Helen, with a better life. Helen, in fact, worked only two days a week as a *funcionária* (civil servant) in a public hospital. Although the name of the post in English may be deceiving, this word is also often used in Brazil to refer to unskilled positions such as cleaners or doorkeepers in public institutions. Flávia was particularly concerned because Helen was not even entitled to health insurance through her work. As in most cases among *cotistas*, Flávia's mother had been left by her husband when Flávia was a little girl. Helen became the head of the household, facing a precarious financial situation. Flávia's father, a bus driver and *pagode*[18] player, started a new family with another woman and contributed almost nothing to his daughter's care. "When I asked him for financial help for university, he told me that he has to provide for his new family and that my mother and I have to sort our lives out (*ele falou que temos de nos virar sozinhas*) . . ." Flávia complained. A female-headed household was a typical situation for my lower-class informants, with worse circumstances when the head of the household was an Afro-Brazilian woman like Helen, with few technical skills to use in the job market (Lovell, 1999: 149–150; Goldani, 1999: 193).

Although the university's socioeconomic questionnaire is not devised to highlight this aspect of students' lives, family structure and contact with both parents may become indirectly visible in other ways, for example, when a relatively significant number of quota students do not know the education level of their fathers, but have better knowledge of their mothers'. This, in my view, suggests that many students do not have frequent contact with their fathers, with figures that can be broken down by opening and course (table 2.3).

In the accounts offered by students, their mothers were described as people to protect and empathize with. It was not by chance that Flávia and other female students decided to study law and that their decision was clearly gendered. In this sense, law is not only seen as a chance for social mobility but also, as Flávia told me, as "a way to avoid other people taking advantage of us and violating our rights, two vulnerable women" (*para que ninguém se aproveite de nós, duas mulheres sozinhas*).

At the same time as empathizing with the vulnerability of their mothers (or that of female relatives and neighbors), Flávia and other students want to take a very different pathway. They look for financial independence from men and see decisional power as an important

Table 2.3 Socioeconomic data about classified candidates in vestibular 2008 (NR: total number of respondents to each question by category and course)

	Nonquota	(NR)	Pub. sch. quota	(NR)	Black quota	(NR)
% students who did not know the educational levels of their fathers						
Law	0%	(145)	11%	(66)	21%	(58)
Education	11%	(302)	15%	(27)	8%	(12)
% students who did not know the educational levels of their mothers						
Law	0%	(145)	2%	(66)	3%	(117)
Education	3%	(303)	7%	(27)	0%	(16)

goal, something that Helen and others like her could not really achieve. While for lower-class boys, social mobility was more typically described as a general way to achieve a better life and become reliable breadwinners, for girls this was consistently seen as a way to shift unequal gender relations, which they had often experienced in their households. "For girls, access to university is extremely important," Daisy said, "because, in the end, it's always the man who leaves the household." In relation to this, a significant fact is that all female quota students in the first-year law class were childless and did not live with a partner (*não casadas*).[19] During interviews, most informants highlighted their single and nonparental status as a *sine qua non* to achieve their professional life projects. "Most girls of my age in the Baixada," Daisy stated, "are already married with kids. If I was in the same situation I could not be studying here."[20]

This information suggests the importance of data about motherhood in relation to age, school, and class (Heilborn et al., 2002; Almeida et al., 2006; Goldani, 1999).[21] Heilborn et al. (2002: 17) discuss that while the general fertility rate in Brazil dropped between 1965 and 1995 (from six children per woman to just two), the adolescent fertility rate increased its share of total fertility from 7.1 percent in 1970 to 14.1 in 1991. These authors also analyze the different impact that adolescent parenthood has in terms of schooling over gender in different social classes (particularly affecting lower-class women). In a similar vein, Almeida, Aquino, and de Barros (2006) argue that motherhood is the first reason for lower-class women to leave their studies. The same pattern is not really observed among women of school age whose per capita family income exceeds the national minimum salary (180 *reais* in 2006) or among young women whose mothers have completed at least secondary education. In addition, among less deprived class groups, it is observed that women have their first experience of sexual intercourse later in life and that they are more likely to have an abortion in the case of an adolescent pregnancy, while eventual childbirth will not greatly affect their educational and professional trajectory. Furthermore, Almeida, Aquino, and de Barros (2006) show that women with lower school education are in any case more likely to have babies in their teens. This would suggest that schooling, along with better income, has an effective impact in preventing adolescent pregnancies. To complete the picture, these authors demonstrate that people with an irregular school trajectory are more likely to be black (or brown), even when the class variable is kept steady. These data can be useful when combined with

Goldani's observations (1999) that black and brown young women are more subject to adolescent motherhood (18.3 and 19.9 percent, respectively) than white young women (13.8 percent). It can therefore be deduced that quota students often represent an exception within their class and racial/color group, and it becomes quite understandable why few of them have children.[22]

Another factor that deserves some attention is age. All the previous considerations about the different social status of quota and nonquota students are in fact reflected by the age at which they manage to enter a public university. According to socioeconomic data of vestibular 2007, there is about a three-year age difference between quota and nonquota freshmen in the Law Department at the UERJ (the average is 21.97 and 18.30 for these groups, respectively). This gap is even more significant when taking into account gender, and especially when looking at the difference between the average ages of female nonquota students (17.75) and male quota students (23.37). These data are probably explained by the greater effort that quota students have to make in order to prepare for and pass the entrance examination, and to save enough money to survive during courses. Alternatively, the gender gap might be justified by the fact that, as some informants argued, female students are more studious, or by the fact that the male labor force is more immediately required by the market and is more crucial to household survival than women's less paid work. Some students confirmed that girls are allowed to stay in the family for a longer time (and therefore presumably allowed to study), while boys are encouraged to become breadwinners or to otherwise leave the household. A hypothesis confirmed by the interview process at the UERJ anyway shows that some among the more persevering girls and boys manage to go back to their studies after several years of underpaid jobs and hard preparation.

University socioeconomic data and interviews highlighted that quota students are usually the first members of their family to have access to university. The attitude of the family in relation to the student's enrolment at the UERJ, however, seems to be ambiguous. Flávia, like many *cotistas*, stated that most of her relatives discouraged her from applying to university.

> In their view, I was wasting my time because getting into a public university and doing law was impossible for people like us. Nobody believed in me. My father was particularly against it because I decided to quit my job to study for the vestibular exam. He said I was crazy and that he would never help me . . .

In this sense, Flávia represents a typical example of a *batalhadora* (Souza, 2010) who is striving to emerge from a *ralé* environment with which she does not identify in terms of life projects and which, at least in a first instance, actually works as a constraint to her dreams. This situation, however, was subverted when Flávia passed the admission examination. When this happened, all the extended family (father, aunts, and grandmother) suddenly became relatively supportive. They even started offering occasional small contributions for the purchase of books or the payment of household bills, making Flávia's life easier. This pattern, which I observed in relation to many other quota students, shows that after overcoming the discouraging process exerted by the family, lower-class students may become a sort of collective investment for the entire group. On passing the vestibular, many students become a reason for pride and an example for other young family members. Flávia, for example, was asked to counsel her aunt when one of her cousins had legal problems. In addition, she advised several members of her family about their studies. This increased popularity in terms of status, however, is often accompanied by skepticism about the course choice, unless it is promising in terms of job prospects like in Flávia's case.

Ultimately, social networks in the family are indispensable for student survival at university. Although the vulnerability of the household might in itself represent an incentive for change, motivational and financial help is crucial. The structure of the household, in this sense, is not a completely neutral factor. From interviews, I noticed that even in those cases where both parents or other relatives financially contributed to the household, law *cotistas* were often the only child, or had only few siblings. In cases where the family household was large, on the other hand, *cotistas* usually had close older relatives and siblings who could play the role of breadwinners in the household. This condition more easily allowed for family investment in the education of a younger member. The help received from upper-class patrons and local churches also emerged as a relevant factor.

"The poor need God to buy": the Role of Neo-Pentecostal Churches in the Social Ascension of Quota Students

One aspect that struck me in relation to the quota students is that most of them had some involvement with Pentecostal and neo-Pentecostal churches, commonly understood as *igrejas evangélicas*, as opposed to more historical protestant churches such as Baptist, Methodist, and Presbyterian churches. Pentecostalism is a derivation of classic Protestantism and was imported to Brazil from the United States at the beginning of the last century. Its main doctrinal pillar is believers' direct experience of the Holy Spirit after baptism.

A number of social scientists have dealt with the spread of Pentecostal and neo-Pentecostal movements among low social strata in Rio de Janeiro and Brazil (Ireland, 1991; Mariz, 1994 and 2000; Lehmann, 1996; Burdick, 1998; Souza, 2010), although the phenomenon has also interested Latin America in general (Escobar and Alvarez, 1992). In the suburbs of Rio de Janeiro, these faiths seem nowadays to represent a large proportion of total church involvement, although they are more or less present all over the metropolitan area (including in wealthy Zona Sul). In this regard, Flávia stated that of ten churches she could think of in Fazenda Botafogo, eight of them were *evangélicas*, whereas only two were Catholic. This presence is strikingly visible on the street and in more private spaces. For example, I noticed stickers of the "I am evangelical" sort outside several doors in the block of flats where Flávia lives.

Most literature about Pentecostalism in Brazil highlights the connection between these religions and social mobility, a fact that is extremely important for my study and which I cannot avoid mentioning. Since all quota informants agreed that evangelical churches generally were a lower-class phenomenon, I was interested in exploring why. According to Glória, a first-year law quota student, "It's because the poor need God to buy, the rich don't. When the rich want something they just go to the shop and they will have it. Am I wrong (*não é isso*)?" Mesquita (2007) and Alvito (2001) mentioned that many neo-Pentecostal churches (in particular the *Igreja Universal do Reino de Deus*—IURD) champion the "theory of prosperity" (*teoria da prosperidade*). Unlike traditional Lutheran asceticism, where heaven is guaranteed by material renouncement, the theory of prosperity defends the idea that adepts can achieve economic well-being in their earthly lives (Mesquita, 2007: 131). In this sense, followers do not have to renounce the desire to improve their lives in a material way; they are instead encouraged to be economically proactive (Mesquita, 2007). I attended some ceremonies in the IURD Catedral da Fé in Del Castilho in Rio de Janeiro, and realized how much emphasis was given to money during sermons. Poverty and illnesses were described as being the result of distance from God, a distance that followers might narrow not only by behaving morally and attending church, but also by giving. The idea of giving is that, in order to receive from God, believers should donate to the church a *dízimo*, which corresponds to a tenth of their monthly income. The donation is in theory voluntary but is more practically treated as God's law (Mesquita, 2007: 125–126). The *dízimo* may even create family problems, especially regarding family members who are not *crentes* (believer, evangelical). Helen, Flávia's mother had found out that, at a time when she and her daughter did not even have the money to pay the bills (*que nem dava pra pagar as contas*), Flávia had made an offer of 70 *reais* to her church, the Renovated Baptist Church. The two had argued animatedly. The episode was remembered with some hilarity and the account was followed by laughter during one of my visits to Fazenda Botafogo, although Flávia was still put out by the fact that her mother had invaded her privacy.

The theory of prosperity is often described as a form of adaptation of Pentecostalism to consumer society and is sometimes used to differentiate neo-Pentecostalism from original Pentecostalism, which is commonly said to put a stronger emphasis on moral conduct and downplays materiality. However, as Mesquita (2007: 119) argues, the theory of prosperity does not directly encourage wild consumption, but legitimates the human desire for material goods. In this sense, it is a way of moralizing desire (*o querer*), because not longing for material things is unrealistic and leads to demotivation. Neo-Pentecostal churches follow this pattern by emphasizing the concept of saving (*poupar*). In a way that is actually common to traditional Pentecostal groups, believers are encouraged to rationalize their expenses, investing in improving the household well-being and cutting out personal, unnecessary, and earthly items such as drinking, smoking, drugs, and gambling (Mesquita, 2007: 123). These are all aspects highlighted in Weber's analysis of Protestantism (2001), where material success is considered a sign of divine approval of people's moral and religious behavior, including aspects such as moderation, caution, self-control, and hard work. In fact, Pentecostal and neo-Pentecostal prosperity is not just an economic fact. It is rather a mixture of economic wealth, family well-being, health, and respect. This might also explain why students never talked in a greedy way of the money that the field of law could offer them. Their references to social mobility were usually quite controlled and indirect, for example, when students said that they had avoided specific undergraduate courses because these would keep them poor. The moderate approach that law *cotistas* have to money can be seen in the way they answered questions on this subject in the vestibular socioeconomic questionnaire (2008). At the question of whether applicants in law were encouraged to choose a specific career by the average salaries in that field, the percentage positive answers was lower for black (59 percent) and public school (60 percent) than for nonquota students (64 percent). These data surprised me, since during interviews and normal socializing, quota students clearly highlighted money aspects more than middle-class students. However, religious morals might encourage evangelical students to retain some moderation when asked about this subject.

In general, the existence of a sharp doctrinal distinction between Pentecostal and neo-Pentecostal churches is not always clear, as there are both similarities and differences within and between churches of the two groups. Souza (2010) however insists on two aspects that can help differentiate Pentecostal and neo-Pentecostal churches. One of them is the fact that neo-Pentecostal churches significantly rely on mediatic tools of communication and evangelization. The second is that neo-Pentecostalism tends to make emphasis in the magical power of faith to change the life of believers quite immediately, mixing magic and therapeutic elements that are clearly (albeit this is not officially recognized) drawn from Afro-Brazilian faiths such as *candomblé*; Pentecostalism would instead focus more on the change of the believers' future by a hard discipline in the present. Because of these characteristics, Souza also tends to describe neo-Pentecostalism as better feelings of hopelessness within the *ralé*, while Pentecostalism would be a more typical faith among the *batalhadores*. Premised that I identify the situation of many of my quota informants as something in-between *ralé* and *batalhadores*, especially due to the family cultural environment shaping the life of many of them, the distinction carried out by Souza broadly speaking fits the reality I studied but cannot be applied to it systematically. Many of my informants did frequent neo-Pentecostal churches such as Igreja Universal, even though they were generally uninterested in (or even criticized) the magic aspects of these faiths. In addition, a high number of informants had frequented many different churches across the time and seemed quite open to the possibility of changing again.

Having provided these clarifications, I suspect that there is a reciprocal positive interaction between idealized moral precepts, dreams of moving up, and faith. This faith, it is worth saying, was found in the church even when the family seemed to be skeptical about the success of the students' academic dreams. As Flávia said, "At a time when nobody in my family believed in me and I felt like giving up, the people of the church gave me a lot of strength and support. Some of them were also studying at university and were sympathetic towards me." In some cases, this support was not limited to general motivation but also implied material support, as mentioned by Glória.

"The church helped in several ways. It wasn't just a fact of faith. When I had to stop working to prepare for the vestibular exam and my mom was unemployed, the church provided a *cesta básica* (family food basket) for a while. We could at least live on that." Especially in neo-Pentecostalism, an immediate strength is given by the rationalization of finances and the reallocation of the household budget to more important items. Mesquita shows that most of those interviewed used this logic to invest in long-term projects, such as the house, or on gathering savings to be spent for emergencies. These religions encourage improving life, starting from the consolidation of the actual scarce resources owned. Improvement should be done sensibly while avoiding biting off more than one can chew (*não dar um passo maior que a perna*), for example, without getting into impossible debt. While the theoretical and practical interpretations of these precepts vary among believers (many of them tend to bite off more than they can chew, hoping that God will understand), the link between this orientation and that of the Weberian ethic of capitalism is clear. This fits a concept of social mobility through honest hard work and rational planning. The efforts my student informants make in order to be at university, in my view, should also be understood in these terms: a form of Christian *prosperidade*.

There are also other points that might justify relations between my informants' social backgrounds and evangelical religions. First, the church becomes an important space for leisure in poor neighborhoods (Mesquita, 2007; Souza, 2010), and also a cultural and educational opportunity in the absence of cultural alternatives. This concept was mentioned clearly by Flávia:

> When I joined the church, I liked the environment there. I was taught the Bible. I read it and discussed it with the other people. We also talked about philosophical things like theology, and other stuff like general social problems . . . There is no theatre or other cultural places here. The closest cinemas just screen very stupid and commercial films . . .

The Catholic Church, on the other hand, does not seem a valid option because it exerts less control over people's souls and is more flexible about attendance. "The Catholic Church is different . . . nobody explains anything there; nobody cares if you go or you don't go to church. This is why people generally say that they are Catholic when they don't go to church (Flávia). When explaining the strong presence of Pentecostal churches in their neighborhoods, students also pointed out the problem of vulnerable social situations in those areas, along with the opportunities for redemption and recognition offered by religion. Considering the impact of drug dealing and criminality in the suburbs, Pentecostal groups carried out very important social work by improving the self-esteem of the marginal and carrying out a moralization mission.[23] As Glória said, "These churches are open and offer redemption to people of any sort, even prostitutes, criminals . . . the Pastor says to them, 'look, God is asking you to do this and that' . . . so they suddenly feel important and good as they have never felt in their lives." In other cases, the church was more clearly described as a chance for socializing by avoiding the street (*a rua*), which is full of risks and bad role models (Souza, 2010). The *rua* is often associated with various bad habits that might lead people to social failure.

> I started to go to church because there was nothing else to do where I live. What else could I do? I never liked wandering in the street (*ficar na rua*). People of my age are involved in the drug traffic . . . they want the easy money. They are into *funk* [music], they drink and go for women. I never thought to follow that way (*nunca quis pegar esse caminho*) because it leads you to nothing. That's like a spiral; it's going to kill you (*isso vai acabar contigo*). (Jamerson)

Note that the idea of *funk*, the favela music that has little to do with US funk, is associated in common imagery with a number of other bad habits like drinking, drug dealing, and casual sex. These are all things—among others—that evangelical churches consider as expressions of the devil (*coisa do diabo*) and earthly (*coisa do mundo*). In my specific ambit of analysis, these temptations would trap people into a negative cycle that, in one way or another, would keep them from long-term and more decent projects such as university. The contrast between the easy money of the drug traffic, which leads to failure, and the money that comes from hard work and sacrifice should be noted. This can be implicitly embodied by the university project and by a Christian kind of morality. Students like Jamerson expressed these concepts through a direct knowledge of their reality. During my fieldwork, Jamerson was concerned about the fact that his 15-year-old brother spent too much time on the street. This boy was killed one year after I left Brazil, apparently due to his involvement with local petty criminality in São Gonçalo.

The risky model that Jamerson describes is valid not just for boys, the ones who are more typically and directly involved in the traffic, but also for girls, subject to becoming the bandits' women in popular imagination. In fact, the image of women portrayed by *funk* is never very rewarding. Not only do lyrics describe women as lascivious and completely sex-addicted, or as bitches (*cachorras*), but the outfit that girls are expected to wear for *funk* music concerts (*os bailes funk*) is very provocative, displaying their legs as well as the curves of their breasts and bottoms very distinctly. The sexual lasciviousness symbolized by *funk*, mixed with alcohol, drugs, and criminality, not only hampers moral respectability in the view of some informants, but is often associated with risks of unwanted pregnancies and paternities. Several female quota students complained that *funk* depicts women as sexual objects, something that for them is in contradiction to the image of honest, highly professional workers and breadwinners they are trying to build through their university careers.[24] Pentecostal churches, in this sense, become a strong ally due to their emphasis on morality, hard work, family, and postponing sex until after marriage.[25]

Nonetheless, none of my informants claimed to follow all religious precepts in a particularly strict way. As a possible consequence, many of them moved constantly in and out of a stable involvement with church groups. These students seemed much more flexible than the official position of their churches on premarital sex, as well as tolerance of homosexuality and leisure. Leisure, in particular, for many Pentecostal groups should be limited to religious activities, demonizing earthly things such as samba music and dancing in general. Informants seemed to use such precepts as an ideal model that, despite representing something good, can be negotiated, maybe so far as it does not represent a constraint to their moving up project. Many informants actually highlighted negative aspects of the church and even made fun of it ("We're evangelical . . . you know . . . that religion that steals money from people . . ."). Some of them declared that they used religion in their own way (*do jeito deles*) and concluded that this is normal because, as Eliane said, in the end, "no religion is perfect." In this sense, religion is not passively absorbed. It is strategically adapted by students in their process of social ascension, keeping people on the right path to social mobility and helping them resist in a hard place.

"UERJ: A (PUBLIC) DREAM IN MY LIFE"— WHEN STATE MEANS SOCIAL PRESTIGE

On Orkut, the ultrapopular online Brazilian social network, where most students display their profiles, keep in touch, and post photos online, Thalita writes: "UERJ: my present, my future. Law at UERJ— the best in Rio" (*Direito UERJ: a melhor do Rio*). This heading is accompanied by the logo of the university in this student's photo section. Next to the UERJ logo, there is an interior shot of the university (with the building ramps clearly visible) captioned "UERJ, a dream in my life" (UERJ, *um sonho na minha vida*). Most law quota students described their presence at UERJ as a dream. Eliane, for example, had failed to get into law at UERJ in the past and had had to divert to a less prestigious private university for a year.

> Any time I passed UERJ by train I got sad because I knew that UERJ is the best . . . the private university (*a particular*) was OK . . . more or less . . . but you know, it was here that I wanted to be. It might be that the building is run down, and that the institution is constantly on strike, but UERJ is UERJ!

For lower-class students, the UERJ is not just a good university; it is soaked in additional symbolism. Despite its many possible defects, the UERJ is public and, as a public institution, it represents the state, a body that has often looked away from certain metropolitan areas. In this sense, the UERJ is not just a possible step to a better life, but also a way to shift hierarchical patterns of human geography in the city through a personal experience of national (public) communion. This fact can be exemplified by Flávia's dream to leave her neighborhood for something better, but also by the fact that entrance to a public university, among good-quality universities, was traditionally and paradoxically more difficult to achieve for lower-class students. It can thus explain why public university clearly had more prestige than private academic institutions at the eyes of these students. On the other hand, it is important to stress that the something better that Flávia is looking for is not imagined through collective empowerment of a suburban community, Fazenda Botafogo. It might happen, instead, through the physical approximation of suburban individuals to an idealized "center." This is represented by areas that count more in the city such as the administrative and historical city center, and also by the middle-class residential and leisure areas in Zona Sul. Lower-class neighborhoods, in contrast, are seen as a peripheral space that excludes one from wealth, information, and prestige; a sort of trap, which is well reflected by the low-paid jobs to which Flávia and other students had felt condemned.

Roberto da Matta (1983) describes Rio de Janeiro's Carnival as a ritual of temporary subversion in a country where places in the social pyramid are highly crystallized. It is (only) during Carnival, the author explains, that underpaid *empregadas* (house-cleaners) and anonymous low-profile workers manage to distinguish themselves as awesome queens of the parades or skillful *passistas* (samba dancers).

Access to university may have some parallels with this subversion of hierarchy, but in a way that could be more concrete and durable than a Carnival dream. What quota students aim at through a university degree is not a temporary evasion of reality but a search for a stable, better place in society.

The particular relation between *cotistas* and the state is also underlined by the kinds of jobs that these students would like to pursue in the future. A significant number of students mentioned that they were interested in achieving a good position in the police or in getting institutional positions with high symbolic status such as *defensores públicos* (public attorneys), *promotores de justiça* (lawyers who defend society against major social offences), *procuradores* (public prosecutors), and *desembargadores* (high court judges). This peculiarity of the *cotistas* was noticed and highlighted by some nonquota students and teachers, often becoming an element of differentiation between lower-class and middle-class students. As Victor, a final-year nonquota student, said,

> *Cotistas* are usually interested in these [aforementioned] public positions. These jobs might be less well-paid than others in the private sector, for example as solicitors in big companies; however, their prestige is higher. I think these positions would make lower-class students feel more important, probably because of the vulnerable social environment where they come from.[26]

There is a related point that I would now like to address. For lower-class students, the symbolic status of studying at the UERJ is not simply in having access to places that represent the state. In fact, the public schools where many of these students previously studied had often become a reason for stigma and exclusion by automatically disclosing their lower social condition. The UERJ's higher symbolic status is increased by the fact that this space has been traditionally disputed by the middle and middle-upper class, and was quite exclusively occupied by the elite. Quota student Zezinho, at the time of research in his second year, highlighted how the fact of studying law at the UERJ made him feel more welcome and respected everywhere. He mentioned that a couple of weeks earlier he had wanted to buy tickets for a major football match but he did not have his identity card with him, as was technically needed for the purchase.

> The man [at the counter] said that in that case he could not sell me the ticket (*a entrada*). So, without many expectations, I showed him my library card . . . I didn't even think it could be useful . . . but at that

point he smiled and said "gosh, man, you study at UERJ!" and he sold me the ticket. You know, people give a lot of importance to it. I'm sure that if I had showed the library card of a minor private university[27] (*uma particular*) the reaction would have been totally different.

This idea, in my view, somehow recalls the distinction that Roberto da Matta (1983) makes about the transition from being an "individual" to becoming a "person." Individuals are people who are undifferentiated in the mass collective to which the law is applied (often unfairly), while persons can exert power through authority and are therefore easily distinguishable from others because they matter. As persons, these people also have access, among other things, to shortcuts and little favors (the popular *jeitinho*) that they would not enjoy in other conditions. Transferred to my informants' context, the meaning of this passage relates instead to a more permanent acquisition of citizenship through social mobility. This citizenship, in my view, does not simplistically fit a universal ideal of being equal citizens. It also specifically means achieving what the middle class has traditionally represented, not just in terms of money but also in terms of prestige and respectability. Nonetheless, the importance of the "public" as an agent creator of status is less striking unless it provides real chances for social mobility. As Daisy said, "[P]eople will by all means prefer to do law at the Estácio (one of the low-standard private universities) rather than studying literature or education at UERJ." This is also why the students I interviewed in less competitive departments at the UERJ seemed to be much less confident about the opportunities of social mobility that university could open to them. Most of these students hoped to move to more prestigious courses in the future. However, in the meantime, they appreciated the differential academic and symbolic capital that a degree in education or social work could bring them, at least within their community of origin.

3

Race between the Class Rows

Urban Encounters and Dis-encounters in the Changing University Space

During my stay in Rio de Janeiro, I often heard that one of the effects of Brazil's racial cordiality is not just its racially mixed population, but also the presence of rich and poor, black and white people within the same spaces. Consequently, any relations between race and use of city space have been somewhat minimized in Rio de Janeiro, aside from the study of more stereotypically racially segregated settings such as the favelas (Oliveira, 2000; Vargas, 2006; Campos, 2006) and the suburbs (Burdick, 1998), or Telles's (2004) comparative research on Brazilian metropolitan segregation.

When I saw black people crowding in São Salvador Square in wealthy Zona Sul, the area where I lived, they were seldom dwellers of the surrounding buildings. Most of them were actually beggars, carers of white elderly, nannies, house-cleaners, shop assistants in the high-class supermarket Zona Sul, street vendors, couriers, and other low-skilled workers. When I asked friends of mine where these people might live, they simply pointed to the nearby small favelas (Morro Azul and Santo Amaro) or the suburbs. If black people actually are dwellers in São Salvador Square, they are exceptions, able to surprise those who are not prepared for their presence. A visiting female friend of mine, for example, almost fainted when bumping into a young black man on the floor of my flat, just outside the elevator. She had mistaken a legitimate tenant for a mugger. The man was dressed according to his middle-class social status and nothing in his outfit looked unusual for a dweller of that building, but for his impressive dreadlocks. In addition, it would have been extremely difficult for an intruder to enter the building without the doorman opening the gate, asking the identity of the visitor, and finally double-checking this information with a dweller. My friend apologized for her feelings but admitted that she did not expect to find a black man (*um negão*) on my floor. The gender of the mistaken mugger is not irrelevant. While middle-class buildings in Zona Sul pullulate with black *empregadas* (housemaids) who hardly scare anybody, the circulation of black men in middle-class spaces is less common, unless their presence in that space can be explained, for example, as builders or other service providers. This expected racial pattern of which my friend gave a spontaneous example sums up a set of social expectations that too often link black men (especially those of a young age) with crime and black women with domestic service in Brazil. These expectations do not necessarily come just from middle-class and white people; they are often confessed by lower-class and black ones also. Such admissions usually come from speakers with a sense of guilt, but they also explain that this is, unfortunately, something naturally running through their heads.[1]

Segregation and racial exclusion patterns should not necessarily be studied by searching for ghettos. Segregation is anything that departs from totally random distribution, and even then, the question becomes about the class- and race-based differentiations within spaces where this distribution exists. Unequal distribution can therefore be found in apparently neutral or mixed locations such as shops, middle-class buildings and flats, means of transport, and streets, where people of different backgrounds and phenotypes circulate and interact. A question, however, is what different people do in those spaces (Freeman, 2002) and how they are distributed there. State public universities in Rio de Janeiro may represent a peculiar example of these diverse locations, especially after quotas increased the access of black and lower-class students to these places and black people do not massively crowd exclusively the security and cleaning jobs at the university. From the first week of my fieldwork at the UERJ, I observed my place of study (the university, the classroom) as a reflection of the unequal urban context in which it is inscribed, with its entire, implicit burden of social unbalances. This discourse is not a simple one, though. At the same time that it reflects unequal spheres of the city, the university is being changed by quotas and in this sense challenges naturalized views of the city itself, and social expectations about the people living there.

If on the one hand the UERJ mirrors Rio de Janeiro, on the other hand it does not reflect it at all. It stands as a utopia, an almost unreal place, where people of different social backgrounds and phenotypes share and use the same space, not along traditional employer-service provider patterns but as equals. It is thus interesting to explore what this artificial social encounter resulting from the quotas produces. On the one hand, the encounter highlights change; on the other, it suggests that change is not radical and sudden but is also apparent and contradictory in many of its early manifestations. It is therefore important to discuss the old and new aspects of Brazilian race relations that are unveiled in the framework of an institutional quota experience. As I will show, old and new aspects often appear intertwined and may consistently feed into each other. This fact hampers a linear understanding of what is really changing even though the change could be, in the end, really significant.

Classroom Geographies: Social Cityscapes in the Mirror

> The *Cones* are those things that you sometimes find when there are works on the road, to show you exactly where you have to pass. We [the *cotistas*] are called *Cones* because we are diligent in class . . . *Cones* are those who do everything very conscientiously (*os que fazem tudo direitinho*). (Eliane)

When I asked first-year law students about their socilizing process in the classroom, several of them asked me back whether I was able to perceive the physical division of the classroom collective into two different groups: the *Cones* (this standing for excessively zealous, swot) and the *Barbárie* (literally, Barbarians). Contrary to what most people might expect from these labels, students understood the division as one between *cotistas* and non-*cotistas*, respectively. What these labels more strikingly implied, instead, was a division between poor and wealthy, suburban and urban students. Lower-class *Cones* were, according to general understanding, those sitting in the first half of the classroom, that closer to the lecturer. Because of this, people also referred to them as *"os da frente"* (literally, those in the front). This term was often imperfectly replaced by *cotistas* even though not all these lower-class students had achieved an opening through the quota system. The wealthier students (the Barbarians) occupied the remaining rows and, consequently, they were identified and self-identified as *"os de atrás"* (those in the back).

When I asked quota and other lower-class students why they clustered at the front of the classroom space, they often explained this by their weaker educational background. They needed to focus on the lessons more than the other students in order to take notes properly and do well. *Cones* also claimed that "*os de atrás*," by and large from wealthy Zona Sul or other middle-class students, were noisy and disturbed their concentration. It is not by chance that this last group of students was called *Barbárie*, a term they eventually appropriated with evident pride. This socio-spatial division within the classroom was not only typical of first-year law students; it was widely visible across all departments and in other elite programs, while it appeared more ambiguously in less prestigious courses where the majority was more consistently lower-class.[2] The observed pattern occurred sometimes with different terminologies and spatial distributions in other law groups. Among the second-year students, for example, lower-class students were not called *Cones* but *Nerds*.[3] In some law groups, in addition, students described the spatial division as occurring between the right and left sides of the room.[4] In the first weeks of the course, the *Cones* had to guarantee their place "in the front" very early in the morning (around 6.30 A.M.), and this even raised initial complaints from other students. *Cones*, in fact, also tended to save seats for lower-class peers who arrived later. After a few weeks, however, rows became implicitly owned according to a sort of common law and no further complaints were raised.

The terms *Cones* and *Barbárie* were appropriated by both groups, with meanings that went far beyond actual dedication to their courses and their quota status. The division was first perceived as a class one but also as geographical, since most *Cones* were from lower-class neighborhoods in Zona Norte, Baixada Fluminense, Zona Oeste, and São Gonçalo. *Barbárie* students, in contrast, were wealthier people from Zona Sul (Laranjeiras, Flamengo, Botafogo, Copacabana, Ipanema, and Leblon, among other places), Barra da Tijuca, and middle-class sectors of Niterói, a city on the other side of Guanabara Bay. Unlike the *Cones*, who were assumed to come from deprived public schools, but some of whom had also attended low-standard private institutions, most Barbarians had frequented exclusive private high schools and had managed to pass the admission examination without being affected by the reduction in openings caused by the quota system. The division thus came to reflect educational background and performance. In the first year, Barbarians scored the highest marks in the class, in spite of their apparent lack of dedication to the course and the naughty allusions implicit in the Barbarian label. The polarization between groups also worked by faith since a significant number of *Cones* declared themselves to be protestant (especially Pentecostal and neo-Pentecostal) while the almost totality of Barbarians described themselves as Catholic or nonpracticing. Both *Cone* and *Barbárie* students stated that they did not socialize much with people from the other group, nor did they apparently show any real curiosity about them. While it took me approximately one month in order to learn all the students' names (70–80 people), students from the two different groups still did not know each others' names after one semester (figure 3.1).

A number of social and academic parameters emerged in the process of differentiation between the two groups of students in the first-year law class. Reference to the dominant phenotype of the two groups in this sense was marginally made by informants, even though the Barbarians were prevalently white-looking, whereas a good number of the *Cones* looked brown or black. What I am describing here is obviously a generalization, and such statements pose anyway the question of how I could ever assess the color of the students, a very sensitive topic in a country where racial/color ascriptions are considered to be extremely subjective. I initially based my observations on my subjective process of categorization, which represented an observational beginning. Afterward, I came to rely totally on the color/race self-identification that students disclosed to me in person, or that they had ticked in the socioeconomic questionnaire at the time of the vestibular. Having said this, I observed that most of the darkest- and brownest-skinned students—girls above all—clustered around the

Figure 3.1 A group of informants at the UERJ.

very front row of the room. I could also say that about 80 percent of the people who at some point identified as black were sitting in the front, most of them in the first row or close to it, by the door. The remaining black students tended to occupy the very margins of the classroom, for example sitting individually or in small groups by the windows, or unnoticeable in the very back row, right behind the *Barbárie*, with whom they had no visible interaction. Such a racial division of space seldom appeared in the accounts of informants, according to whom the obvious division was actually based on class and opening type, as implicit in the model *Cones-Barbárie*. However, I observe that certain remarks scaled down the overpowering role of class at drawing social divisions; in fact, as a student pointed out, the actual distribution of black students in the classroom was not random, not even among the *Cones*:

> Black students are in the [very] front [rows]. However, there are some of them sitting at the margins of the class, by the door, or even hidden in the very back of the room, right behind the Barbarians . . . then, there is a group of three black girls who sit together by the window and—I can't say why—they don't relate to anybody else. (Gabriel, nonquota student, self-identified as lower-class and white)

Black-quota student Jamerson endorsed this view by defining the students at the classroom's edges, which he also occupied, as being more dark-skinned, poor, and shy. He added that even when they did not sit in the front, these students were still perceived as *Cones* since they managed to socialize only within this group, while being largely ignored by the spatially closer Barbarians.

A stronger and more politicized race relations reading of these data emerged when I discussed classroom spatial issues with law students who were politicized through the Black movement, most of them in their final academic years. In these cases, racial patterns were magnified, as Jurema shows:

> I've attended courses with people in different years and I can tell you that if you see a black person, there are always other blacks sitting next to him or her. This is because you won't sit close to somebody who might not accept you . . . people who, if you ask them the last word that you've missed in the lecture, pretend that you don't even exist . . . (Jurema, Denegrir militant)

Although I noticed a general division in the classroom space as roughly suggested by informants, and this reflected processes of differentiations that become relevant in the everyday-life shaping of social expectations and discrimination, my impression was that students tended to overemphasize differences through a simplified process of categorization. In particular, I noticed that a number of nonquota students sitting in the second row were naturalized as *Cones*, even if they were not *cotistas*. These students came from relatively good private schools and performed quite well, but were of modest backgrounds as was also made clear by their geographical origins (the suburbs), their outfits, and, more generally, by their spatial, social, and behavioral closeness to *cotistas* in the classroom. These students were identified and self-identified mostly as light brown or white.

Very few *cotistas* sitting in the first row self-identified or were identified as white within the class. Due to their social background, they spent most of their time with the other brown and black *cotistas* or, more generally, with other *Cones*. However, as will emerge more clearly later, they enjoyed slightly better status (or mobility) by stepping more easily into the middle-class social space. Some of these students also seemed to make greater efforts to match the middle-class group in terms of outfits. The few remaining white *cotistas*, presumably having a better income in comparison to the others, were actually absorbed straight away by the *Barbárie*. These students, however, were often identified by other *cotistas* as fake quota students who had studied in the best public high schools (especially Pedro II, Cap UERJ, and Cap UFRJ)[5] or who had managed to pass as black-quota students by self-declaration, even though they were light-skinned and therefore had little to do with the rest of the black *cotistas*.

These examples are not the only ones showing how imperfect the division of the classroom was, at least in comparison to students' generalizations. The fact that all *cotistas* were very dedicated, for example, was a kind of myth, although even less-studious *cotistas* were automatically considered *Cones*, or excessively disciplined, due to the physical space they occupied in the classroom and to their social network. The group of Barbarians, in addition, was also quite heterogeneous, divided into subgroups along lines of gender, dedication to the course, school of origin, and neighborhood provenance. For example, the students from the wealthy part of Zona Oeste, Barra da Tijuca, on deeper observation represented a group substantially separate from the Zona Sul crowd. A group of very studious Zona Sul girls also represented another separate block but still consistently interacted with the core Barbarians, namely, a group of naughty and cool guys (*playboyzinhos*) sitting in the back. However, having been explained these imperfections, I found the process of group polarization deployed by first-year law students very insightful. This was not only because their observations were not completely random or wrong, but also because this process reflected how certain stereotypes may be created and reproduced in everyday life, along with their implicit burdens of errors, drawbacks, and risks of essentialization. Similar processes of essentialization, in the end, may be used to explain why a black dweller in a middle-class space can often be mistaken for a servant or a thief, or why somebody with a look identified as *suburbano* or *favelado* might easily be expected to be intellectually deprived or involved in illicit activities. What struck me even more was how the social divisions observed in this and other classrooms quite faithfully reflected the social structures and distribution within the city. However, even this is a generalization, as while the pool of quota students was typically lower-middle or even extreme lower class, they were never completely deprived in terms of social, educational, or financial capital. In order to be at university, quota students needed to have a high-school degree and enough knowledge to pass the difficult entrance exam even if benefiting from quotas[6]; these students also had to count on supporting networks in their families or neighborhoods and, even more crucially, had to be exceptionally motivated for their studies and/or for social ascension.

Social Affinities and Symbolic Reversals: Socializing and Differentiation between Groups of Students

When I asked the *Cones* and the Barbarians why they tended to socialize only with people from the same group, they always pointed out that this depended on a process of internal affinities (*afinidades*) playing out within both groups, the kinds of physical and metaphysical places that students already occupied in Rio de Janeiro and which were reflected in the classroom's spatial distribution. Particular social conditions do not suddenly disappear in the apparently democratic space created by quotas, but emerge quite clearly in opposition to wealthier students. Stigmas are reproduced in the new context and even add to the identity of quota students as a separate group.

Gabriel stated that the main obstacles to intergroup socializing in the classroom were economic factors, which, according to him, were embodied in the geographical origin of students. In this sense, transport becomes one of the many representations of these affinities or differences because, as Gabriel said, "students with money don't go by train . . . the train is what poor people take (*trem é o que pobre pega*).

Those with money go by car, by tube or, perhaps, by bus." The train is in fact considered a typical form of transportation for poor people, connecting Central do Brasil in the center of Rio de Janeiro with the suburbs. It is therefore an expression of both class and geographical divides. Reference to transport as a dividing element was also made by students in less popular courses, such as education, where the student group is by far more socially homogeneous and typically less affluent than in the Law Department.[7]

> I don't see much division in my classroom . . . but sometimes wealthier people react in a strange way when I say that I go by train . . . when I said that, a colleague stared at me, almost horrified . . . she then wanted to point out to me that she goes by car instead . . . you know, it's as if she wanted to distance herself from me. (Regina, education)

In analyzing relations between *Cones* and *Barbárie*, Flávia and Daisy argued that they had made some effort to foster extragroup socializing, but they did not see any interest on the other side. As Flávia said, "[T]he problem is not about shutting ourselves out but about not being accepted . . . I tried to talk to 'them' but I didn't feel considered." She then jokingly added, "[C]an you see? This is not a pre-conception; it's a post-conception!" (*não é um pre-conceito; é um pós-conceito!*). "However," Flávia concluded self-critically, "I must confess that the poor are sometimes ashamed of their own condition."[8] Transport, again, emerges as a powerful metaphor of social distance:

> The other day, for example, the *Barbárie* people were organizing the *trote* [freshmen's prank day]. They needed sweets (*balas*) as material for the jokes . . . it was then when Eliane [quota student] offered to buy the *balas* on her way home, off the railway, because they are sold cheaper over there. She said that this would be easy for her since she and other students use the train every day. At that point, Rafael [another quota student] called her aside and said "Are you crazy? Why have you told them that we use the train?! Those guys are from [wealthy] Zona Sul!" (Flávia)

This is an example of how self-isolation and shyness may represent a defensive strategy by lower-class and especially quota people: being ashamed of being poor and less deserving, these students limit interaction with wealthier classmates because they were afraid of being discriminated against. These feelings are understandable, since many quota students enter university with the feeling of being in a place they do not really deserve and where they are not welcome.[9]

Further reasons were offered to explain the lack of socializing with wealthier students. On several occasions, for example, *cotistas* mentioned that nonquota students go to very expensive clubs and can even spend 150 *reais* in one night. "Some guys were saying that they go to clubs where drinks cost 15 *reais* . . . this is much more than my daily expenses for transport to university!" Jamerson stated. Daisy and Murillo, interestingly, made a detailed list of all the clubs in Zona Sul where wealthy students go, with annexed costs including admission fees, drinks, and transport. As for having meals at university, most quota students used the Restaurante Popular do Maracanã, a state canteen for poor and street people charging one *real* per meal (0.40 Euros at the time of my fieldwork), beside the popular football stadium. Alternatively, some quota students would reschedule their lunch for when they were back home in the evening. In addition, the few times quota students gathered outside the university, this happened in inexpensive venues. I sometimes joined them to visit free art exhibitions and museums in town, or to attend plays at affordable prices in the Banco do Brasil Cultural Centre. They also organized sporadic trips to the beach. Birthdays were often celebrated in modest but popular venues such as Parmé, off the Uruguaiana area, or in Norte Shopping, the most appealing shopping mall in the suburbs.

A number of authors have explored the use of jokes as the weapon of the weak. A classic example is James Scott's theory of hidden transcripts, or forms of indirect and subtle (if not unconscious) resistance different from organized political actions and uprisings. Similarly, Goldstein (2003) argues that laughter and black humor or irony from the oppressed is often the only way to resist, resignify, and deal with imbalances of power. These kinds of issues can also be explored with *cotistas* and their process of adaptation at university. For example, Eliane made her peers laugh several times by launching a fake campaign that addressed the solidarity of *Barbárie* students: "[P]lease, adopt a *cotista*! Take one of us to clubs (*leve um pra boate*)!" In spite of this being just a joke, tragicomic humor is often used to stress the way *cotistas* see and experience their financial distance from the middle class. Indeed, this is also a form of consolidating group identity as poor. Other references are made to the leisure time of nonquota students. Daisy and Yara, in this sense, laughed about the fact that three wealthy girls from their class had spent the Christmas holidays in France, while a number of other students had traveled abroad with their parents. This sounded like a joke to Yara. With ironic self-commiseration, she was reminded of how some *cotistas* had had to cancel their trip, organized far in advance, to the nearby town of Petropolis, because they could not find the money for the coach ticket.[10] Eliane's and Yara's jokes set out, at the same time as scaling down, difference by ridiculing the other or making their own situation less tragic (Goldstein, 2003).

Nonquota students were perceived as people with an easy life, who live in Zona Sul, studied in the most exclusive high schools, do not need to work to pay for their studies, and, indeed, do not use the train. Their parents were imagined as highly skilled professionals in the field of law, such as *procuradores públicos* (public prosecutors), *promotores de justiça* (lawyers who defend society against major social offences), or *desembargadores* (high court judges). In spite of this, I noticed that *cotistas* in general made a bigger effort to dress more formally. In contrast, many nonquota students dressed quite simply, and it was not unusual to see wealthy boys attending class in Bermuda shorts and flip-flops. Eliane confirmed my observations:

> *Eliane*: Something you'll see for sure in the class is that the poor dress better . . . whereas people from Zona Sul don't bother at all . . . They go very informally dressed (*largados*), wearing flip-flops (*chinelos*) and Bermuda shorts (*shorts*) . . . all beach stuff (*roupa de praia*) . . . Have you seen Carlos? Have you seen how he goes [badly] dressed? He lives in Ipanema [wealthy area]! And Laura . . . have you seen her? She's from Zona Sul as well. The poor go better dressed (*de outro jeito*). For example, look at how well-dressed Lucileidy is. She's from Nova Iguaçú [a poor area], in the Baixada [laughing] . . .
>
> *Me*: So, do you have any explanations for this?
>
> *Eliane*: Of course! It's enough that we are poor . . . can you imagine if we also went dressed poorly? What would people think of us? [in a very playful tone]

What Eliane pointed out is that quota students have to make the effort to overcome a number of stigmas when they start university. In this case, clothes were used by my lower-class informants to balance prejudices and to confer some legitimacy, at least in terms of outfit, to their presence in the academic setting.[11] This is just one factor, because formal dressing is also something encouraged by evangelical faiths as a symbol of Christian morality and *prosperidade*.[12] Other quota students, however, drastically reinterpreted Eliane's impressions. According to these other *cotistas*, a more formal clothing style does not necessarily balance the appearance gap between wealthy and poor students:

> What Eliane told you is just what it seems like! They [the Zona Sul boys] might even wear Bermuda shorts and flip-flops . . . but it's all

finely-branded stuff (*roupa grifada*). I can clearly see the difference between those who buy in proper shops (*nas lojas*) and those who do so in the *feirinha de São Gonçalo* [lower-class market in a poor area]! These [Zona Sul] girls have better-quality clothes . . . but it's not just that . . . they are lighter-skinned; they have good skin (*a pele é boa*) and finer features. They look better. If you don't see that, you're blind![13] (Glória)

When Flávia was explaining to me the way she came to socialize with the other quota students, she mentioned that she did not know how it had happened. "We did not know that we were *cotistas*, but a mysterious thread linked us . . . It's as if we spontaneously recognized each other," she said. Glória, instead, suggests that this happened due to the similar look of lower-class students, and that this may also relate to phenotype (as she also suggested in her aforementioned quote):

> *Glória*: The day we received the new freshmen,[14] Gabriel [lower-class student] looked at the new group; with his finger he pointed with high confidence at those who were *cotistas* and those who were not. Having a look at them was enough! You know . . . we even had a laugh, but it's actually sad . . .
> *Me*: So, what did they [the new *cotistas*] look like?
> *Glória*: They were people of humble profile . . . like us . . . with browner skin (*mais escuros*), people who don't talk very much (*calados*), shy, people who seemed to feel out of place (*fora de lugar*) . . .

Glória's accounts suggest that phenotype, and not just outfit, can be an important and at least more immediate and general difference in delimiting boundaries between (very broadly speaking) the *Cones* and the *Barbárie*. The reference to phenotype is always implicit and often silenced, but never completely hidden from observation. Eliane's statement that "the poor cannot go badly-dressed," after all, echoes the common saying that "a black person cannot go badly-dressed" (*negro não pode andar mal vestido*), or the similar saying "we are blacks but we're not pigs" (*somos negros mas não somos porcos*), as some black people stressed during my fieldwork to show how a nice outfit was important to them in order to fight stereotypes. According to Brazilian ideals of appearance, black people start from a very disadvantaged point. Outfit, as a consequence, is often used as a means to redress naturalized imperfections and partially rehabilitate people from specifically racial stigmas. If being lower-class is then penalizing, a dark phenotype is an amplifier or an aggravating factor of this constraint (Souza, 2010: 196).

The fact that race played an aggravating role in the construction of group affinities/differences among students could also be seen in the fact that the only black student among the Barbarians, formally a *cotista*, was highly gossiped about by *Cones* of all colors. *Cones* gossiped about how the profile picture of this student on Orkut[15] was on top of a very expensive motorbike, something he proudly described as his (*a minha moto*). Even though some other students in the *Barbárie* were *cotistas*, they were white and, consequently, much less gossiped-about by the *Cones*. In some cases, they referred to this black student as the "*cotista* of the *Barbárie*" or as "*o negro da Barbárie*" (the Barbarians' black). On the other hand, they must have felt a special and inexplicable affinity to this classmate, otherwise I could not explain why they seemed to be less affected by being ignored by the white Barbarians than by somebody who was much darker (*mais preto*) than most of them. The *Cones* had somehow perceived something bizarrely wrong and out of place in the location of this black student within the wealthier group. He was thus sometimes referred to as the slave (*o escravo*) of the other Barbarians. He would be the one who carries things (*o que carrega as coisas*), drives the car (*o motorista*), puts the music on at parties (*o DJ*), and does everything to please and amuse (*o palhaço*) his (white) Barbarian friends. Some students also joked about the fact that other Barbarians accepted this black colleague so they could show to the world that they were cool and tolerant. To complete the picture, some doubts circulated about whether this student was invited to the house of other middle-class peers, or whether the parents of middle-class girls (*patricinhas*) would be pleased to have him as a son-in-law. These comments reflected very imperfectly the class-based division that all students described as the real cause of missed socializing with the opposite group.

The case of the *negro da Barbárie* is certainly useful to question the popular saying that money whitens in Brazil. As Telles (2004: 98) argues, this rule often works imperfectly, especially when a phenotype does not look racially mixed and ambiguous enough to make the life of a person as easy as that of his white middle-class peers.[16] This means that there are contexts in which race is more clearly *not* disguised by class. The "*negro da Barbárie*" case is also crucial to the topic of jokes and their possible function to negotiate social differences. Students deployed differentiation from and approximation to this wealthier black student within a substantial process of negotiation with the other; in this case, like that of others, lower-class students interact with the object of laughter by pointing out the paradox of differences through a mixture of ironic self-commiseration and certain hilarity about this person's power and privileges.

More generally, there are aspects in this ethnography that might explain how processes of categorization and exclusion occur in the city, the social complexity of which is better reflected in the classroom following the introduction of quotas.

A first aspect to draw attention to is how processes of generalization and polarization happen. For example, it seems that the existence of a group of very dedicated poor (especially female) students and the dark phenotype of many of them has the power to extend these characteristics to a *Cone* group, which is actually quite diverse both in terms of phenotype and academic dedication. A similar process happens with the Barbarians, whose identity is mainly reinforced by a group of naughty middle-class boys sitting in the back. A different proportion of black students in each group, rather than totally homogenous composition, is what in the end makes the *Cones* a substantially black (or darker) group and the Barbarians white in students' understandings. This logic resembles very much how specific colors are generally ascribed to poor suburban areas and to wealthy Zona Sul; and it also shows how the presence of black people in middle-class spaces ends up subverting expectations if this presence is not explained by traditional patterns of subalternity. If in the city there are natural spaces (physical and metaphysical) where black people would normally be expected to be, such expectations survive in the classroom (and more generally in the university), although resignified within the quota system.[17]

A second crucial aspect seen in this ethnography relates to the game of somewhat carnivalesque subversions that the encounter between groups triggers. The way these groups occupy a particular space in the classroom, appropriate identitarian labels, as well as their behavior and outfit styles, might be unexpected, giving the clear impression that students actively play to subvert stereotypes about each other at university and in society. The fact that *Cones* are from suburban areas but most of them are in the front in the classroom is a typical example. This happens through an ideal and attempted approximation of what the opposite group is supposed to be, without really avoiding distancing. More practically, reversals barely occur because original class gaps are still deeply crystallized by place of residence, annexed lifestyle, and actual academic performance. All these factors still play an important role in driving quite separate socializing processes among students.

Do Quotas Have Their Color?

Although scholars teach that racial/color identifications are quite subjective and shifting in Brazil (Sheriff, 2001; Fry, 2005), I arrived at the UERJ after months spent socializing with people of different social backgrounds and becoming more familiar with formal and informal patterns of racial/color classification in Rio de Janeiro. As a consequence of this familiarization, I immediately perceived that there were a good number of people who might be considered black, or who might be black-quota students at the UERJ. However, I could not compare this scenario with the prequota situation. By carrying out interviews with the administrative staff of the university, I was more commonly informed about the general impoverishment of university users and the building itself, while race did not emerge spontaneously as the subject of the conversation. A retired education teacher I met among the administration staff remembered with a touch of nostalgia that in the past more students came from Zona Sul and many of them came in flashy cars. "Believe me, my students even used to tease me because I just had a *Fuska* (Beetle)! I cannot see many flashy cars in the parking area anymore." Other staff informants remembered the prequota epoch as a time when people at the UERJ had overall nicer clothes and the university enjoyed better prestige in Rio de Janeiro. Some interviewees noted the change in university users by pointing to other particulars, such as: "[B]efore, the libraries were always empty. Now they are full of *cotistas* . . . you know, this is because they don't have the money to buy books and need to study here." Some of the staff also pointed out that bars and canteens at the UERJ had had to cut their prices after the arrival of less-affluent university users. In some cases, I was told that this decline of the university had started before the introduction of the quota system and coincided with a general decline of the public sector in Brazil. However, most interviewees believed that the quota system had contributed to fostering such decay.

Only following more direct questioning, most academic and administrative staff from several departments clearly stated that they had noticed an increase in the number of black students, especially in the morning shift where these students had been traditionally less common.[18] I was also told that the difference was more visible in specific programs such as law, medicine, and journalism, since these courses are more competitive and therefore usually inaccessible to the lower classes. Conversely, I was told that in history, social sciences, and education the change was also visible but less striking, because these courses were less appealing to the elite, and had therefore automatically represented the most achievable option for lower-class students. As an interesting detail, speakers automatically tended to identify the *cotistas* as black- or brown-skinned students, even though the public-school quota is not informed by any color/racial basis.

> *Me*: Have you noticed any change in the student collective since the introduction of quotas?
> *PG* (teacher): Of course I have.
> *Me*: So you know who the quota students are . . .
> *PG*: I don't, because the information about the *cotistas* is confidential.
> *Me*: In that case, how can you state that the student collective has changed?
> *PG*: Look, I studied in this department myself. There were no black students in my class.
> *Me*: You mean brown and black-skinned students?
> *PG*: There are also more brown students but I was referring to the typically black-looking ones (*os que são negros mesmo*).

By virtue of these considerations, I was not surprised that black people have been tacitly naturalized as *the* users of quotas at the UERJ. This might have happened in ways similar to those by which middle-class students were seen as the "natural" university users before the introduction of quotas.

The increase in black students after the introduction of the quota system was also confirmed by students who had experienced the transition at university. Some of them started studying before 2003 but due to one problem or another had to delay their studies, catching up with those classes that enrolled *cotistas*. The graduation picture boards hanging in the corridors of the university speak clearly. Until the early 2000s, there are very few photos of black students. Black people seemed to have become slightly more common from the 1980s but nothing comparable to the way the Law Department looks today. This change is usually estimated primarily in visual terms and proved by the presence of black students.

Being a black student generates a series of expectations about being lower-class, and therefore probably a *cotista*. Such a view was confirmed by white nonquota students, who tend to assume that black students are *cotistas*. Black students, especially politicized ones, claim they suffer the *cotista* stigma even when they are not *cotistas*, while white students from the public-school quotas *passam batidos*, meaning that they tend to pass disguised within the rest of the (white) student collective. When I asked a law teacher about this matter, she reinforced this view by saying: "[W]hite students may be *cotistas* but it is more difficult to say . . . black students may not be [*cotistas*], but it's quite easy to think that they are." Many nonquota students endorsed this view as well. In addition, some teachers in different departments stated that they sometimes had to reconsider their initial assumptions about who might be the quota students in the class. More commonly, the modified assumptions related to black students: "I have a black student who is particularly clever and participates a lot in the class . . . I cannot be completely sure but I've come to think that he must not be from the quotas." This student must have looked like an anomaly to the teacher for reasons different but somehow also similar to those regarding the black Barbarian in the first-year law class.

It is important to point out that although the most immediate way that teachers identify quota students seems to be based on their phenotypes, other elements become relevant afterward. Once teachers start interacting with their students they gather additional information, for example, in relation to provenance.

> A student told me "Prof, I arrived late for the class because I live in Olaria," a poor neighborhood . . . so I assumed she was a *cotista*. Others might mention that they studied in a public school . . . because they expect you to be more flexible with them . . . or maybe only to justify educational weaknesses . . . in that case, again, I might be wrong but I tend to assume that they are quota students. (Penal law teacher)

On a couple of occasions I was also told that the use of Portuguese language in exams is clear evidence of the social status of the student. In other cases, it is clothing style that helps teachers in their heuristic process, although some of them, especially when older, are less sure about this aspect, arguing that young people use an undifferentiated global style (*globalizado*). Despite the presence of typically class-related characteristics to identify the *cotistas*, students' phenotypes come out again as a striking element in specific situations. For example, when asked about her feelings at university following the introduction of quotas, a teacher said:

> Frankly, I feel better . . . but this might just be my personal view because I do not feel comfortable in a social space where there are just whites. I go to church a lot, and there are people of all kinds (*de todo tipo*) . . . when I am on the street, I also see people of all kinds . . . so, why should this be different in a university? I feel more comfortable in a mixed environment (*onde tem mistura*). (Penal law teacher)

In the end, racial characteristics seem the most immediate way to make considerations about quota status and, indirectly, about class. Although white lower-class students had also not been typical of the Law Department before the introduction of quotas, the markers of the change were visually more striking by looking at the black students. If seen from this angle, quotas are typically "black."

The "Polite" Voices of Racial Censorship

If associations between blackness and quotas emerge very often in private interviews and indirect discourse, public racial references at university are usually avoided for reasons of courtesy. This kind of silence, as Robin Sheriff illustrates, is no less effective than language in shaping (unequal) political and cultural landscapes. Sheriff describes this silence as a form of cultural censorship which she separates from state-sponsored censorship, as it does not rely "on explicit coercion or enforcement."

The first day I attended classes with first-year law students, I felt rather surprised when the teacher of Direito do Pensamento Político (law of political thought class) started a discussion of quotas with his students.[19] However, very few students, all non-*cotistas*, shyly expressed their opinions. These few students pointed out the discriminatory value of quotas and mentioned that access to university should be based on merit. The discussion generated some constraints among *cotistas* and none of them said a single word. What struck me the most was that no mention of racial quotas appeared in the debate, even though the entire attention of the Brazilian media and intellectuals actually focuses on this kind of measure. A couple of months later, another very interesting event happened. During one of their courses, first-year law students had to organize group presentations on the topic of culture and rights. This was a promising research opportunity for me, especially considering that two groups of middle-class students chose to present about hip-hop, and I wondered how they would deal with the racial aspects implicit in their subject. Both groups described hip-hop as having emerged from ghettos in the United States, highlighting the social contestation value of this musical genre. However, to my surprise, both groups cleverly managed to bypass concepts and words such as "race" or "black" in their presentations. It was also interesting that, perhaps in order to make their talk more authoritative, one of these groups had invited a speaker from outside the university, a black hip-hop musician whose blackness was strengthened by copious dreadlocks and a reggae outfit.

In the second group of presenters, racial silence was instead paradoxically downplayed by a different fact. All of the members of this group sat on the stage except for the aforementioned Barbarians' black student. This boy remained on the sidelines, working with the stereo equipment and changing the hip-hop music that functioned as a soundtrack for the presentation. This racial situation might have been random and was probably unintentional on the part of the other participants. However, within the general framework of Brazilian race relations in which it was inscribed, this scene sent a powerful message that made any language fairly superfluous: the only black student of the group stood out as an expert able to select tracks of a somewhat racialized musical genre, while he emerged less clearly as a resource for the intellectual aspects of the presentation.

In leaving racial issues implicit, middle-class students were probably trying to be polite to their black classmates, or perhaps they did not feel legitimate enough to talk about a reality perceived as not really theirs. Most black students, in fact, had entered university through quotas and carried the stereotype of being less capable. It would therefore be inappropriate, if not cruel, to remind them of this, especially since this fact might hint at something supposedly wrong in their biology or ancestry.[20] After all, defining hip-hop as having come from US ghettos and bringing a black speaker onto the stage might have sufficed to compensate for the careful deletion of racial terms by the speakers.

In my everyday life at university and in Rio, I seldom heard any explicitly racist or race-related language from middle- and upper-class people. On some occasions racial references emerged only through very tortuous paths and were always solidly tied to concepts of space and class. At a party to which only nonquota students happened to go, two young Zona Sul men mentioned that women from lower-class Baixada Fluminense "are ugly and have large hips." These women were also defined as *gostosas* (tasty), in apparent contradiction to the first statement, but for the fact that *gostosa* implies being sexually lascivious and thus not *finas* (elegant, graceful). It is clear that, to wealthy boys, these women do not represent a target in terms of potential partners, although they might represent a fairly easy sexual choice. In deepening conversations, I also found that these boys preferred certain dance clubs where they could find "amazing" girls. These girls were never described as white, but as very well-dressed, wealthy, from Zona Sul, and attending the Pontifícia Universidade Católica (PUC), the highest-standard private university where the elite study in Rio de Janeiro. When I asked these boys whether they frequented other, relatively cheaper clubs (e.g., Maruzinho in the Cinelândia area), they stated that only women from the Baixada go there. They repeated that those women were not attractive, although no reference to their skin color was made. However, when I expressed my desire to go to one of these less-exclusive clubs, one of my middle-class informants jokingly said, "[A]h, now I understand . . . you like *mulatas* . . . I like *mulatas* too . . . we can bring you there another day . . ." In that case, some reference to mixed race and black features was made, albeit in an indirect and not very positive way. The link between the *mulata* and the racialized sexual preferences of wealthy boys comes out indirectly, first by references to the Baixada, a poor area where women would be ugly and have large hips, the last being a racialized characteristic typically ascribed to black women in Brazil; second, by the fact that the women from the Baixada are tasty but, despite being a presumably easy sexual option and probably embodying the archetype of Brazilian women abroad, are never fully desirable as partners.[21]

Some silence about race, I emphasize, was not only typical of middle-class students in public situations. In fact, none of the quota students who attended the presentations of hip-hop by their wealthier classmates pointed out the oddity of racial silence in these talks, showing that there was an implicit contract of courtesy that made further explanations superfluous and undesirable to all participants. In this vein, Sheriff rightly observes that silence differs from speech by requiring the cooperation of a plurality of actors who enforce its maintenance without any formal coercion. However, actors' cooperation in silence is driven by different reasons and unequal power relations, since, according to Sheriff (2000: 114), this cultural censorship is inevitably governed by the political interests of dominant groups. To middle-class students, the silence was an expression of politeness and tact, presumably working to hide the subaltern's vulnerable situation, although it also worked to conceal the speakers' enjoyment of social privileges.[22] In the case of black-quota students, on the other hand, the silence fulfilled their wishes for invisibility. Such a wish, as mentioned earlier, can be explained by the fact that most black-quota students felt they were in the wrong place at university, since they made use of a policy advantage that ambiguously hinted at academic incompetence, social theft, and racial inferiority.[23] Silence, I observe, does not necessarily imply a lack of consciousness or knowledge. According to Sheriff (2001), in fact, the practice of silence can be "simultaneously a public form of accommodation and a private (if at the same time communal) form of resistance." In any case, the silence of black students could be seen as a passive form of this resistance, a means to avoid both suffering and active contestation. Resistance from the audience certainly would have been quite different had there been members of the student black movement attending these presentations.[24] As I realized from several interviews during my fieldwork, black activists openly contested situations of racial silence, targeting them as relatively common ways in which racism in Brazil perversely worked and was automatically reproduced in the university space.[25]

Discussing racial cultural censorship among the middle class should not give the impression that middle-class students feel completely at ease about public comments on matter of class and spatial differences even when race was not clearly the topic under discussion. At one point of the academic year, the whole class of first-year students was invited to visit the Federal Court where one of their teachers worked. The Court was located in Baixada Fluminense, in Nova Iguaçú, and we had to catch the train, standing without any air-conditioning for more than one hour on an extremely hot day. The journey back was incredibly interesting for two mains reasons. The first reason is that this journey highlighted quite powerfully the way the same class, race, and space relations that I was exploring in the classroom also interlace more broadly in the metropolitan map. Most lower-class students got off in suburban train stations before reaching the centre of Rio de Janeiro, as these stops were closer to their homes. I instead reached Central do Brasil with the wealthier students and from there I took the underground to Zona Sul with many of them. By the Central Brasil, where the train line connecting center and suburbs ends, the group of students came socially (and racially) filtered, having lost the almost totality of its lower-class component. The second reason that made the journey back from Nova Iguaçú particularly interesting is that I had the chance to understand the impressions of some middle-class students about their day out. On the one hand, these students were pointing out how unattractive Nova Iguaçú was and how uncomfortable the local train had been, which most of them had used for the first time while it represented the normal daily form of transportation for many of their lower-class colleagues. On the other hand, the same students also showed some interclass solidarity gossiping about a fact that had shocked them during the visit. As soon as the group had arrived at the Federal Court, a *Cone* classmate had greeted the teacher by saying: "Prof, you work at the end of the world!" (*Profe, você trabalha no fim do mundo!*). According to these wealthy students, the comment had been completely inappropriate because some people in the class were actually from Nova Iguaçú. Such solidarity, however, was privately deployed, and private was also the breaking of the class/space censorship, a fact that for these students seemed particularly inappropriate only when done in public at the presence of lower-class colleagues. When class censorship from middle-class students was broken more publicly, in fact, this usually came unintended and under the form of gaffes. For example, when students were collecting a 20-*reais* fee for the *choppada* (beer party usually held at the beginning of academic semesters) and quota students stated that the fee sounded quite expensive to them, a middle-class colleague reminded lower-class colleagues that, in the end, 20 *reais* is not a big sum. This fact did not pass unnoticed by *Cones*, who gossiped about the unfortunate remark for weeks. It is important to observe that the impact of such comments is completely different in the eyes of lower-class students depending on who say them. What might sound funny when said by a same-class person, might instead sound really offensive if said by somebody who does not share similar urban environments and comparable levels of social deprivation. When I spoke to the *Cones* from Nova Iguaçú about the unfortunate comment describing their district as "the end of the world," they broke into a loud laugh and observed that it was completely true!

Race to the Surface (or Maybe Not): Nonblack *Cones* and the Breaking of Racial Silence

A question that arises is whether avoiding racial language or deploying censorship in general is something especially typical of the middle and upper classes. I discussed this topic with some friends of mine who had grown up in the suburbs but who had finally managed to move up socially. In my friends' understanding, when looking for the racism of the middle class, you should not look at their direct language but to something more indirectly embedded in people's behavior: you should simply look at the middle class's lack of conviviality with people of different colors outside the subordinated role these people fulfill, for example, as servants in their houses. Such conviviality, conversely, is more common among the lower classes and typical to the suburbs; along with this may also come racist language. According to Juliana,

> In the suburbs, there is a good amount of black and white people living next to each other and you see lots of mixture. However, you mustn't assume that race relations are necessarily more relaxed over there. I would just say they are more explicit. I remember that when

I brought home a black high-school classmate, my father called me aside and warned me, "look, if that *macaco* (monkey) makes trouble in my house, you'll see!" . . . If you're middle-class, you're less likely to hear your parents saying things like that . . . This kind of language would be seen as a lack of education and style among middle-class people . . . discrimination from the middle class does not pass much through language but through actual behavior and exclusion.

There might then be two different forms of interracial socializing in Rio de Janeiro. One of these forms could be defined as "vertical," as ideally represented in social intercourses of the employer/servant type, ruled by the middle and upper class; the other could be defined as "horizontal" because it implies less hierarchical relationships between white and black lower-class people.[26] Class represents the main factor of differentiation between the two models because, while wealthier white students have very little in common with the black lower-class people, the white poor at least share living spaces and economic deprivation with a high number of black neighbors. Perhaps because of this, the only white students who brought up racial topics during my fieldwork were almost universally lower-class. Although this does not mean a lack of racial silence among white *Cones*, these students seemed to enjoy more freedom in talking publically about race, much more than their wealthier colleagues could ever dare.

At the beginning of 2008, Gabriel's difficulties with his grandmother, with whom he had been living in Realengo (Zona Oeste), came to an end. Ultimately, Gabriel had to move out to Cosmos, further away in a rural area, where his sister lives. A group of quota students and I were having lunch in the canteen on the 11th floor while Gabriel was running his grandmother down.

> Just to be harsher on me, she even asked my sister: "have you seen him? I guess he's dating (*namorando*) that *pretinha* (very dark-skinned little girl)[27] with such hard hair!" (*de cabelo duro, duro, duro!*) . . . Can you see how racist is she? (Gabriel, white lower-class student)

The girl in question was Eliane, with whom Gabriel had become very good friends at university. At that point, a discussion started about whether Gabriel's grandmother had been as racist as he was trying to suggest. To my surprise, the other students did not share Gabriel's view.

> *Fábio*: I don't think this is being racist. Just because she doesn't like the black [phenotype], this is not being racist. It's matter of taste.

> Look at me, for example . . . I would never date . . . let's say . . . a Japanese . . . I don't find Japanese girls attractive!
> *Gabriel*: You're wrong. I promise you that I know my grandmother and I know she was talking in a very racist way!
> *Flávia*: Maybe she was just making a comment about Eliane's hair but she didn't want to be racist or say that she didn't like her. Did you mention that to Eliane?
> *Gabriel*: I did. The worst thing is that I hoped she would hate my grandmother for it. Instead, she laughed! She said that my grandmother was right! [Everybody laughs]

I did not really know what to think of this conversation. I was struck first by Fabio's hesitation and probable substitution of the word in question, "black," with "Japanese," possibly to avoid being impolite to Flávia and Daisy, both girls, and the only persons present who could have been considered black in that context. Second, I was obviously surprised that everybody was so unsure about the demeaning intentions of Gabriel's grandmother, while Flávia's reaction sounded as if she was trying to deny racism to avoid diminishing herself as a black girl by offering an improbable interpretation of facts.[28] This case is interesting because it demonstrates a lot about Brazilian race relations: first, in terms of how race is imperfectly hidden by lower-class students, and how racial references can emerge more clearly in moments of conflict (between Gabriel and his grandmother, for example); second, the fact that Flávia's censorship should not be interpreted as similar to the one deployed by her nonblack colleagues. This idea recalls Sheriff (2001: 83) very strongly, when she argues that the practice of silence is "simultaneously a public form of accommodation and a private (if at the same time communal) form of resistance."

In other cases, censorship was easily broken in normal conversations with *cotistas* self-identified as white or at least as nonblack. These conversations usually took place when no black colleagues were present. I wanted to discuss with Yara (a white *cotista*) the fact that none of her black colleagues mentioned experiences of racial discrimination at university. Yara misunderstood my statement. She thought I was stating that her black classmates had never felt discriminated against in their lives.

> What? If they say that, it means that they never put their feet outside their houses! . . . The other day, a black girl from the [law] evening shift told me . . . "when you finish university, finding a job will be easier for you, because you're white" . . . I didn't know what to say for

shame (*morri de vergonha*), because the sad reality is that she was right! (*porque a triste realidade é que é assim mesmo!*)

White non-*cotistas* and other informants in Rio also commented on jokes that people (of course which they themselves did not) might use to offend black people in everyday life, or which might even be used by the same black people in certain situations.

> Do you know when is the only time that a black (preto) can move up in life? When the shack blows up . . . Black people (pretos) are like sparrows; they take everything and give nothing back . . . I don't drink coffee to avoid mixing with preto . . . Why are there no chiromancers in Africa? Because pretos don't have any future . . . Why do pretos [or negros] go to evangelical churches? To call the white "brother" . . . I knew she/he was a preto/a (tinha de ser) . . .[29]

On the other hand, I have already pointed out that most white lower-class students established good friendships with black-quota students of the same social background. In the group of lower-class students I spent most time with, at least four of them self-identified and were identified as white. I never noticed any real racial tensions from these students, who were usually extremely careful to avoid any references that could directly affect their relationship with their friends.[30] If white lower-class students raised racial topics, this always occurred in the form of jokes. When her black friends asked her to do some chores for the barbecue (*churrasco*) at Daisy's place, white *cotista* Andréia pointed out that "the owner should always pay the white slave better . . ." This comment raised a laugh of convenience, although I missed exploring how Andréia's black friends really processed it.[31]

WHITE CONES AND THEIR ACCESS TO MIDDLE-CLASS SPACES

White, brown, and black *Cones* had similar social backgrounds, a fact that increased intrasociability and also made the group quite mixed in phenotypic terms, despite the nonrandom distribution of black students in the class. Having said this, an aspect I grasped during my fieldwork was the easier mobility of these white lower-class students into the Barbarians' spaces. In this sense, race and class emerge again as factors that should not be too broadly mixed together.

Lower-class Gabriel, whom I have already mentioned several times, represented a special case. This student did not have access to quotas since he managed to study in a good private college through gaining a scholarship and is white. He therefore achieved a place in law by merit, scoring very well in the vestibular. Although Gabriel repeatedly stressed (at least until the second semester) that race is not a crucial basis of division in Brazil, even when admitting his grandmother's racism, it is interesting how he described the achievement of his scholarship:

> My teacher saw that I was a very promising student and organized for me the opportunity of moving to a better school . . . you know, with a scholarship. But I can tell you . . . if I hadn't been a *loirinho de olhos azuis* (a cute blond boy with blue eyes) I don't know if she would have felt so moved by my case . . . sometimes I went to her house and she said racist things against black people (*piadinhas racistas contra os negros*) . . .

This comment reminds me of some of Sheriff's (2001) remarks about Morro do Sangue Bom, and of comments I heard during my time in Rio. In some cases, even black people tended to consider a white in a bad situation even more unfortunate than themselves.[32] These are comments such as, "poor girl . . . she died of cancer . . . a little blonde girl with blue eyes . . . (*uma loirinha de olhos azuis . . .*)." In addition, Gabriel's account recalls Telles (2004: 158), when he states that "many teachers, consciously or not, invest in lighter children because they believe that those children are more likely to succeed, and thus a good education will be more beneficial to them."

Another relevant fact is that, at the very beginning of the semester, Gabriel received much attention from the Barbarians, who had provisionally been his closest friends at university. Gabriel's cleverness and charisma must have favored this interest. However, I cannot disregard his phenotype, which increased his chances of being naturalized within the middle-class group. Gabriel was invited to take part in all aspects of *Barbárie* social life before realizing (indeed very quickly) that this was out of his reach. He then gradually merged into the social group of my main quota informants, among whom he was the only nonquota student at the time of my research.

> They always invited me to go out, but I couldn't because I didn't have the money and I also lived too far away . . . I constantly told them that I was too poor to join them. At that point, Laura [from *Barbárie*] even told me . . . "Please, stop reminding us all the time that you

are poor! . . . Can't you just avoid saying that? Just hang out!" . . . But I realized that I didn't have much in common with them . . . they talked of things that for me were superficial . . . their problems are not of the kind that they don't have the money to catch the bus . . . I identify much better with these other [quota] people (*esse pessoal cotista*) . . . we even laugh a lot together about being poor . . .

To make his point stronger, Gabriel made me notice that he had even moved from the *Barbárie* group spatially a few weeks after the start of the course, joining the front rows of the classroom. In doing this he was not forgotten by the people "in the back," with whom he maintained substantial interactions, or at least much more than the other *Cones*. Gabriel's case is probably the most striking one, although there were a number of other less successful cases of status mobility in the class among white lower-class students. Andréia, for example, sometimes managed to keep one foot in the Barbarians' camp and made some visible effort to dress according to middle-class standards, although she was not completely successful in raising their interest. This story strengthens the view of Black militant law students in their final years, according to whom, "white *cotistas* usually have to struggle in order to be included by middle-class students; however, at least they are more easily considered than black ones" (Jurema, Denegrir militant).

AN UNEXPECTED MIDDLE-CLASS PERSPECTIVE: THE IMPORTANCE OF QUOTAS AS A FACTOR OF SOCIAL MIXTURE

In previous sections, I highlighted how the diversification of the classroom collective among law freshmen reflects, and paradoxically even stresses, class and racial divisions that were less evident when the Law Department was more predominantly white and middle-class. Such an account is quite unfair without observing that quotas also are vehicles for very important contacts between students of different backgrounds. I noticed that boundaries in the classroom were less rigid than students described and I saw, on several occasions, *Cones* and Barbarians joking with each other or having a chat in the law corridors. Flávia and Glória, in this sense, were pleased when an upper-class colleague lent them expensive text books. Flávia also appeared very happy when a female Zona Sul classmate addressed her in a friendly manner when they met in the Direction Office. Although many students had felt directly or indirectly discriminated against or uncomfortable in certain situations during their academic life, similar feelings were also experienced in extrauniversity daily life as typical manifestations of Brazilian class and race relations. To be honest, most of my quota interviewees had expected more confrontational and racist attitudes from the wealthier students at university than they actually realized, especially considering the alarmist information widely diffused by the mass media and fomented by some literature in this regard. According to research carried out by José Luis Petruccelli with 557 university teachers across several Brazilian universities, 77 percent of the interviewees said that race relations did not change negatively at university after the introduction of quotas; and 80 percent thought that it was important or very important to have racial diversity in their courses.[33]

Most Barbarians declared themselves to be middle-class or on the way to becoming upper-middle class (*classe média* or *classe média para média-alta*), while they denied being the "rich" people that their lower-class classmates imagined they were. "I don't think there are particularly elite people here," nonquota student Mariana said. "Some people might be relatives of lawyers who already have a good name, but I guess there are not many people here whose parents are high court judges (*desembargadores*) . . . my father, for example, is the first person in his family to have a university diploma and is just a common solicitor." As with Mariana, most nonquota students pointed out that the rich people were not at the UERJ but at the PUC,[34] while the *very* rich were probably not even studying in Brazil, and instead studying in places such as the United States and Europe. Middle-class student Beatriz provided a similar account of why she had opted for the UERJ:

> My mum could have made the effort to send me to PUC, but why pay up to R$ 2,000 per month if I can study [a top-quality program] here for free? However, most of my friends went to PUC . . . they said I was crazy because this place is far from Zona Sul, the building infrastructure is in precarious conditions and the area is dangerous[35] . . . they also said that the prestige of the law course at UERJ would go down because of *cotistas* . . . Anyway, it's enough that I live in Ipanema and I studied all my life at the Santo Ignácio school, one of the most exclusive ones here . . . can you imagine if I were studying at PUC as well, now? Well, that would mean completely fitting the stereotype of the *patricinha* (spoilt rich girl)! . . .

Interviews revealed that nonquota students did not just choose the UERJ because its law course was free and highly regarded. Other factors were also mentioned, including the point that studying at the UERJ was valuable to many of these students because of its mixed and diverse student body, as well as its ability to offer the challenges and skills necessary for adapting to a rough environment and decaying infrastructure.

A fact is also that a surprising number of middle-class students and teachers, during my fieldwork, expressed satisfaction about sharing the same space with the lower class. Some middle-class students appreciated that they had black and lower-class classmates for first time in their lives and that this made them more aware of realities they had always considered rather alien to them. Others added that, as an effect of quotas, their classroom reflected the diversity of Brazilian society more fairly. Further comments also referred to the fact that *cotistas* were in the end very dedicated and, generally, good students.[36] As a consequence, many non-*cotistas* and teachers declared that direct experience had changed their minds favorably about quotas after being initially quite critical of these measures. Such feelings were expressed even though the majority of the interviewees stated that the best strategy would be to improve the standards of public schools, and that quotas should be accepted only as a temporary solution until this objective was achieved.[37]

Like Beatriz, a number of middle-class students eventually stated that they had chosen the UERJ to step away from the comforts of Zona Sul and to look less stereotypically spoilt. The appropriation of the name Barbarians, their location at the back of the classroom, and their (at least apparently) simpler outfits, after all, may not only have represented a jocose inversion of reality by certain social actors; these elements also may have expressed a more or less conscious attempt to question social boundaries and stereotypes, and to enjoy the social mixture promoted by inclusive policies. This mixture arguably is well-matched to a pool of meanings that are crucial to Brazilian national identity and cultural ideals of social and racial democracy.[38] It is also interesting that a good number of nonquota interviewees, in addition to studying law at the UERJ, also managed to attend different undergraduate programs in other public universities where quotas were not implemented at the time of writing; for example, the UFRJ (Universidade Federal do Rio de Janeiro) and the UFF (Universidade Federal Fluminense). In comparing the UERJ to the other public universities they also attended at the time of my research, these students described the environment of these institutions to be more elite and, therefore, less cool (*não é tão bacana*). People in other universities were also described as looking all the same and stuck-up, while the environment was generally defined as more boring than at the UERJ.

In the experience of most nonquota interviewees, quotas worked as a factor of diversification of the social collective, acting therefore as a positive assessment of how certain policies of social integration might have a good impact if applied on a larger scale. The novelty, I reiterate here, is not about the circulation of poor and black people in the same spaces as the middle class, but about the role they take on there. In spite of the mentioned social frictions and racial dynamics occurring in the classroom (including both social censorships and covered racism), these aspects already exist in society and are not the product of quotas at the UERJ. As an important aspect, wealthier students at the UERJ often seem more open to social diversity than lower-class students might suppose, and in fact ascribe to a quota-implementing university the possibility to create such diversity. In addition to this, the presence of lower-class and black students who do well at university not only challenges stereotypes about these groups but also shows that paradoxes in access to the public university system have led to a waste of human resources, and represent a crucial obstacle to the social mobility of the lower class.

I actually noticed several situations in which middle- and lower-class classmates could interact outside the university. Among these were the *choppadas* (beer parties) and barbecues organized at the start of each semester, as well as get-togethers promoted by the academic staff, such as visits to juridical institutions in the city or other extrauniversity gatherings. Over the last few years, on Orkut (and more recently on Facebook), I noticed an increasing number of photographs picturing smiling law students from varied social backgrounds standing next to their teachers in some stylish bars of Rio de Janeiro. I also noticed increasing numbers of online friendships between lower- and middle-class students, while the entire first-year law collective during the time of my research already had been keeping in touch about administrative and academic aspects of their courses through mailing lists and blogs on Orkut. Finally, the mixing of presentation groups by teachers, according to some interviewees, proved very helpful in increasing social interaction and reciprocal knowledge between students from different backgrounds.[39]

Having said this, I also observed that the occasional sociability and interclass empathy observed in my ethnography was more typically bounded by the perimeter of the university. A common opinion among final-year students I interviewed in 2008 was that contact in the classroom does create some empathy and increases mutual understanding; what I could not see, however, was a drastic shift in patterns of socializing. Considerations of this kind were quite typical among Black-activists I interviewed between 2007 and 2008, as expressed by Denegrir militant Jurema:

> Some wealthy people in the class are nice to me and hold me in high esteem . . . they see that I'm a smart girl . . . that I make good comments in class and that I dare to wear an ethnic hairstyle [braids] . . . however, these same people have never invited me to a party in their houses . . . they may like me, but at the same time they must feel uncomfortable and there is never any real fusion . . . (Jurema, final-year law student)

She then continued,

> Most of these people are used to interaction (*lidar*) with *negros*, but just because they have a doorman or a maid . . . because, in fact, we [black people] have been in their space for a long time . . . but just in a position of subordination . . . Then, the moment that you get into a place as an equal (*de par à par*), things really change . . . it's then that they feel uncomfortable. They might think . . . how can I sit next to Maria,[40] that woman who mops my floor . . . at whom I'm used to shouting all day? How is it possible she's sitting here studying law or philosophy, getting good marks and even saying interesting things?[41] (Jurema)

Space sometimes returns to the surface as a powerful and perhaps "polite" reason to explain the lack of further socializing. When I asked a final-year nonquota student whether he would invite any lower-class colleagues to his birthday party in a club in Zona Sul, he said, "well, it is very far for them to get there . . . they would have problems going back home afterwards . . ." No reference was made to the fact that these students might not have the money to reach Zona Sul, to enter the club, and to buy drinks. Such comments do not allow for understanding whether students from the Baixada and other poor neighborhoods are also seen as not matching the Zona Sul environment or the social milieu of the middle-class person having the party (perhaps in terms of phenotype or way of speaking), possibly even potentially causing some embarrassment to other guests. Such considerations are made unnecessary, being cordially implied in and silenced under the concepts of place and space. Middle-class students explained, similarly to what quota students also said, that they chose their friends on the basis of affinities (often implying area of provenance in the city and—tacitly—its attendant lifestyle). It is interesting that affinity in anthropological parlance takes on slightly different nuances from general similarity. It implies, for example, marriageability and family ties. It might then imply attraction, sharing of common interests, and probably "natural" empathy and sympathy. All this suggests something that may come from deep inside and does not need to be deeply thought through. This is a naturalizing discourse of class, space, and race.

I was able to reflect more deeply on the apparently contradictory messages contained in this ethnography when, in 2011, I carried out further socializing and face-to-face interviews with my original freshmen informants. In 2011, the first-year students I had met in 2007 were close to concluding their undergraduate programs; I was then very curious to discuss with my informants whether classroom socializing patterns had substantially changed over time. In a first instance, the totality of the students interviewed stated that the division between *Cones* and Barbarians was still very significant. However, all of them agreed that social intercourse was still fairly cordial and had actually slightly improved. Some of my lower-class informants also confessed that, in spite of the generally persisting group separation between *Cones* and *Barbárie* in the classroom, they had been able to foster rather stable friendships with a few wealthier colleagues outside university; this fact also included frequenting each others' households and social networks in specific occasions. These data show that even though quotas do not have the power to shift the patterns of interclass relations radically at the UERJ, at least they potentially favor social *urban encounters* that could be even enhanced by specific teaching strategies and academic activities.

Other Facets of Mixture at UERJ: Middle-Class Appropriation of Plebeian and "Black" Roughness

Limited extrauniversity socializing with *cotistas* was not the only element that made me partially reconsider the benevolent attitude of middle-class students to quotas. A fact is that the appreciation for the environment of a decaying and old-fashioned building, which was also socially diversified, was described by many of these students as a truly Brazilian and democratic experience. It is in this sense that being at the UERJ became somehow even more valuable than attending other universities for these middle-class students. The name Barbarians, their famed naughty behavior, and the space they occupied in the classroom suggests some desire among middle-class students to mystify social assumptions about their status and expected place in society. I cannot avoid observing that this middle-class ideological appreciation for a social (and racial) mixture that is never concretely achieved in practice finds some parallels in Freyre's (1961) celebration of the triumphant adaptation of the Portuguese man to the inhospitable tropics. With the concept of Lusotropicalism, Freyre reacted to the negative view of racial mixture that eugenic thinkers promoted at the beginning of last century and transformed it, at least on paper, into a comparative advantage for Brazil. In Freyre's imagination, unlike other European colonizers, the Portuguese man had been successful in adapting to a difficult environment, strategically appropriating the knowledge and qualities of a subalternized African and Indigenous other. A similar point does not try to minimize middle-class appreciation for social mixture at the UERJ; it wants instead to suggest that some shades of this appreciation remain ambiguous, especially when they are not followed by effective inclusion.

As an example of such ambiguity, some wealthy UERJ students pointed out not only how people in more equipped universities lived in a middle-class bubble; they also remarked that passing the vestibular at the UERJ had become even more difficult because of the introduction of quotas, as 45 percent of openings were now reserved for *cotistas*. Beatriz and other middle-class people commented that PUC students are not very dedicated and just think of clubbing: "Their parents will find them a very good job in some prestigious legal studio, so they don't bother at all about studying hard . . . after all, they are paying!" Through similar accounts, UERJ middle-class students stand out not just as cooler but also as substantially more capable than middle-class students in other institutions.

This seems to fit a discourse of middle-class and white masculinity that transcends the actual gender of the speakers and somehow raises an aspect that could be contested to Freyre: the domestication (feminization) of indigenous and black populations by the extraction of their wildness and primitive wisdom (and masculinity), which serves finally to enhance the power of the white man (see Wade, 1999). The *Barbárie/Cone* model recalls similar aspects within the classroom, where the phenomenon of symbolic reversals seen earlier converts the *Cones* into a substantially domesticated and in this sense feminine space; this happens at the same time that middle-class students are steeped in barbarian, black, and—by fusion—*mestiço* power. Exactly as in Freyre, the mixture experienced by middle-class students does not necessarily erase certain established social and racial hierarchies in the constitution of the social collective, although it might appear tropically democratic (Wade, 2005).

Additional ethnography better exemplifies the racial subtleties of this reasoning. Every year, the UERJ Law Department faces law departments from other universities in athletic competitions (Jogos Acadêmicos Jurídicos); mainly for economic reasons, these Jogos have become a substantially middle-class, and thus reasonably white, space. Students, in fact, had to pay for accommodation and food in a faraway resort over several days. An interesting fact is that, in recent years, supporters of the other universities at the Jogos started labeling the UERJ as "Congo" (with clear reference to the racial quotas), a term that middle-class UERJ students ended up appropriating with clear pride. Informants of different backgrounds referred that UERJ students started turning up at the Jogos Jurídicos with the Congo's national flag, composed a fake Congo national anthem, and replied to the Congo joke/offense during competitions by shouting slogans like "yes, we're Congo . . . [because of this] we have a [big] black dick!" (*sim, somos Congo, temos piroca de negão*).

When I asked lower-class informants whether *cotistas* also appropriated the word "Congo," they stated that it happened more rarely, whereas it was strikingly typical of the *Barbárie* in their activities of showing UERJ pride at the Jogos. "Have you seen their [online] profiles on Orkut? . . . They always write "Country of Origin: Congo, Zimbabwe . . ." Eliane said. "Have you seen them? They are white . . ." she concluded. This argument echoes Moutinho's (2004: 302, 324–329; see also Wade, 2009) considerations about the notorious sexual power (both physical and athletic) of black men in the gendered and racialized Brazilian imagination. It also recalls examples of white male appropriations of Native American masculinity in the United States (Clark, Tyeeme, and Nagel, 2000; Nagel, 2003), or of rugged and plebeian *mestizo*/indigenous masculinity in Mexico (De la Cadena, 2000: 145–151; Irwin, 2003: 194). By referring to black sexual attributes, these students might be celebrating racial democracy, but they are also strategically borrowing sexual and physical power from a rougher, racially inferiorized other. These black symbols are more clearly appropriated by middle-class students in order to stress their intended differentiation from elite students at other universities, so that outsiders stand out as properly and unfairly wealthy and spoiled, if not emasculated. By this reading, people would therefore be less good than the UERJ *mestiços* as a symbol of national masculine prowess and, indeed, Brazilianness.[42] This kind of ideological appreciation of *mestiçagem*, it is clear, has not really prevented the perpetuation of racism in Brazil even when solidly championed as national pride.

The use of a racialized discourse from the middle class at the Jogos is apparently justified by its collective use in the context of university pride and by its apparent racially affirmative character. It might anyway be an example of how the white middle class could embrace a discourse that has less to do with racial solidarity or antiracism, and seems more clearly functional for institutional and self-celebratory reasons. It seemed in any case to emerge only in primarily nonblack settings such as the Jogos, where censorship would have less reason to be enacted due to the relative absence of black students. Racial censorship had instead been clearly deployed during the debate about quotas in the classroom and the presentations that non-*cotistas* had made about hip-hop in the law of political thought course. Read in this light, it seems that the interclass and interracial encounters favored by quotas still share much of logics that have allowed for the perpetuation of many racial democracy myths in Brazil. However, it seems that, in their own way, *Barbárie* students at the UERJ are also experiencing a form of less neatly hierarchical contact with a socially disadvantaged other. The quota system is then a potentially crucial means to build interclass and interracial contacts on more equal premises from how they usually occur in Brazilian society.

4

From Race *or* Color to Race *and* Color?

Ethnography beyond Official Discourses

The relevance of racial quotas in Brazil goes well beyond their implementation in Brazilian universities. These measures have increasingly become the ground for contending views of the nation, as appears polarized in the claims of quota skeptics and quota supporters. A significant part of public opinion, particularly following certain academics, ascribes to quotas the negative power of biracializing society after a US model, reproducing many of the problems that these measures seek to redress and creating even more racism and exclusion. A minority of public opinion follows instead the Black movement and some academics, according to whom racial affirmative action is a promising chance to redress historical inequalities. These sympathizers also defend the idea that some polarization of Brazilian race relations would be healthy in order to counteract the concealing and perverse mechanisms steeped in the myth of racial democracy.

This chapter begins to engage with the anti- and proquota discourses, unveiling their complexity and how they relate to the history of race relations and racial terminology in Brazil. My final aim is to explore how the experiences of the beneficiaries and of the quota system in general fit these opposing views and some of the related assumptions. The ethnography of the UERJ displays information about trends in people's identifications that diverge from political and official discourses of race/color categorization but potentially also bridge the same discourses to some extent. Although deeper research and discussion should be necessary in order to assess the level of applicability of these findings and reasoning to the broader Brazilian context, this ethnography is relevant as it suggests the possibility of thinking alternative patterns of classification that could be tested in the future.

Racial Terminology and Racial Categories in Brazil: A Debate on Flexibility and Fixity

Marvin Harris (1952, 1963, and 1970) has extensively discussed the massive number of racial/color terms that Brazilian people use for everyday identification, pointing out the high subjectivity with regard to this matter and the lack of consensus among his informants. Robin Sheriff (2001) strengthens this point by adding that terminological flexibility is strongly influenced by the different contextual framework in which people interact, but she also scales down such fixity in many of its connotations. According to Sheriff, the preferred use of mixed race terms in comparison to clearly black ones often responds to cultural censorship and courtesy more than reflecting the actual view of the speakers.[1] Terminological variability and flexibility in Brazil, in any case, also consistently depends on age and region, which means that some terms and concepts might be used in different ways by younger generations (Sheriff, 2001; Sansone, 2003) or may vary in their use in different geographical areas (Sansone, 2003; Telles, 2004; Petruccelli, 2007: 40). Nevertheless, Sansone contends that, as an effect of Black politics and the media, spontaneous racial classification is becoming gradually more homogeneous across different regions, as also noted by Kottak (1995).

The idea of flexibility in terms of racial/color language and identity has constantly led to discussions of the use of racial classification systems in Brazil. The IBGE (Instituto Brasileiro de Geografia e Estatística) has traditionally used a racial/color question in demographic surveys and censuses (Nobles, 2000) and, in the 2010 census, most of the Brazilian population was still divided into three main color/racial categories (*branco*, *pardo*, and *preto*).[2] These categories comprise over 98 percent of citizens, adding to the less statistically significant *amarelo* (yellow)[3] and *indígena* groups.[4] This division, as Petruccelli (2007: 13–14) observes, has remained substantially similar since 1872.

The presence of three main racial/color categories might seem somewhat limiting when considering the richness of Brazilian racial/color terminology in everyday folk language. In a Datafolha survey (1995), for example, 135 terms were used in open-ended questions about racial/color identity over a sample of 82,577 people. However, as Telles (2004: 82) points out, 95 percent of those interviewed used just six categories,[5] and three of these were actually contained in the IBGE standard classification. The people in the sample were finally given the chance to reclassify themselves by using only IBGE categories, showing general agreement on how subjective labels could fit a fixed and simplified institutional model. In this sense, Fry (2005: 194) might be right when he says that the IBGE classifications are an acceptable reduction of a multiple model of race relations into an official classification system. This official and simplified multiple model is actually in itself rather fluid and preserves ambiguity by the presence of the *pardo* (brown) category, which basically encompasses anything lying between extreme white and black poles (Nobles, 2000: 126) and embodies much of Brazilian *mestiço* national pride.

Other voices have more directly scaled down the flexibility of Brazilian race relations. As far back as in 1971, Sanjek pointed out that, despite any terminological complexity of self-classification, Brazilian people tend to label varieties into simple prototypical categories such as white, black, and indigenous. Sheriff (2001) makes similar considerations about the relatively structured character of Brazilian race relations. After observing the variability of racial/color terminology, Sheriff argues that her informants in a carioca favela understand a number of terms indicating black and brown skin (or racial mixture) as black (*negro*). She notes that, according to a popular Brazilian *ditado* (saying) that social scientists have too often overlooked, "all that is not white is black" (*tudo que não é branco, é negro*).[6]

Another debated question is whether the language used by official classification systems matches more popular uses of racial/color terms. Harris et al. (1993), for example, ask in particular whether the term *moreno* should be preferred to *pardo* since it is widely employed by brown people when answering open-ended questions about racial/color identification. Telles (2004: 84) scales down this possibility by noting that *moreno* is also commonly used by people who self-identify as white in multiple-choice IBGE surveys and this pattern is particularly observed in the variant *moreno claro* (light *moreno*) (Petruccelli, 2007: 34). As I realized during my fieldwork in Rio, the term *moreno* is often used as a polite way to address very dark-skinned people (Sheriff, 2001; Sansone, 2003: 49). Apart from this usage, it is typically employed to indicate brown- or olive-skinned individuals with softer hair and finer features than people seen as more "typically-African," or more simply to express brown color.[7]

There were a number of other color/racial terms I commonly heard during my fieldwork. Among them were *escuro* (dark), the use of which both as a polite and offensive term I noticed mainly among elderly and lower-class people away from the academic environment; *mulato/a*, which mostly refers to black and white mixture[8] but is widely seen as having negative connotations of hybrid people and sexually easy women, and is especially rejected among Black activists; and *caboclo*, which my informants used specifically to stress perceived indigenous ancestry by phenotype, for example, those people with markedly brown skin and straight dark hair.

Some specific space in this discussion is to be granted to the terms "*negro*" and "*preto.*" In popular understanding, these words are still somewhat interchangeable, even though their value has shifted over time. Sanjek in 1971 related that the word *negro* was still considered highly offensive and was often replaced with *preto*. However, as more recent literature points out, *preto* has gradually become more offensive than *negro* due to the political empowering of the latter term through Black politics (Sansone, 2003), and *negro* is particularly preferred within middle-class and intellectualized environments (Maggie, 1991).[9] Sansone (2003: 47) draws some difference between *preto* and *negro* not just in terms of positive and negative. He argues that *negro* is generally used to refer to a "Negroid phenotype,"[10] while *preto* tends to refer to the actual (deep) black color; and *pardo* is more commonly used for the brown color. Telles (2004) and Sansone finally agree that, although the term "*negro*" is still preferred by people at the darkest end of the color scale, this word is also being increasingly appropriated by people who are not markedly dark-skinned in Brazil.

As a further, crucial detail, the term "*negro*" is now increasingly used at the official level to mean the sum of *pardos* and *pretos*. This usage has been strongly influenced by the work of Hasenbalg (1979) and Silva (1985). These authors have started a trend where social analysis gathers *pardos* and *pretos* into a single social group (*negro* or nonwhite), since the socioeconomic performance of these groups is quite similar and both suffer discrimination.[11] This reasoning has become one of the ideological pillars of the Black movement. Since the 1980s, Black activists have lobbied to change both the structure and the terminology of the IBGE classification system (Nobles, 2000: 121). They argue that IBGE demographic samples should be more simply divided into *branco* and *negro* (or nonwhite), encompassing the *pardos* as members of this black group. According to the Black movement, in fact, the traditional division of the Brazilian collective into the three main color categories is detrimental and divisive for blackness, which is instead a sociohistorical reality common to both *pardos* and *pretos* (Benedita da Silva, 1999b).[12] It is not by chance that American scholars such as Skidmore (1993), Winant (1999), and Hanchard (1999) have noticed the gradual bipolarization of Brazilian race relations following a typical US model. Hanchard, in particular, takes the popular story of the "black Cinderella," the case of a mixed-race Brazilian woman who suffered racial discrimination in an upper-class building elevator despite being the daughter of the governor in the state of Espírito Santo. Hanchard (1999: 73) used this case in order to show the inconsistencies of the Brazilian multiple model of classification, criticizing Degler's widely known theory of the mulatto escape-hatch and praising the politicization of blackness in Brazil.[13]

Favor toward a more bipolar view of Brazilian race relations has started becoming visible in the Brazilian government. In a public speech in 1996, the Brazilian president, Fernando Henrique Cardoso, invited the IBGE to gather together *"mulatos, pardos* and *pretos* as members of the *negro* [black] population" (in Telles 2004: 86). These recommendations have never been adopted by the IBGE, whose censuses still divide the Brazilian population into five categories (*branco/pardo/preto/amarelo/indígena*), although a bipolar approach is sometimes used to systematize certain survey outputs for *pardos* and *pretos* (IBGE, 2007). The institutional popularity of a bipolar approach to race relations has grown consistently. In Rio de Janeiro, the first law of quotas (3.708/2001) addressed *pardos* and *negros*[14] as student beneficiaries of racial quotas for *negros* in public state universities in the State of Rio de Janeiro. Although the revision of the first quota law, in 2003, addressed more generally *negros*, without making any reference to *pardos*,[15] the understanding of *negros* as the sum of *pardos* and *pretos* was officially restated at the federal level by the Statute of Racial Equality approved in 2010 (law 12.288/2010). This law, which sets a number of principles to be addressed by further legislation in matter of racial equality, defines the *negro* population as "the whole of people who self-identify as *pardas* and *pretas*" (art.1) according to the IBGE classification and those who use a similar self-definition.[16]

Racial Quotas as a Threat to *Mestiçagem*

In the introduction to this book, I mentioned that the implementation of racial quotas has created much alarmism within the public opinion and among social scientists. Peter Fry (2005) and Yvonne Maggie (2005 and 2006b) have dedicated much of their recent work to discussing the perils of the racial reasoning entailed by quotas.[17] Maggie (2005 and 2006a, b) talks of racial pedagogy from the state, wherein people would be taught about supposedly biologically existing racial differences and encouraged to feel black.[18] People, in the end, will arguably be influenced by state intervention to choose between a black and a white identity, with social policies working as an incentive to make people "black." This possible identity shift seems particularly realistic for those who are already classified as *pardos* in demographic surveys and in everyday life. Other critiques relate to the impossibility of defining who is black in Brazil and the risk of reinforcing genetic ideas of race that have already been refuted by science (Cavalli-Sforza, 2003) and proven counterproductive in history. Such a process of racialization, for example, would sadly recall systems implemented in South Africa during apartheid[19] or in the United States during Jim Crow.[20] Fry is concerned by the fact that people would have a biracial US-style model imposed upon them and that this does not take into account the high flexibility of racial/color ascriptions in Brazil, where *mestiçagem* represents a crucial component of national identity but is also an expression of the intense racial mixture in that country. In this sense Bourdieu and Wacquant (1999) see the prospect of the bipolarization of racial identities and categories in Brazil, supported by Hanchard, as a form of American imperialism or ethnocentrism, which does not take into account the specificities of the Brazilian context. The actual fear, in Brazil, is that quotas represent an antecedent of and a justification for something more radical for the future of the nation. The Brazilian Parliament is in fact deliberating on a number of measures that might lead to institute university racial quotas at the federal level, with their possible extension to the whole public sector, including, for instance, education, health, and politics.[21] These anxieties are well-expressed in the so-called Manifesto Contra as Cotas (Folha online, 2008a), signed by intellectuals, civil society organizations, and private citizens and addressed to the Supremo Tribunal Federal (Federal High Court) in May 2008. The objective of the Manifesto was asking the Federal High Court to declare the unconstitutionality of quotas:

> [Racial quotas are] the more visible representation of an official racialization of social relations that threatens national cohesion . . . In Brazil, this [quota system] means radically revising our national identity and renouncing the possible utopia of the universalizing of effective citizenship . . . The jurisprudential decision [of the Federal Court in relation to quotas] will have historic meaning because it may create jurisprudence about the constitutionality of racial quotas not just for higher education but also for public competition in general. This decision [by the Federal Court] also has the potential to send an important message about the constitutionality of racial laws. (Author's translation)[22]

Making traditional readings of Brazilian race relations more complex, Peter Fry (2005: 183, 195) admits that Brazilian people already rely on bi-racial models of classification in folk parlance and that this is not exclusively due to quotas. He notes that, depending on the context, a biracial approach is freely alternated (but, as I understand it, never considered and used simultaneously) with multiple models, which better reflect the complexity and ambiguity of Brazilian color/racial identifications in everyday life. The problem with Black movement politics and language, which are implicit in quotas,[23] Fry suggests, is that they impose on people the use of a biracial means of classification as the only one possible. In doing so, they prevent Brazilians from choosing freely between models of identification. This militant biracial model, according to Fry, is quite different from the one used by ordinary people ("popular bi-polarity"), which can instead coexist with the "multiple" style of identification (Fry, 2005: 195; see also Schwartzman, 2009).

It is clear that the quota debate has raised more general questions about official classification systems in Brazil. Whereas until the 1940s official color classification was aimed to assess the stage of whitening of the Brazilian population, if not directly to whiten it (Nobles, 2000: 101), in more recent times classification has been used to describe the multiracial character of the country, or more simply to assess how different population groups fare in socioeconomic terms, without this implying any practical consequences in terms of racial policies. The use of official color classification has therefore been accepted to a degree in Brazil, aside from having been briefly withdrawn during some periods of the military regime—when stating racial divisions was interpreted as conspiring against national unity—and finally reintroduced in the 1980s at the time of the *abertura democrática* (104). Racial/color classification has again become more controversial as people have realized that it can be used as a basis for racial policies, a fact that supposedly threatens the traditional *mestiço* and antiracist constitution of the nation.

We are here at a crucial point. As Wade (2004b) observes, Latin American scholars have often been overoptimistic in celebrating *mestizaje* as an antidote to racial absolutism and racism. In fact, the two concepts can coexist rather well. This is because *mestiçagem* feeds itself from the origins on which racial absolutes rely. These origins, I add, already respond to hierarchies that are historically constructed and that Freyre's fable of the three races does not really unsettle.[24] In my view, this fact implies not only what Wade suggests but also that there are *mestiços* and *mestiços*, and that their location on an imagined discrimination scale might depend on how much they resemble a specific pole or origin, which is widely perceived negatively in society.

In this sense, some people might fit well into the *mestiço* category but more imperfectly than others due to their deeper resemblance to certain racial absolutes. A question, for example, is whether the ideal type of the Brazilian *mestiço* is after all rather "African-looking," or instead quite whitened. This fact is relevant to discuss the inclusion of *pardos* as *negros* because a frequent tendency is to overgeneralize and oversimplify mixedness.

Another question is whether racially based affirmative action—at least in the way that it is implemented at the UERJ—is racializing the student collective through the effect of a quota choice. In this regard, I should clarify that associating the racial quota system at the UERJ with a system of racial classification is not quite correct. In the case of quotas, students of all colors might decide to use racial quotas by self-identifying as "*negros*" but are not asked to decide between different color/racial groups in order to fill a quota.[25] In fact, students who use racial quotas are technically still allowed to self-identify as "white" (*branco*), "brown" (*pardo*), or "black" (*negro*) in question 25 of the socioeconomic questionnaire ("*como você descreveria a sua cor?*") filled in during the vestibular. Students who identify their color as white in the socioeconomic questionnaire can nonetheless apply for a black quota and achieve it by self-identifying as *negros* for reasons that might transcend color. This is possible because neither the quota law nor the university give instructions to help students understand what being *negro* means, leaving it open to interpretations that rely on phenotype, ancestry, or other social identification factors. The term *negro* is thus made, deliberately or not, potentially including of different color identifications. In this sense, the quota system differs very much from the system of IBGE classification because, in IBGE categorization, people must choose between different color/racial categories and the chosen category automatically excludes the others. In addition, the terms *pardo* and *preto* used in the IBGE are less controversially understood as referring to skin color in Brazil, whereas the term *negro* is much broader and its interpretation may go well beyond color shades, depending on who is using it and when.

The Black Movement's Mainstream Discourse and the Contending Understandings of race in Brazil

During my fieldwork, I interviewed UERJ Black activists to understand the new political tendency that gathers *pardos* and *pretos* together as *negros*, and finally reflect on its possible meaning for quotas.

Me: Why does the law now talk generally of *negros* to address the beneficiaries of racial quotas?
Jurema: Before we said color . . . we said *pardo* and *preto*. Now it's all just *negro* to us. Black (*negro*) is race. It is the fairer one and the darker one . . . let's say all Afro-descendants.
Me: So, do you think that *pardos* are *negros*?
Jurema: I do, because we have a view of black (*negro*) being everybody who is not white. We have a popular saying here that "all that is not white is black." However, some people are lighter-skinned due to our [Brazilian] miscegenation. There are blacks (*negros*) who are quite dark (*escuros*) and others who are quite fair-skinned (*claros*); there are *negros* whose hair is curly (*cacheado*) and others whose hair is rather kinky (*bem crespo*) . . . but there is no doubt that all of them are *negros* . . . (Jurema, final-year law student and Denegrir activist at the UERJ)

Explanations also recalled Hasenbalg and Silva's comments about the similarities in economic performance of *pardos* and *pretos* (Hasenbalg, 1979 and 1985; Silva, 1985; Telles, 2004). "The fact that *preto* and *pardo* are merged into the same *negro* category is due to the economic factor. *Pardos* and *pretos* perform very similarly . . . The *pardo* is much closer to the *negro* than to the *branco*" (Renato Ferreira, director of PPCOR—Politics of Color—UERJ). Renato Ferreira highlights a reading of race that reflects gaps in the understanding of this concept between the pro- and antiquota movements. He reiterates a common point within the Black movement that race is not really something genetic, due to the general miscegenation of the Brazilian population between people of European, African, and indigenous descent.

Ferreira: . . . Biology is very important but is not always useful in discussing social problems. Race has meanings which are historical, social, political and cultural but they are not related to the genetic question. We are all of a human race . . . we already know . . . however, what we are discussing is not inequality in the genetic field but in the social one. Perhaps you have more African genes than me, who knows? In spite of this, my African genes are phenotypically translated in a way that makes me *negro*, whereas you look white . . . genetics is not so relevant in social matters. If you said that you are superior because you descend from a group which is more intelligent, etcetera, you would be talking about genetics. However, we are not talking about [genetically] superior and inferior here . . . we are talking about poor and rich . . . We say race because this concept includes people of different color [shades] . . . Race is the universe of these people.

This point is crucial because it shows that the discourses of pro- and antiquotas start from quite different assumptions. There are in fact two main views of race that are presently debated in the framework of Brazilian quotas. The first view is essentially scientific in a genetic and biological sense and has been widely refuted by science. One of its typical effects would be the "one-drop rule" ascribed to the US situation, which gives importance even to very distant African ancestry. The other view sees race as a social construct that derives from the general differentiation of a specific group of people in the social collective due to the way that their appearance is commonly read and generates certain expectations, for example, about class and behavior (Wade, 2004a: 157–159). Such a construct is not only social but also historical, because processes of perceived difference are rooted in particular historical processes. In fact, as Segato (2007: 25) argues, it is not correct to say that race *can be seen*; what can be seen, instead, is the history transcribed on the relativity of the body and which, consequently, "cannot be fixed in identities emptied of the historic game that produced it." Visual meanings are culturally created and negotiated through a multiplicity of factors; for example, through certain black aesthetics that find increasing space in the media, which represent new antihegemonic models and may shift the dominant ways in which the black phenotype is read in society. According to Segato, color is the most immediate and stronger aspect that leads to a process of otherification and subsequent exclusion, by recalling the historic defeat of the African people by the colonial forces and their relative enslavement. This is also why, even in the case of some black people who are not related to slave history, the sign they hold will basically be read in the context of such history (134).[26]

These two approaches to race may have variations and should never be understood as absolutes. In particular, the second approach often tries to emphasize socioeconomic indicators more than appearance and it is commonly said that this approach is social, not biological; however, it seems that it cannot escape biology *tout court*. This happens not in the sense of the body as a given scientific reality, but in the measures that biology and especially phenotype (what one sees on the outside) can be socially constructed through socially constructed vision.[27] Also, as Osorio (2004: 92) adds, certain aspects of this vision are still determined by a number of genes able to produce certain phenotypes or "visible differences." In a similar vein, Sesardic (2010) highlights how certain biological aspects of race resist in science in several ways, contradicting attempts of scientific and social deconstructivism from the same scientists and from scholars in the social sciences.

If the socioeconomic approach ends up downplaying biology more nominally than practically, a parallel impasse affects those who more actively claim the nonscientificity of race. The introduction of quotas, ironically, coincided with a new emphasis on scientific genetic studies in Brazil to prove Brazilian miscegenation, the unclear correspondence between genes and appearance, and which, consequently, undermine the logics of racial quotas (Alves-Silva et al., 2000; Pena et al., 2000). In this vein, Santos and Maio (2004: 75) cite scientific research illustrating that 60 percent of the genomic map of self-declared white Brazilian men is composed of indigenous (33 percent) and African (28 percent) genes in the matrilinear line (Santos et al., 2009). Almost paradoxically, these scientific studies that aim to scientifically deconstruct race somehow recreate it by very similar means. While they try to prove mixture, this mixture is still presented as being formed from discrete categories such as European, African, and Amerindian, which sound racial implicitly or otherwise. In addition, genomic research might not be so revealing if, as Telles (2004: 93) shows, 52 percent of white Brazilians admit non-European ancestry independent of any scientific tests. This acknowledgment of one's mixture, he observes, does not necessarily prevent people from being racist or enjoying privileged treatment in society due to their fairer skin or "finer" features.

Race as a concept for quotas is in any case contested not just due to its lack of scientificity, but also due to the fact that this idea historically served to annihilate, subordinate, and segregate groups. There is therefore an assumption that the word race cannot escape the negative and dangerous meanings that history has conferred to it, that its signs cannot be reinterpreted over time, and that any attempt of the social movements to use it in order to claim rights is somehow wrong and should be contested. Another mentioned risk is that the originality and flexibility of the Brazilian system of race relations would be unsettled by foreign (US) models that use ancestry or the one-drop rule in order to decide about somebody's blackness.

On the other hand, while antiracializing discourses in Brazil subtend extremely complex layers, the Black movement's efforts to merge the *pardo* and *preto* categories into *"negro"* do not simply match a description of things; they are instead quite normative and imply, at least potentially, huge political consequences in terms of statistics and policies. It is enough to consider that, according to the IBGE, *pretos* (black-colored people) comprise just 6.9 percent of the Brazilian population, whereas *pardos* (brown-colored people) comprise 42.6 percent, and *brancos* 49.7 percent (see PNAD 2009 data in IBGE, 2010).

By combining the first two groups, the *negro* population would magically rise to about 50 percent of Brazilians.[28] A similar mathematic operation might contribute to raising racial consciousness, the weakness of which, according to militants, is also due to the availability of the *pardo* category as a possible escape for people to avoid blackness. In this vein, Black activists also hope that black affirmative action will consolidate the racial identification of the black group, because this action widely draws on a biracial philosophy of classification.

Are All *Pardos* "*Negros*"? Blackness and *Mestiçagem* in the Discourse of the Black Movement

> *Pardos* are not all the same thing, because in Brazil it's enough that you have straight hair and fine features so you won't be that discriminated against. (Patrícia, social sciences)

Until this point I have artificially emphasized the unity and coherence of Black militant discourse about the encompassing of *pardo* people as *negros* in Brazil, as this is widely presented as *the* view of the movement in Brazil. Fieldwork data, however, problematize such unity since a number of activists expressed some tension between blackness and mixedness. In this sense, mixedness (or brownness) is often indirectly or directly recognized as something separate that cannot be automatically encompassed as blackness. These ambiguities emerged in my interview with Renato Ferreira:

> Who is black in Brazil? The *pretos* like myself, and the *pardos*. In Rio de Janeiro, the *pardo* is *negro* . . . I am *negro* and *preto*. My brother has lighter skin and despite having negroid features (*feições negroides*), he might be seen as non-*negro*. For example, if he wore a hat, he might be seen as *moreno* [because his kinky hair would be disguised by the hat]. *Pardos* and *pretos* will always be considered *negros* in specific situations. In others, they might not be seen as *negros* but this doesn't mean that such a vision saves them from stigma in absolute terms . . . When looking for a job I might be discriminated against, whereas my brother might not . . . however, if you [as a white person] compete with him for the job, he might be discriminated against and you not. So, both my brother, who is *pardo*, and I, as *preto*, are *negros* . . . they are degrees that can be noticed in specific situations . . . It is possible that a *pardo* never suffers discrimination, or that he feels *negro* only at the time of getting a quota or amidst white people. A *pardo* [person] is somebody from the Baixada Fluminense [a lower-class area],

with tanned skin and less straight hair (*de pele bronzeada e cabelo menos liso*) . . . if this person goes to [wealthy] Zona Sul, this person will be considered *negro* . . . at least, in Rio de Janeiro.

Me: Does *pardo* include *moreno*?

Ferreira: Yes, but [some] *morenos* can say that they are white in Brazil, light *morenos* (*morenos claros*). However, the *pardos* are *negros*, at least in Rio de Janeiro and in the [Brazilian] South . . . Some of them may be lighter-skinned and have straighter hair . . . however, for those who are looking at them . . . these people are *negros*. They might not suffer discrimination but they are *negros* . . .

This interviewee stresses that *negros* may have curly or kinky hair (never naturally straight), while the skin has to be at least *bronzeada* (tanned, brown). The word *"negroide"* is used in order to point out particular features that make some people more *negros* (or typically "African-looking"[29]) than others. However, accessories such as hats and certain aesthetics may push somebody toward one pole or the other of an imaginary color/race scale and therefore expose people to more or less discrimination. Considering *pardos* and *pretos* as beneficiaries of the same racial policies is, however, not so simple. Although Ferreira tends to minimize this fact in the first stage of his interview, at one point he states that brown-skinned people (*pardos*) are discriminated against less and in fewer situations than darker-skinned people (*pretos*). He also adds that some brown people, especially certain *morenos*, might not suffer discrimination at all. Ferreira's distinction between *pardos* and *morenos* should in any case be taken carefully. It was seen that 54 percent of those people who self-declared as *morenos* in open-ended questionnaires of the 1998 PME (Monthly Employment Survey)[30] in fact chose to reclassify themselves as *pardos* in the closed questionnaire with the traditional IBGE format of *branco/pardo/preto/amarelo/indígena* (Petruccelli, 2007: 35). This fact necessarily raises questions about whether it is possible to distinguish between *pardos* and *morenos* on a terminological basis. It also raises questions about the meaning of a *negro* political category if this is simply created by combining the *pardo* and *preto* IBGE categories.

Black militant Carlo Alberto Medeiros dealt with this point further at a forum for the implementation of the Estatuto da Igualdade Racial (Statute of Racial Equality) held by the Partido dos Trabalhadores at Leopoldina Station in August 2007. He argued that people like Camilla Pitanga, a popular (and self-identified *negra*) Brazilian actress, should not be entitled to use racial quotas. Pitanga, as Medeiros observed, was allowed to play the role of an Italian girl in movies: the light brown color/phenotype of this actress was not (black) enough to expose her to discrimination in Brazil, although she was not identified as white either by the speaker.[31]

In interviews collected by Alberti and Pereira, Medeiros observes that if one of the problems with racial quotas is establishing who is *negro* and who is not due to Brazilian miscegenation, it would still be possible to address at least—or first—those *negros* he defines as *indisfarçáveis* (unambiguous).[32] These points highlight the fact that *mestiçagem* is directly or indirectly considered within the Black movement, and sometimes even excluded from blackness, in spite of this fact often being minimized in the movement's official discourse. On a rather similar note, Renato Ferreira finally concluded that

> [t]here are *pardos* who do not descend from *negros* and people whose close ancestors are *negros* but whose phenotype does not lead to discrimination . . . [This is why] it would be important to discuss further the concept of *mestiçagem* within the [Black] movement in order to understand what could be accepted as *negro* and what could not, establishing measures for this. (Renato Ferreira)

Problematic aspects about *mestiçagem* within the Black movement do not emerge only in formal interviews but also more crucially in the live experiences of students. An informant complained that when he joined the activities of the Black student movement at the UERJ for the first time, somebody expressed reserves about him being black. This student was quite fair-skinned but he identified as *mulato* due to family history. A fact is that although militants with relatively fair skin are present at Black student events (albeit in a minority), they usually balance a less-clear black phenotype with aesthetics, for example, massive black-power grooming or dreadlocks, whereas the student I mention did not use any ethnic accessories or style. A question is whether militants considered this student white, or maybe just not black enough. If this informant had been quite dark-skinned or had had stronger black features the questioning of his blackness would have been less likely within Black political circles, even in the absence of a Black-ethnic outfit. *Mestiçagem* is therefore more clearly included as black by Black activists, outside the discursive realm, only if some black phenotypic or aesthetic criteria are also observed. In this vein, some activists demonstrated that a darker skin generally confers more authority or legitimacy within the Black movement, even doing so with humor: a Black-militant at the UERJ used to tease lighter-skinned activists by saying that they were not as "pure juice" as he was (*puro suco*).

Similar conclusions emerged during interviews with students at the UERJ research organization Proafro, which is linked to the Black movement, and where some integrants were very fair-skinned or had olive skin with naturally straight hair and looked, roughly and stereotypically speaking, Southern European. On the question of whether he identified as *negro*, Tullio had some hesitation but finally stated that he did in a political sense. In physical terms, in fact, he did not identify either as *negro* or as *branco* but just as *pardo*. This black identification, even if partial, raised copious laughter from several of his colleagues who categorically dismissed Tullio's chances of being *negro* without identifying him as white either. Another student, who was very light-skinned, concluded that *negro* identification was in many cases not so relevant "because, in the end, you can be really *negro/a* only if you look and people in general consider you as such."

Finally, *mestiçagem* within the discourse of the Black movement is to be considered for another reason. A number of first-year female law nonquota students who were commonly identified as white by classmates self-identified as *pardas* in interviews. Other interviewees stated that they self-identified both as white and as *pardas*. They explained their *pardo* self-identification either by awareness of their mixed ancestry, or by comparison to more Anglo-Saxon models of beauty (particularly blonde hair and blue eyes), which find a privileged space in Brazilian mass media.[33] At the same time, these students do not automatically stress any clearly shared ground or feelings of discrimination with darker and more typically "African-looking" people.

> It's because [almost] nobody is really white in Brazil. The real white is somebody like Xuxa[34] or Gisele Bündchen,[35] you know . . . blonde people with very fair skin, blue eyes and straight hair. I'm not like that! My skin is more *morena* . . . and guess what . . . I'm not even going to the beach! (Viviane, first-year law student).

Racializing the UERJ? Self-Identification and Beneficiaries' Use of Racial Quotas

Something that really struck me during fieldwork was that most nonpoliticized quota informants I interviewed at the UERJ used the system but considered it unfair and acceptable only to balance, on a temporary basis, state redistributive failures. "Quotas should not be a permanent system. I agree with them only if they are used as a provisional solution, in the meantime, while the state ensures good public education for everybody" (Daisy, *negra*, black-quota student). Informants' negative attitudes to quotas can also be generally explained by the fact that these students are allowed to enter university with a lower score, which is commonly interpreted as a lack of merit. Racial quotas are considered particularly negatively and even as threatening to racial harmony, while public-school quotas are preferred as a lesser evil.

> Why should I have used the black quotas, considering that I studied at a public school? I really disagree with racial quotas. They discriminate against people who are not black . . . Now tell me something: is it not true that the poorest people in Brazil are *negra*s? . . . where are they studying? They study in the public system, right? . . . In that case, the public-school quotas would automatically address all needy people . . . (Flávia, *negra*, public-school quota student)

It is important to clarify that the public-school quota option is not always available to students. Eliane (*negra*) did study at a public school and complained about the ethical foundations of racial quotas. Having said this, she had to fall back on the racial system due to its simplified bureaucracy.

> The only thing that candidates need to apply for black quotas is a high-school diploma and a written statement of black self-declaration [at the time of the vestibular] . . . In order to use public-school quotas, however, you have to show that you did most of your studies in public schools . . . however, one of my previous [public] schools was on strike and I could not access my certificate [to apply for public-school quotas] . . . this is why I had to use the racial system . . . (Eliane, black-quota student)

One year after she had started the undergraduate course in law with the help of racial quotas, Eliane was still unhappy about having accessed the Law Department as a black-quota student:

> I've always said that I'm *negra*, but I don't accept the idea of applying to university by skin color . . . skin color should not be important . . . why should I be less skillful than other students just for being *negra*? . . . I felt very bad when I had to apply through the racial quota system . . . Anyway, when looking at my score in the vestibular exam I realized that this was similar to that of public-school *cotistas* . . . this still cheers me up a bit . . .

Flávia and Eliane disliked the racial system because it reinforces inferiority stigmas for black people and somehow stamps a certificate of demerit on students. The same students, however, would not feel equally diminished by using the public-school quota system. This channel is in fact perceived as color-blind and as a better match to universalistic approaches of redistribution and equality. Public-school quotas are presumably justifiable due to state inefficiency, which is external to students and is, therefore, presumably less directly related to their biology.

As with Eliane and Flávia, Daisy was not enthusiastic about the racial quota system either, although she had eventually relied on it. Unlike the other students, however, Daisy explained her choice by the fact that the ratio of applicants/openings for quota students in the Law Department had been lower for racial quotas in previous years and therefore she expected to have more of a chance to pass through this system. Daisy also disagreed with the idea that the public-school quota system really is color-blind. She mentioned that wealthier students who study in better-standard public institutions, and achieve most public-school quota openings, are by and large light-skinned.

> Public schools are not all the same . . . some of them are good and reach part of the middle class. For example the Pedro Segundo, the CAP UERJ . . . the CAP UFRJ . . . they are federal or state schools which are good. Users are people who cannot pay for very elite private schools but might have a better economic situation than people who come from cheap private institutions . . . black people are not really common there![36] (Daisy, *negra*, black-quota student)

Daisy's opting for racial quotas also had other practical reasons. Since she had studied in a low-standard private school, she could never apply through the public-school quota system.[37] Daisy's situation was actually quite common among black-quota law freshmen, the majority of whom came from low-standard private institutions.[38] In this sense, racial quotas at the UERJ are rather inclusive. Not only can they be used by a wide range of people with different skin-color identifications due to self-declaration, but they also avoid excluding an important number of low-income students who come from low-standard private schools.

Quota statistics might add interesting information about the appeal that black quotas have for students. In 2007, people used 85 percent of the public-school quotas available, whereas just 40 percent of racial quotas were filled. This is an average that does not reflect the situation in any specific courses. In elite courses (law, medicine, industrial design, journalism, etc.), where competition for access might be harsh and the admission score notoriously high, 100 percent of racial quotas were used. In contrast, this system is very little used in courses such as physics, math, and education (only 25 percent of racial quota openings in education, and 5 percent in physics were used in 2007). In these courses, the ratio of candidate/opening is rather low, and access is relatively easy even without quotas. In the socioeconomic questionnaire for candidates in 2008, 14 percent of *non*quota students in education and 12 percent in physics identified their color as *negro*[39] (against 5 percent in law and 0 percent in medicine); this suggests that a good portion of these students could probably have applied for quotas (if matching the low-income parameter) and therefore might represent missing applicants for black-quotas.[40] In courses considered less prestigious the percentage of public-school students who self-identify as black-skinned in the socioeconomic questionnaire is even higher: 30 percent in education versus just 11 percent in law and 5 percent in medicine in 2008. This shows that although self-identified black students generally try to avoid quotas—more specifically racial quotas—the pressure to use the quota system might be even lower when the course is less popular. Having said this, when the quota system is used, the incentive to use racial quotas is much lower if students are eligible for the public-school quota system.[41]

The data presented also encourage considerations about whether the use of racial quotas reflects people's identification and in what way the student collective would be racialized. On the one hand, many self-identified black students avoided or tried to avoid racial quotas. On the other, the self-declaration used by the racial quota system at the UERJ implies that students of all colors can apply, although they have to write a self-declaration to explain their black identification, for example, by color or ancestry. It follows that the allocation of quotas does not provide a clear insight into the actual distribution of color/racial identification of the student population at the UERJ and, consequently, of its racialization. The color declaration in the socioeconomic questionnaire at the UERJ, similarly, is only partially useful in understanding everyday identification. This is, first, because it is never clear what *pardo* is and how students interpret this term in the questionnaire, and second, because students who apply through racial quotas might feel the incentive to identify as *negros* in the questionnaire to avoid looking incoherent with their planned quota choice. By accessing the Vestibular Office database of how first-year law students in 2007 answered the socioeconomic questionnaire, I achieved some interesting information in this sense. I realized that many of my informants who had used a black quota but stated themselves to be non-*negros* in our everyday socializing had ticked *negro* in question 25 of the questionnaire, the question about their color. In interviews, some of them stated that they had chosen that identification because it was more coherent with their quota use, or that they had been afraid that some process of information cross-checking by vestibular officials could reveal this "inconsistency" and thus exclude them from the racial quotas. I cannot overlook the fact that the racial/color language used in the questionnaire might also have influenced students to answer in specific ways. If question 25 had used *preto* (which is more strongly associated with dark skin and black-racialized phenotypes in Brazil), instead of *negro*, to express color identification, many students who had identified as *negros* in the socioeconomic form might have ticked *pardos*, since the word *preto* would more clearly be at odds with their lighter skin and perceived mixture.[42]

Racial Quotas and Their Influence on the Identity of Brown Students

A question that I have not yet addressed concerns the influence that racial quotas might have on candidates, especially on brown people who might start to self-identify as black through using racial quotas. In this regard, I noticed that a number of brown students who were using black quotas continued self-identifying as *pardo*, *moreno*, or *mestiço* (brown/mixed) during my fieldwork at the UERJ. Blackness was suddenly stated by these students only when I asked them why they had used black quotas.[43]

On a first informal interview, I asked Glória, a black-quota student, about her identification.

> *Me*: Do you consider yourself *negra*?
> *Glória*: Me? I don't. I'm *morena*! I'm *parda* . . . *Negro* is something different. It's something more African, like him [pointing to another—very dark-skinned—student]. My father is white and my mother is brown (*morena*) like me . . . there must be a bit of everything in my family . . . even indigenous blood (*até indígena deve ter na minha família*).

On a different occasion, I met Glória for a formal interview. I was intrigued by the fact that this student had used black quotas—and had filled in a self-declaration for this—but had never described herself as *negra* in previous meetings. In this new interview, her answer was quite different.

Look, [I used black quotas because] I'm *negra* (black) . . . even though my features don't show much of it (*embora as minhas feições não deixem ver muito*) . . . the fact is that I had never used this term before because I'm *morena* . . . but some people (*alguém*) told me that I could consider myself *negra* . . . let's say Afro-descendant, OK? Look, white I'm not . . . one day I went to a restaurant with a friend and I felt that I was the only non-white (*não branca*) there . . . My grandmother was descended from a slave woman . . . an Italian found her in the pillory (*a chibata*) and made her pregnant (*engravidou ela*).

A question is whether racial quotas are really changing anything in Glória's self-identification.

The first interview shows that this student still considers herself brown because she does not clearly fit onto a binary black-and-white pole; she uses the term *negra* in phenotypic terms as something corresponding more or less to the color *preto* or, as she says, to a "more African" appearance. In the second interview, on the other hand, Glória's answer was clearly biased because I might have somehow been questioning her entitlement to a black quota. At that point, as other students did, she attached her blackness to ancestry. She had to explain this ancestry in detail in order to be more convincing, presumably because her blackness was not clearly supported by her appearance ("*embora as minhas feiçoes não deixem ver muito*").[44] Another important point is that some people (*alguém*) had to let this student know that she could consider herself *negra* for quota purposes, since this had not previously been clear to her (although she certainly never self-identified as white either, as the episode in the restaurant shows).[45] This black identification was used for the vestibular but never became a solid part of this student's identity, at least during my fieldwork. In other words, I am not convinced that the use of a black quota is bringing out or creating any black identity in this student at the expense of her everyday mixed-race identification preference.

Also in Glória's case—as shown earlier—the school of origin emerges as a crucial (but very often silenced) reason for the use of black quotas.[46] Glória had studied in a low-standard private institution, a fact that would exclude her from public-school quotas. Unlike Glória, several public-school quota students who self-identified as *moreno* and *pardo* felt freer to consistently deny any blackness during my fieldwork.

Me: . . . Why didn't you use a black quota?
Rafael: It's simple! Because I'm not *negro*! [Looking surprised]
Me: So, how do you classify yourself?

Rafael: I'm *pardo*!
Me: Could you say *moreno*?
Rafael: Yes, if you prefer. *Negro* I'm not.
Other student: He's *moreno* . . . You can see how his features are delicate (*finas*) and his hair is not hard (*duro*).
Me: Then, for people you would never pass as *negro*?
Rafael: No way . . . (Rafael, *pardo*, law public-school quota student)

This student concluded, "Anyway, I did not have any reason to use a black quota . . . I come from a public school. It is enough that I don't like quotas . . . can you imagine how much I would like racial ones?" In countertendency to my findings, Francis and Tannuri-Pianto (2010: 15), who researched shifts in color and racial identity among students at the University of Brasília, concluded that there was an increase of almost 6 percent in the percentage of self-declared *pardo* students who also identified racially as *negros* in comparison to the prequota period.[47] This increase, however, does not seem to be striking in terms of possible racialization, both in terms of percentage and also because the prequota data available to these researchers for comparison concerned just one semester before the implementation of the quota system at the University of Brasília. In addition, Francis and Tannuri-Pianto ascribe this percentage shift to the (positive, in their view) racializing effect promoted by quotas. However, it is not clear to me whether part of this variation could be also and better explained by the increasing fashion that, more generally, *negro* identification enjoys among some young generations as a consequence of Black politics and affirmation, or due to the black confidence that students might develop at university because of contact with politicized students and the exposure to certain academic topics.[48]

IDEAS OF SIMULTANEOUS PHENOTYPIC IDENTIFICATION AS "BLACK" AND "BROWN" AMONG QUOTA STUDENTS

What has been said earlier may unfairly suggest that no brown UERJ students genuinely self-identify as *negro* other than to justify, very contextually, their use of racial quotas. In fact, several brown-skinned students who self-identify as *negros* independent of quota usage and Black-politicization also see themselves as *pardos* and/or *mestiços*, a fact they usually explain through mixed ancestry, their relatively lighter skin, and less "typically-black-African" features. These students simultaneously use blackness and *mestiçagem* as two concepts that are neither systematically antithetical nor simply coincide. In fact, they use and combine these concepts in different ways depending on how much they believe they carry black-racialized features.

> *Flávia*: . . . We went to a '60s music event in the Circo Voador in Lapa and I saw only very few *negros* there; probably four including me . . . some of them were *mestiços*. I was with Elder but he's not *negro* . . . he's just *mestiço* . . .
> *Me*: So, he's just *mestiço* but you're *negra* . . .?
> *Flávia*: Well, I'm *mestiça* too . . .
> *Me*: But . . . you just said that you're *negra* a few seconds ago!
> *Flávia*: There is mixture in my family . . . the family of my father is white. Look at my color [rubbing the skin of her arm]. It's *parda*. Look at my hair . . . so, how is it possible that it is not as hard as that of the other girls (*não é duro como o das outras meninas*)? *Negro* is somebody more [with embarrassment] . . . how to say . . . African . . . like that [referring to another student]. I actually know people who are even worse (*pior*) than that [still referring to the other student]. Sorry, I wanted to say darker (*mais escuro*) . . .
> *Me*: . . . You mean that people don't consider you *negra* in Brazil? . . .
> *Flávia*: Of course people will see me as *negra*! My race is *negra* but my color . . . Wait! Are you asking me about my *race* or my *color*? [looking rather uncomfortable] . . . What I wanted to say is that I'm *parda* because my skin color is lighter than that of other people . . . because I'm not *preta* (very dark) and my hair . . .

Flávia's case is complicated by the fact that she uses the term *negro* in two different ways. The first is closer to the sociohistorical interpretation of race formally used by the Black movement and is generally expressed through black ancestry; however, it is also broadly visual, encompassing people who occupy different places on the color/racial scale (*pardos* and *pretos*) but who can also be visually recognized as *negros* (a few people at the concert). The second interpretation of *negro* used by Flávia is even more strikingly visual and closer to *preto*, which is a much darker or more typically "African" than *pardo* (brown).[49] Looking at it in this second way, *negro* more specifically appears to be something "worse" (*pior*), setting blackness as something to feel rather uncomfortable about. Terminological ambiguity apart, I could conclude that Flávia self-identifies as both *negra* and *parda*—which also entails feeling mixed, *mestiça*—at the same time, implicitly articulating two concepts that are semantically different, as she expresses in the question: "Are you asking me about my race or my color?" Because she is mixed, Flávia's hair is not as "hard" as that of other girls but might still be hard and curly enough to make her black; her skin color is not *preta* but probably dark enough to easily fit into a black category. In addition to close black ancestry, Flávia not only seems to acknowledge the visual existence of a black sphere that encompasses different shades of blackness (skin color and more or less marked black features); she also ascribes to these shades a specific value on the beauty scale, on which she believes that she enjoys a more privileged position than darker-skinned or more typically "African"-looking girls. It is also interesting that Flávia ends up ascribing blackness to herself, whereas the same identification is denied to her *mestiço* friend ("he is not *negro* . . . he's just *mestiço* . . . "), for whom this articulation of blackness and *mestiçagem* does not seem to work equally well.

Regina, an education nonquota student, offers a similar example of articulation of blackness and *mestiçagem*. In the same interview, this student self-identified as black (*negra*) but also as brown (*morena, clara*). "I'm *negra* but I have never felt much discrimination in life because I'm like this, *morena* . . . rather fair-skinned (*porque a minha pele é assim, morena . . . bem clara*)." However, as she remembers,

> When I went to primary school in Campo Grande [a poor area of Zona Oeste], my mom was afraid that I might be discriminated against . . . because I have black features (*porque tenho feições de negra*). She actually prepared me for this risk and always said "look, if somebody calls you *macaca* (monkey) you should reply 'Do you know why toilet paper is white? To clean black people's shit!" (*pra limpar o cocô do preto*).

The exposure to being called "*macaca*" (monkey), a very stereotypical insult for people with a black-racialized phenotype, is what, contextually or not, relegates Regina to a *negro* group. This is relevant even though, as she said, her color is lighter and this spares her from the more automatic discrimination that affects darker-skinned people with black-racialized features. *Negro*, in this case, is something very visual and perfectly compatible with a brown color. The word *preto*, used in the prepared formula to counteract racial discrimination, highlights the forced and inescapable inclusion/relegation of this student into a black group.

It is important to clarify that neither Flávia nor Regina, at the time of the interviews, had any connections to the Black movement, the politics of which, in their view, was too extreme and somehow also inversely racist (*racista às avessas*). Both Flávia (public-school quota student) and Regina (nonquota student) had avoided racial quotas due to the moral questionability of these measures and their being at odds with the Brazilian ideal of racial harmony, which ideal they paradoxically scale down through their accounts.

Another interesting example of articulation is represented by Eliane, a brown-skinned student who generally referred to her skin color as *parda* but started self-identifying as *negra* from an early age, even though she disagreed with the rationale of the black quotas and was rather skeptical of Black politics.[50]

> *Eliane*: Why do I have to say that I'm *morena* or *parda* (brown) if I'm *negra*? I've always considered myself *preta*, ever since I was a little girl. I remember that a primary school classmate of mine was used to saying that he was *pardo*. I always teased him and said "look, how can you be *pardo* if you're darker (*mais preto*) than me? You're *negro* too!" . . .
> *Me*: But what does *negro* mean, in the end?
> *Eliane*: It's very simple. *Negro* is features, lips, nose and especially [hard] hair. *Pardo* is nothing . . . it's just color . . . [pointing to the skin of her arm] I'd use this term just for somebody who is my skin tone, *pardo*, but who doesn't have any black features (*que não chega a ter feições de negro*), or when you don't really know what this person is because he or she is a mix of everything, like the real *mestiço* (*o mestiço verdadeiro*) . . .
> *Me*: And *moreno*?
> *Eliane*: It's the same. A *moreno* might be my skin color, not very dark (*que não é [da cor] preta*), but with fine features and straight hair (*as feições são mais finas, o cabelo é mais liso*) . . .
> *Me*: So, in the end you say that you're *negra* but you also said that your skin is *parda* . . .
> *Eliane*: That's because we're all mixed here . . . [suggesting that there was not contradiction between the two things]

Eliane offers an understanding of being black as having certain black features—nose, lips, and especially hair—which are significantly racialized in Brazil. Color, as in the other cases, is more typically used to refer to skin tone (Sansone, 2003: 47) or to the intensity of a person's features between ideal white and black aesthetic poles. Such a skin tone, however, is not crucial in producing black identity because other people with brown skin might be phenotypically excluded from such identification; on the other hand, skin color is still relevant in providing specific details of this student's appearance (see Sheriff, 2001). By this usage, Eliane articulates *mestiçagem*, a fact that explains her brown color, with blackness, which explains something typically black, stamping black fixity on her mixedness. The use this student makes of the word *preta* at certain points of the interview is

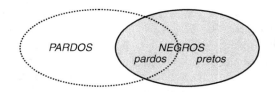

Figure 4.1 My visualization of the possible relationship between blackness and mestiçagem/brownness as described by Eliane.

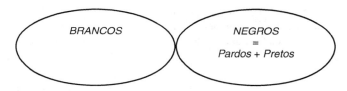

Figure 4.2 Relationship between blackness and mestiçagem/brownness as proposed by the Black movement.

deployed not to describe her actual skin tone but to contextually reinforce her black identification and differentiate more clearly between her and other *pardos* who do not have typically black features.

I visualize here Eliane's view of the possible relationship between blackness and *mestiçagem*/brownness (figure 4.1).

This scheme substantially differs from the one more officially proposed by the Black movement and subtended by racial policies (figure 4.2). From the Black-movement perspective, the pardo category would be altogether encompassed under negro along with preto, but for those pardos who, given the biracial choices, might prefer white identification.

Pardo and negro, in Eliane's explanation, are not just two different shades of an identical concept because pardo refers more strikingly to brown skin color,51 whereas negro entails more specifically certain racialized features that are perceived as black in Brazil. As a further difference from the political and social view officially championed by the Black movement, Eliane talks of blackness as a predominantly visual idea that she may have built through her experiences of discrimination in life or through feelings of inadequacy in terms of beauty.52

On the other hand, the dissonance is also clear between this student's identification and both the linear multiple model embodied in IBGE official categorization and the color labeling used in the vestibular process. In fact, *negro* is still an absent category in IBGE official statistical outputs (but for representing, sometimes, the aggregation of data concerning the *pardo* and *preto* categories) while this term simplistically replaces *preto* (dark colour) in the vestibular socioeconomic questionnaire at the UERJ. In Eliane's view, *negro* is not simply imagined as the sum of the *pardos* and *pretos* accounted by IBGE; it includes, instead, *pretos* and some *pardos*.

I should conclude this presentation of ethnographic data about race and color by pointing out that brown-skinned students such as Flávia, Regina, and Eliane were not the only ones to deploy articulation between blackness and *mestiçagem* (and/or brownness). Several darker-skinned informants who self-identified as *pretos* (black colored) also stressed mixture as a crucial aspect of their family identity and transversally (or metaphysically) encompassing the overall Brazilian color scale.

> I say that I'm *negra* because I don't have any choice to say that I am anything else. I would say I'm *morena* if I were so, but I'm *preta*. However, my origin is very mixed . . . there are Portuguese, African and indigenous ancestors in my family history, you know? This is Brazil . . . (Janaina, history student)

What Janaina says is crucial because at the same time as she clarifies the presence of certain racial/color boundaries (she is neither white nor *morena*), she also legitimates Brazil as a *mestiço* country (her origin is very mixed).

Articulations between Blackness and *Mestiçagem*: An Academic Discussion

The ethnography presented here and its relevance for my point really needs further discussion in order to become fully comprehensible. In the discourse of informants like Flávia, Eliane, and Regina, mixture emerges not merely as ideology, as some Black activists would propose, and not even simply as lived experience, as some popular language tends to depict Brazil (Wade, 2005). Admitting that mixture is also lived experience in Brazil, of course, does not refute the idea that there has also been a "mixture pedagogy"[53] in this country; neither does it mean that the way people experience mixedness can be considered totally separately from ideology. However, it should not be necessary deciding between racial pedagogy *or* mixture pedagogy when analyzing the processes of racial identification in Brazil; both these processes intersect and manifest in constant tensions, shaping what most children learn in Brazil about race, and explaining many of the contradictions explored in this book. Such tension between pedagogies is enacted in part by the mixture people experience in their families and communities, by the celebration of mixture as a means of national pride, and by the silencing of historicized racial hierarchies under a multiple set of cultural censorships in everyday life, school textbooks, and in the city landscape. On the other hand, this tension also significantly draws on the discrimination received from socially dominant others, which varies according to the perceived strength of certain racialized characteristics. The same tension can therefore also be sustained by the politics of difference that some groups now deploy to counteract systematic invisibility and marginalization, despite their apparently central place in the democratic fable of national construction.

It is important to reiterate that mixture is not really a democratic and romantic space of sameness for various reasons: first because, as Wade (2005) points out, it implies some exclusion at the same time that it includes people; and second, because hierarchies still deploy their power within such mixture, depending on how much of its founding components can be seen. The naturalized values of these racial components do not simply dissolve through the fact of mixing together. In this sense, a *mestiço* with clear black features might be considered worse (*pior*, to use Flávia's words) than one closer to a white (or even indigenous) idealized pole. Also, as Eliane notes, there might exist a the *mestiço verdadeiro*—one who better fits this ideal and probably whitened model, which is less discriminated against—and another kind of *mestiço* who is instead a more imperfect fit with this model (Gomes, 2006: 277).[54] What I say here does not intend to overlook the way that class aesthetics impact on the discrimination suffered by people in Brazil. The weight of racial considerations over class, however, will vary greatly, depending on the perceived intensity of certain racialized features that can also exist independently of skin color.

Most literature dealing with race relations in Brazil has widely used the terms "race" and "color" as synonyms (Moutinho, 2004; Telles, 2004; Petruccelli, 2007). It is undeniable that these terms overlap in usage and are often employed interchangeably in common speech. This ambiguity is also reflected by modern institutional language in the IBGE, which asks people about their *raça ou cor* (race *or* color).[55] However, in looking at my ethnography, many non-Black-politicized students often suggested that race and color are not quite the same thing. Black militants, after all, also make some conceptual distinction between these ideas when they argue that color is divisive—thus nonuseful—for the black collective, whose unity is instead ensured by the idea of a black (*negro*) race. Quite differently from mainstream activist discourse, students like Eliane, Regina, and Flávia have a view that, far from being political, implicitly restates the importance of color in terms of shades to define which black person they try to describe.

In anthropology, I have found only a few authors who, more or less explicitly, deal with the distinction between race and color in Brazil. Robin Sheriff states that her informants in a carioca favela understood terms such as *pardo*, *moreno*, and *preto* as *negro*, as this term either worked as a synonym for the other terms, or encompassed all of them. Having established this, Sheriff (2001: 44) also mentions that, according to several informants, "*preto* is color, *negro* is race." She therefore argues that race is something conceptually broader but also more fixed according to her informants, whereas color is more fluid and represents the "polite surface of speech" (46). Her informants, in this sense, do not use color terms such as *pardo*, *moreno*, and *preto* as clear means of racial identification, but as ways of better describing themselves or others in particular contexts. Sheriff finally notices that intermediate chromatic terms in particular, such as *moreno*, are often used in order to deploy censorship when speakers politely try to avoid any references to blackness (51–52).[56]

I argue that carrying out some distinction between race and color is exactly what allowed my informants to articulate blackness and *mestiçagem*. *Negro* would then be a broad term of reference intersected by intermediate (or mixed) colors to better define one's place within the black group. Having said this, unlike Sheriff, I am more skeptical about the fact that brown-skin shades automatically imply feelings of belonging to a black racial group for Brazilian people. In fact, mixedness can also work as a rather independent category from black and white in Brazil.[57] I would also add that, after one year of socializing with students at the UERJ, I noticed that the articulation between blackness and *mestiçagem* was not so randomly deployed. This is especially true when considering that the presence of different contexts that may influence the use of certain terms in particular ways is not necessarily proof of the flexibility and ambiguity of racial/color categories in Brazil. In direct contrast, the contextualized use of diverse identity labels may conceal a relatively solid coherence in the way students understand themselves and others.

In my ethnography, race and color often emerge as two different concepts that are both flexible and fixed, depending on the situation. By self-identifying as *negras*, Eliane and Flávia relate themselves to a wide racial reference group, while by using the terms *parda* and *mestiça* they fix their positions within this group. At the same time that color is employed to fix the location of these students within the black group, blackness fixes what kind of brown students they think they are, for example, by drawing the line for other people who might be brown-skinned but general *mestiços* without clear racialized markers, and for this are not *negros*. Black activist discourse, I previously observed, also deploys some articulation of race and color, with the only difference being that one of the terms of this articulation (color) is downplayed in order to emphasize a social identification (race) that is politically functional, and to strategically play down phenotypic differences between *pardos* and *pretos*. In some cases, color can also be contained within race as different spheres inscribed on one's identity and useful to describe the self, for example, to express something of the sort "I am brown-skinned but I am also black; I'm a brown-skinned black."

My point does not intend to overlook the ambiguity existing between concepts of race and color in Brazil. These are in fact often confused and interchanged when used as individual concepts, with meanings that do not always correspond depending on users and contexts. However, in particular contexts where these concepts are used simultaneously, they might be semantically divided and, because of this, articulated. Moreover, where there is terminological ambiguity, as seen in Flávia's double use of the word *negro*, it is the understanding of these different contexts that explains how the merging/overlapping of race and color often is only apparent.

A similar idea of articulation also emerged when I asked some informants to compare the terms *negro* and *preto*.

Me: So, saying *negro* and saying *preto* is the same?
Daisy: . . . It's different because *preto* is the color [she rubs the skin of her arm] while *negro* is the race [she passes her hand close to her face as if to refer to facial features].[58]
Me: But what is race?
Daisy: Race is race. It's your . . . origin [pointing at her face again].

The word "origin" (or ancestry) seemed to be in contrast with Daisy's body language, which was instead pointing to the overall of one's facial features by which such origin can be visualized, perhaps evoking the image of an African slave and, consequently, potentially leading to situations of discrimination that color alone could not explain.[59] In this case we could also talk of articulation of race and color, although this appears less obvious by the fact that the terms *negro* and *preto* semantically overlap more automatically in Brazilian folk usage and might even—deceivingly, in my view—be presented as redundant.[60] Daisy's point complements views of race and color seen with other students such as Eliane, Flávia, and Regina. In general, all these testimonies show that even though a dark skin color often is used as crucial elements for racial categorization, their weight never is necessarily determinant, depending on how these phenotypic aspects combine with the overall of one's face features (Gomes, 2006: 285, 296).[61]

From Race *or* Color to Race *and* Color? Ethnography beyond Official Discourses

In this section, I have discussed how self-identified black quota-students use black quotas, and the way that these students relate to ideas of race and color. Through ethnography, I questioned a number of assumptions, especially about the power that administrative use of affirmative action would have to racially divide the student collective at the UERJ. I also questioned whether these measures necessarily "blacken" people's identities at the expense of feelings of racial mixture. In contrast to what quota supporters hope and what quota skeptics fear, students seem to be little interested in racial quotas. They actually try to avoid the racial quota system unless it is strictly necessary in order to access an opening. At a different level, it seems that those students who use racial quotas do not clearly shift their identity in a black sense by the fact of using a quota. Depending on their everyday system of identification, these students might still self-perceive as mixed, a fact they highlight through the varied and complex racial/color terminology that relates to Brazil's rich history of race relations. I have also shown that, independent of quotas, many informants articulate blackness and *mestiçagem* as two concepts that do not exclude each other. Such articulation is possible because many of these people contextually deploy a conceptual difference between race and color, two terms that have been widely treated as synonymous both in social statistics and academia.

At a first glance, it seems possible to agree that there is some tendency toward bipolarization in Brazilian race relations (Winant, 1999; Sansone, 2003; Telles, 2004), a process that policies may accelerate but which is happening anyway in Brazilian society through the media and Black politics, also with the help of transnational channels. However, this tendency should not be overstated, considering the transversal role that *mestiçagem* and a multiplicity of color labels continue to play in personal (and national) identifications in Brazil. It is quite hard to believe that despite any possible biracializing tendencies in Brazilian society, people will renounce the variety of terms they traditionally deploy for racial/color ascriptions with regard to themselves and others (Sansone, 2003: 56). My impression is that, more than biracializing Brazil, affirmative racial politics that promote a better image of blackness (e.g., in the media) *might* especially encourage a number of *pardos* with features that are broadly racialized as "black" in Brazil to self-identify more consistently as *negros* in everyday life, or to be identified more consistently as such. This tendency, however, should not be seen only as an effect of Black movement's "racial pedagogy" but also, more positively, in the sense that some people are gradually feeling less ashamed to use certain identifications. If seen this way, the growth of black consciousness might produce as much freedom as it actually produces conceptual and terminological impositions of race and colors on potential users. On the other hand, it is clear that long-term comparisons in terms of race relations between Brazil and the United States have often presented these systems as radical opposites. Against this view, a number of authors (Winant, 1999; Daniel, 2006; Telles and Sue, 2009) suggest that the US official model of classification is gradually becoming less bipolar, in part due to the presence of ethnic communities, of which Latinos represent an important component.[62] This fact does not mean that the "American" model can or should simply be implemented in Brazil, as Ferreira da Silva (1998) and Segato (2007) point out, considering the different history of race relations in these countries.[63]

The ethnography presented here takes my questions further. Racial quotas have often been understood as a sort of official classification that is able to produce biracialization in Brazil. According to Fry (2005), in particular, a view of blackness that encompasses brown people substantially imposes a reasoning that works at the expense of the multiple ways of identification to which Brazilians are accustomed, and tends to split society into black and white. My findings at the UERJ, however, suggest different conclusions. I have shown that, according to several students, a bipolar model can not only be used *alternatively* to the multiple one, as Fry states, but also *simultaneously*, through a complex process of encompassment/articulation between blackness and *mestiçagem* (an idea for which a brown color only works as a form of approximation). In virtue of this, I am not convinced that establishing a black (*negro*) category that gathers *pretos* and (at least some) *pardos* of the IBGE classification system would necessarily require a biracial model in order to be used in official classifications

Figure 4.3 A virtual classification system that would reflect my findings at the UERJ.

and policies. My ethnography shows that classification systems that are alternative to those traditionally discussed could be also imagined, although their relevance and applicability should be obviously studied beyond my pool of informants. A virtual classification system that reflects my findings at the UERJ could be represented as follows:

Acknowledging that no clear-cut divisions are possible between the three groups represented in figure 4.3, and that the categories/groups presented should never be interpreted as reified truths, the scheme here suggests something important. It is based on the idea that skin tone is not necessarily determinant in defining general racial and phenotypic identifications (uppercased in figure 4.3). This fact is also suggested by the fact that some people self-identifying with a range of shades of brown and mixture in open-ended surveys reclassify as "white," "mixed," or "black" when asked to use the IBGE system of categorization (Petruccelli, 2007). It should be also noted that "mixture" in Brazil is not something confined to the IBGE mixed-race group and phenotype; as informants pointed out during my fieldwork and most Brazilians would agree, mestiçagem is something both concretely and ideologically transversal to Brazilian society. Awareness about one's own mixture, nevertheless, does not prevent certain people with a mixed ancestry from being generally considered (and treated) as white or as black in Brazilian society.64 Being treated as a member of a group or the other, for these people, will largely depend on how the white and black constitutive elements of their mixture are generally seen and judged in local and/or national contexts.65 Clarity and homogenization of terminological and conceptual use, one could observe, are odd concepts when dealing with racial categories. However, shared understandings might gradually increase and categories might become more defined in people's usages over the next few decades. This might be possible, for example, because the complex interaction between Black politics, policies, and popular appropriations of certain labels and concepts might produce some terminological/conceptual homogenization and standardization over the time (Sansone, 2003). The way demographic surveys are constructed, it is clear, both influence and accompany this process.

There is now the question of whether the virtual model of categorization drawing on my ethnographic findings at the UERJ could be relevant for a discussion about affirmative action. Without meaning that racially based affirmative action a priori *is* the only or best way to reduce inequalities in Brazil, I observe that these measures could be practically foreseen with a model of race relations either addressing the black (*negro*) category as indirectly suggested by Eliane's in this chapter and recalled in figure 4.3, or, alternatively, by addressing only the darker, *preto*, color category of IBGE surveys.[66] In both cases, a central mixed (or brown) category with no clear racial ascription would still be preserved. In this sense, the classification system would remain multiple without this being at odds with the possibility of identifying a black group as beneficiary of affirmative action.

In any case, a model of the sort of that which I virtually draw from UERJ ethnography may not only be considered for racial affirmative action. Once it is agreed that keeping phenotypic information in demographic surveys can be valuable for assessing inequality between groups, this model intrigues me by simultaneously taking into account: (i) the cultural centrality of *mestiçagem* in the Brazilian system of race relations and the national "originality" of such a system, as shown by the presence of numerous people who consistently self-identify as *pardo*, *mestiço*, and *moreno* without accepting to be reduced to black or white; (ii) the ideas championed by the Black movement about the need for conceptual and statistical revision of the black category due to newly emerging tendencies in identification in Brazilian society; and (iii) understandings of the relations between mixture and blackness, and between race and color, as those that my informants suggested. Such ethnographic considerations, I clarify, should be treated mainly as *one* possible example of the limitations implicit in the two mainstream classification models that are presently discussed in Brazil. Informants, in fact, suggest that other paths are also possible; these paths, in my view, could be explored and discussed more systematically with the help of ethnography and tested statistically as they have much to contribute to present debates about racial classification in Brazil. This point is especially relevant because, as Schwartzman (2009) highlights, the state does not "see like citizens," whereas the citizens' sight might be quite inspiring in order to define policies or discuss how they could be made closer to their users. In the specific case of my ethnography, I show that some people can interestingly conceptualize models that avoid rigid binarization while also being compatible with the politics of difference.

At this point, questions remain about how a racial/color model as the one emerged from ethnography could ever be carried out in statistics and about whether there are shared terminologies ready for this goal. If a *pardo* color subcategory of the *negro* racial group were established for classification, for example, it would be unclear what this should be called. A terminological possibility would be *mulato*, in fact the only word that clearly refers to people with both brown skin and black features (especially hair, and lip- and nose-shape) in Brazil. Teixeira (2003), in her research at the Federal University of Rio de Janeiro, seems to follow similar reasoning when she divides her student sample into *branco, pardo, mulato.* and *preto*, thus distinguishing between two intermediate racial/color categories that are more or less "Africanized."[67] As a drawback, I acknowledge that the term *mulato* is presently contested by the Black movement as something hybrid, and has never experienced a process of political empowerment as the term *negro* has, in addition to the sexualized and therefore demeaning connotations that the idea of *mulata* implies for Brazilian women (Gomes, 2006: 290).

Different uncertainties relate to whether classification in official surveys should be self- or hetero-based, a fact that becomes even more relevant when a classificatory system is used to identify beneficiaries of certain policies. In this regard, Telles (2004) suggests that hetero-classification is more useful because discrimination mostly relates to the way that people are perceived by others. Although hetero-classification sounds like a more useful instrument to assess racial discrimination and implement policy countermeasures, I believe that self-classification should be maintained as it brings about a double advantage when cross-checking information with the hetero-realized information. Among these advantages, cross-checking data of hetero and self-classification may consistently ensure a view of possible misrepresentation between hetero- and self-classification at specific times; and second, it could show the trends of this misrepresentation over time, which might also be a useful way to assess the trends in convergence and consistent use of certain race/color ascriptions in Brazil.

Other questions relate to whether a system of racial classification should be based on ancestry and ethnicity (if not just actual skin tone), instead of relying on general phenotype. In this sense, Nobles (2000: 169) cynically observes that whatever concept or term is used for this kind of demographic classification in Brazil, it would hardly disguise the racializing meanings implicit in any classification system. The model I have discussed here mainly relies on phenotype because this was the more crucial characteristic that emerged in my ethnography with non-Black-politicized quota students in a metropolitan environment, but also because phenotype is quite central when we talk of racial discrimination and certain related inequalities. Adding further cynicism, I would say that in the heads of those people interested in the color data in IBGE surveys, what presumably matters is how people look, much more than their cultural identification. Having said this, surveys that rely on different classification reasoning (e.g., ethnicity and ancestry) might still be used for studies and policymaking where this information is crucial.

As a final consideration, it is probably too early to foresee how official systems of racial classification such as the one implemented by IBGE will develop in Brazil, and which tendencies and actors will prevail in their definition. For now, the increasing discussion about racial classification suggests that this field is far from being static. Anthropology and ethnography should be particularly useful in setting out and analyzing these new tendencies.

5

Narrowing Political Gaps

Black Awareness and University Education as Ways to Be "Central"

I have often highlighted that my main informants in the Law Department were not students politicized under the sphere of the Black movement, although the activist voice has been transversally present in my account for purposes of comparison. This lack of activism among law freshmen was something that I did not foresee when I approached my fieldwork, and it looked initially random and inexplicable. I had assumed that activists would be spread across all courses and years of study. In addition, I had assumed that most black-quota students would be somehow politicized since many of them had presumably had experiences in community prevestibular courses led by organizations linked to the Black movement, such as Educafro. In fact, I noticed that most freshmen (usually between 17 and 24 years old) did not show any political interest at all, whereas many students later develop some political interest at university. On the other hand, I discovered that the majority of Black activists at the UERJ were from the social sciences or other courses considered not to be particularly prestigious in terms of future salary prospects, such as history, education, and social work.

Having said this, from the beginning I realized that focusing on nonpoliticized students might be quite interesting for my study, especially considering that my contacts with the Black movement outside the UERJ were well-established and I was already quite familiar with the political (and not particularly diversified) discourses of Black militants. The black nonpoliticized sphere was less known to me but still crucial, considering that black students without any involvement in Black politics represented the vast majority at the UERJ. In shaping this interest in the nonformal Black-politicized sphere, I felt very much influenced by John Burdick's *Blessed Anastácia*, which I had read well before starting fieldwork. Although I was curious about studying the identity-building process of non-Black-politicized students, other factors surely drove the choice of my main research subjects. In fact, in spite of establishing good relations with activists within and outside the university, especially through Educafro, my position as a white man restricted some aspects of my access to the political life of student activists. The board of Denegrir, the main Black student organization at the UERJ, for example, ultimately refused to release formal interviews to me. I heard that there was suspicion about my research, as some people unofficially informed me, and that was why those who released interviews always clarified that they were speaking for themselves and not in the name of the organization. I was also informed that not all Black-politicized students would be keen to share their suffering with me, due to my white, foreign, and research positioning in that space. It does not go without saying that my intrusive participation in typically Black events at university, albeit never explicitly forbidden, looked slightly odd and raised some cordial skepticism among activists, requiring some boldness on my part.

The extensive lack of involvement of black people in Black politics is something reflected in wider society, as suggested by Hanchard (1994 and 1999) and Skidmore (1974). These authors have largely read the disconnection of the black masses from racial consciousness as the result of alienation produced by the blurred system of race relations in Brazil, where people find it more appealing to self-identify as mixed, rather than embracing blackness. Other voices, such as the "Manifesto against the Quotas," sent by antiquota campaigners to the High Federal Court in 2008, pointed out that the disconnection between the black masses and the Black intelligentsia is also a matter of class. In this document, Black activists are imagined as middle-class people pursuing interests different from those of the poor (Folha online, 2008a).

I have to confess that in looking specifically at the university context, nothing made me see any substantial class differences between Black activist and black nonactivist students. Paradoxically, the fact that more Black-politicized students were from less prestigious courses might suggest the lower social status of activists in comparison to non-Black-politicized law freshmen. I also noticed that almost no law students had attended the community prevestibular courses organized by Black movement organizations. Most law students had invested in higher-standard private preparation courses (*cursinhos particulares*) since the competition to get an opening in law is particularly fierce. Community preparation courses organized by Black and other organizations rely on volunteers who might be very helpful and eager but not always necessarily the best trainers on the market. Nonetheless, from a deeper perspective, no significant social differences were observable between the aforementioned categories of black students. Students who passed into the Law Department might just have been more motivated, or relied more often on savings they had amassed with difficulty through underpaid jobs in order to pay for private preparation courses; in some cases, however, they had the fortune of coming from slightly better schools or counting on some financial support from their networks of relatives, friends, and acquaintances. Not even place of residence or religious faith seemed to be factors of a neat difference: the vast majority of activist and nonactivist black quota students lived in the suburbs and practiced Pentecostal (particularly neo-Pentecostal) faiths. This point brings to my mind literature dealing with black mobilization and religion in Rio de Janeiro. Burdick (1998), for example, mentions how the core of the *Movimento Negro Unificado* (MNU) Black activism seems to gravitate around Afro-Brazilian cults such as *candomblé* and seems for this reason rather disconnected from lower-class sectors of the black population involved in evangelical faiths or popular Catholicism.[1] It is important to mention that many Pentecostal churches are rather averse to Afro-Brazilian cultural practices, largely defined as *"coisa do diabo"* (things of the devil). Having said this, most students, whether activists or not, seemed to be quite tolerant in this regard, declaring that all religions should be respected. In this way, they seemed to reject the typical moral radicalism of some evangelical stances, while none of them showed an interest in the frugal aesthetics promoted by these churches, and instead seemed quite aware of fashion and beauty trends.[2]

In spite of the similarities in background, these two groups also demonstrated some differences. Unlike my first-year law informants, Black-politicized students proudly defended racial quotas as necessary and politically vital ways to redress historical inequalities. Some activists criticized the rejection of quotas by other black students in terms of a denial of black identity and a blindness produced by the alienating power of the "racial democracy" ideology. However, I have already problematized this idea by showing that my main informants did not clearly deny blackness; otherwise it would be difficult to explain why these students self-identified as black even before using quotas or criticizing these measures, and even without being significantly dark-skinned. Rather than denying blackness, my main informants simply did not seem as proud of it as the activists were. In this sense, they did not use this identity as a political strategy to empower a whole group but as a way to accomplish very personal projects. In terms of the political approach, I have also mentioned that my main informants considered activists to be radicals and reverse racists (*racistas às avessas*), if not enemies of ideals of racial democracy and of national communion. In addition, some differences can be seen in the way students experienced their evangelical faiths. Unlike black nonpoliticized students, activists often made reference to black versions of the theology of liberation (Burdick, 2004) or highlighted the African roots of Christianity. For example, some politicized black students referred to the story of the Queen of Sheba, to the location of the Garden of Eden in Ethiopia, and to the importance of Africa in Rastafarian traditions. I should point out that the religious groups of which Black activists are members are not part of the black evangelical churches discussed by Burdick (2005 and 2008), although they seem to carve a niche as black Christians within cross-racial evangelical groups.[3] This fact suggests that even in the circle of evangelical churches with no specific racial approach, followers can cultivate some black consciousness, become militants, and set out certain ethnic aesthetics. It also suggests that the primacy of Afro-Brazilian faiths (mainly *candomblé*) within the Black social movement, as discussed in Burdick, is consistently counterbalanced by the growing racial consciousness developed within Protestantism.[4] Interestingly, I could not find any quota informants involved in *candomblé* or the other main Afro-Brazilian cult, *umbanda*. Without denying their presence, these faiths did not seem very popular among lower-class students. Many *cotistas* admitted that they had had some exposure to Afro-derived cults within their extended family but showed a lack of interest in these kinds of practices.

This preamble helps to introduce and clarify my next steps in this book. My objective is particularly to deal with contact between Black-politicized and non-Black-politicized students, at least as on the potential and immaterial level. I also aim to introduce matters of personal transformation that quotas might favor, although one year of fieldwork may be quite limited to grasp outstanding changes ethnographically. By "contact," I mean the newly produced relationships of my main quota informants with certain spaces and certain people. These spaces are the UERJ and the city itself, which cannot really escape racial readings and the occupation of which should be interpreted along with the dialectic tension between center and periphery. The people to whom my lower-class informants started relating can be roughly divided into two groups. The first group consists of middle-class students who live in wealthier metropolitan areas and with whom suburban freshmen come to share the same university space. The second consists of politicized, lower-class black students with some involvement in Black activism. Since the interaction of my main informants with wealthier students has been closely analyzed in the discussion of classroom geographies, I will now explore more specifically contact with student activists and intersections with their ideas.

The Black Movement at the UERJ: A Growing Presence

The pressure exerted by the Black movement in favor of the implementation of quotas in public universities has boosted Black student organizations. As a crucial factor, the main Black organization supporting racial quotas was Educafro, a network of prevestibular community courses falling under the umbrella of the Catholic Church and devised to increase the presence of black and poor students in university. Educafro's struggle gradually started to occupy the UERJ from within, championing its ideas through students who had managed to enter university before the implementation of the quota system, mostly in less prestigious undergraduate programs. Educafro joined the fight for the actual implementation of Law 3254, which had established quotas for public-school students. At a later time, in November 2001, lobbying from the Black movement influenced the creation of a number of openings for black students. In the early 2000s, when UERJ Direction still refused to implement the quota law, Educafro led an impressive protest outside the UERJ, a fact that was given some coverage in the media. Students chained themselves for several hours to the UERJ's fences, while a Black militant student from Educafro hung himself on a cross as a symbolic black Christ. As mentioned earlier in this book, the quota law was implemented after much contestation only in the 2003 vestibular examination, the organization of which had commenced in 2002.

The Black movement is presently not as centralized and unified as it was at the time when Black politics were dominated and centralized by MNU, presently an overshadowed entity on the Black political scene in Rio de Janeiro.[5] In a paper presented at IUPERJ, Márcio André dos Santos (2007: 6–8) discussed the "NGOization" of the Black movement and its gradual fragmentation into a number of organizations within an altered (neoliberal) framework of political economy. This tendency is also touched upon by Alvarez, Dagnino, and Escobar (1998) and Escobar and Alvarez (1992) when they discuss the diversification of social mobilization through identity politics in Latin America, across lines of class, race, ethnicity, gender, sexual orientation, religion, and environmentalism. Such movements are defined as "new" social movements in opposition to more traditional ("old") class-based ones. Such a process has affected racial mobilization so that the expression Black social movements is rather conventional. To explain this, it is useful to refer to poststructuralist thinkers such as Stuart Hall (1983 and 1996) and Laclau and Mouffe (1985). In a way that seems to articulate very well with neoliberal NGOization, these authors encourage readings of social mobilization and realities as essences "without guarantees," flexible and continuously reshaped through negotiation. In this sense, collective actions may converge at specific times without necessarily producing essentialized entities and identities. As a possible framework for Black mobilization, I also find it useful to refer to Bruno Latour's (2005) discussion of actor-network theory. This author describes social action as a whole with material (people and things) and semiotic (concepts) dimensions in a process of constant reproduction and negotiation. Latour also contends that, at certain times, we tend to look at particular collective social actors (e.g., the state) as coherent wholes and they might even appear as such. However, this apparent unity entails internal conflict and continually produced redefinitions. The Brazilian Black movement today fits particularly well into this framework. Different black groups that normally focus on separate issues (e.g., gender, sexuality, religious faith, university life, art, mainstream politics, etc.) overcame divisions in order to support racial quotas and defend their establishment.[6] There are therefore periods when this Black articulation relaxes before converging again on specific matters and at specific critical moments such as the implementation of quotas. On the other hand, no single group composing the movement should be seen in an essentialized way. Many students involved in Black politics at university, for example, stated that they had left Denegrir's core militancy due to ideological reasons and incompatibilities, which sometimes also implied personal issues with other members. These people, however, continued to gravitate around Black militant activities at the UERJ; this is why I conventionally include them within the realm of Black activism. The use of a poststructural framework, in any case, is also useful for another reason. It shows that despite differences, Black activist and nonactivist students have more in common in their trajectories than one might imagine and that, conscious of this or not, they are part of an antihegemonic sphere that university education reinforces.

During my fieldwork, I spotted at least four different black student organizations at the UERJ. Apart from Denegrir, which is probably the most radical one and exclusively UERJ-based, the other groups were Aqualtune, Coletivo Luiz Gama, and Coletivo Sankofá. The first two groups are transversal to other universities (Aqualtune is specifically a women's group), whereas Sankofá gathers black integrants—not just university students—from all over the metropolitan area. A number of students were active in several groups at the same time, including Educafro and other nonuniversity-based collectives. However, the different groups were in a constant process of interaction, trying to coordinate agendas and actions at public events. In conferences and debates where quotas were discussed, integrants of the different groups were usually seen as being from the same body, since the questions at stake were general and transversal to each group. This is why Black-politicized students tend to inhabit the same social spaces within and outside university, often frequenting the same or similar events and venues. The gathering of these young people also has an important visual impact in terms of aesthetics, since most of them demonstrate black-power and other black ethnic grooming and outfit styles.

Following the introduction of quotas, the Black movement strengthened its presence at the UERJ for several reasons. First, the number of black students significantly increased. Second, since racial quotas initially produced a strong negative reaction within the university and the future of the system looked unsteady, this fostered solidarity and activism among black students. At the end of 2007, just before the parliamentary reexamination of the 2003 quota law, new alarmist voices started circulating in Educafro meetings. Friar David dos Santos, the national leader of the organization, alerted members that racial quotas may be not reconfirmed through a new law, due to the general hostility these measures still faced in the mass media and wider society, despite the good academic results of *cotistas*. A number of public events were organized in order to lobby governors to reconfirm public-school and racial quotas. Denegrir, in this sense, played an important role alongside Educafro; its integrants were always actively present at all public events that aimed to defend or protest quotas in Rio de Janeiro.

Denegrir represents a way for students to get together and discuss topics relevant to the black student collective. During my fieldwork, this group coordinated a number of events at the university throughout the academic year, with special emphasis on specific dates such as Abolition Day (May 13) and Black Consciousness Day (November 20). Other activities and seminars were promoted with the support of the research organizations Proafro, Neabi, and PPCOR,[7] which involve black academics and students and are also an effect of the new black reality that quotas have enhanced at university. Among several activities, I will mention the Curso de Extensão em Historia e Cultura da África and the *Grupo de Estudo* (Discussion Group), where black students gather to discuss Black theorists and racism on the ninth floor at the UERJ, on which history, philosophy, and social sciences classes are held. The group also requested and obtained from the Direction a physical space for meetings, the Abdias do Nascimento Room. All its activities try to involve black people from all departments and are usually advertised in leaflets across the university. Denegrir also coordinates forums and a mailing list, through which black students and activists within and outside the UERJ keep in touch and up-to-date in relation to any topics and events relevant to them. As an example, students discussed Obama's presidential campaign, advertised internships and educational opportunities, reported intolerance against Afro-Brazilian faiths and homosexuality, promoted social (not necessarily racially oriented) protests, parties, graduation viva examinations (the last one I went to was entitled "*Was Cleopatra Elizabeth Taylor?*"), solidarity appeals, and so on.

The Black social movement also had a strong attitude toward highlighting the problem of financial sustainability for quota students during their courses. Lobbying the Academic Direction, along with the mobilization of other Black and non-Black social movements, student activists must have had some influence on the extension of the scholarship for all *cotistas* to the entire undergraduate program at 250 *reais* per month.[8] In fact, the Black movement and black students were more assiduously present than other actors in public events debating quotas. Black activists were often the only voices defending the institution of quotas, therefore also automatically defending the interests of public-school *cotistas* of all colors. Although I knew that a number of trade unions and student organizations were in favor of quotas, their presence was little visible at events debating affirmative action, while it was also uncommon to spot white or light-skinned students in the audience. In the end, in spite of their racial approach, Black organizations not only appeared as an integral part of the broader (nontypically racial) framework of social mobilization, but they often emerged as *the* defending counsels of issues broadly transversal to lower-class people. I also point out that the Educafro pre-vestibulares courses address not just *negros* but also, more generally, *carentes* (needy people). This suggests that the self-segregating approach ascribed to the Black movement is often overstated. Some of the Black activists I got to know, in fact, participated in a number of other social groups. André, among others, in spite of being coordinator of Educafro-Rio, was involved in several class-based events, such as the *Sem Terra* movement's political camps. Several other black students mentioned that they were generally more inclined toward class-based activism, although they took part in a number of activities organized by the Black movement within and outside university.[9] In apparent contradiction with what I am saying, the exclusive participation of black students was encouraged in core militancy and in specific activities where blackness was more directly discussed and whiteness questioned.

In May 2009, after the action of unconstitutionality of quotas promoted by the state deputy Flávio Bolsonaro, which established an unexpected suspension of the system in the State of Rio de Janeiro from 2010, new demonstrations were held at UERJ, with the visible presence of the Black movement. A sentence of constitutionality was finally given by the Justice Tribunal of Rio de Janeiro in November 2009, reconfirming the quota system after 2010.

"These places were not made for us": Displacement and the Occupation of New City Spaces

Between December and March 2008, the break following the first academic term increased my chances to socialize with quota students outside university. This period coincided, for my suburban first-year law informants, with a process of discovering the city and its cultural attractions. I often joined lower-class law freshmen for free visits to local museums and exhibitions, cheap plays at the Banco do Brasil Cultural Centre, film screenings, historic tours of the city center, and sporadic incursions into wealthy Zona Sul. Flávia, for example, was impatient to visit the bohemian neighborhood on the central hill of Santa Teresa, a typical colonial spot mostly frequented by tourists and intellectuals. This process of discovery added to frequent visits to juridical institutions that students carried out as an integral part of their course. The classes of Direito e Cinema (Law and Cinema), for example, took place away from Maracanã, in the Procuradoria Geral do Estado off Praça XV and the Paço Imperial, in the historic hub of the city center. This is an area, between Avenida Rio Branco,

Cinelândia, and the Bay coastline, where the royal family was initially based after its arrival in Brazil in 1808 and which now hosts the main cluster of governmental offices. Although these spaces are part of the city center, they are quite far from the suburbs where my informants lived. Quota students had not had many occasions to visit these areas that were historically important and encompassed some popular nightlife spots, but were also considered dangerous, especially at night.[10] As a consequence of this, my meetings in the city center with first-year law quota informants normally occurred during the day.

Several cultural events were regularly organized in town by groups linked to the Black movement, especially in the Lapa area. Lapa is the sector of the city center where most cultural activities relating to politicized and trendy blackness (among others) take place, with street *capoeira* performances and the clustering of a number of centers for Afro-dancing (*dança afro*) and black culture. This area was the hub for many Black NGOs such as the Instituto Palmares and CEAP (Centro de Articulação de Populações Marginalizadas); it is also a space to appreciate modern black urban grooming and styles. Some of the events in Lapa were advertised on the Denegrir mailing list and I often invited my quota informants to attend. Through political events, I hoped to generate debates around blackness with my nonpoliticized informants and explore their reactions to the ideological points championed by the Black movement. Unfortunately, I was never very successful in this sense because only few suburban freshmen would venture into the city center at night, also considering the cost of travel, the lack of resources to make the most of the night out, and the scarce availability of transport to head back home. In addition, students were clearly not interested in the kinds of events I was proposing. On most occasions, they seemed quite skeptical of Black activism, the ideas of which were considered to be "reversely racist". However, the negative comments I constantly heard about the Black movement were quite vague; a sort of superficial and a priori rejection, which did not rely on substantial knowledge or a deep discussion of the questions identified by Black activism. The university space might obviously prompt contact between students with and without some Black political consciousness. Exploring these dynamics ethnographically at university was rather complicated in the short term, due to the size of the UERJ, its vertical divisions into departments by floors, and my more specific focus on the elite Law Department, on the seventh floor.

At the beginning of 2008, something unexpected anyway happened. Flávia showed up at a couple of events organized by Black movement groups outside the university and suddenly became more open to discussing racial matters. These were issues that, until then, she had only touched on implicitly and rather briefly. In fact, despite Flávia's comments on race that have already been reported in chapter four, I had constantly noticed the embarrassment of this student when discussing race with me. In February 2008, Flávia surprised me for the first time by turning up at the screening of *Compasso de Espera*[11] (1969–1973), a film starring the black actor Zózimo Bulbul and gathering a number of black university students in the Afro-Carioca cineclub in Lapa. The screening had been widely advertised by Denegrir and other Black student organizations in Rio de Janeiro. Flávia looked a bit nervous and chose a seat in the back row of the small and crowded room, whereas I sat on the floor, just by the screen. The film in question, as the same Bulbul (the director of the cineclub) presented it, was the only cinematographic work by play director Antunes Filho and had faced several problems in relation to censorship at the time of the Military Regime. As Bulbul clarified in person, the movie was finally released in 1973 but never widely distributed. The plot narrates the story of an impossible romantic relationship between middle-class black intellectual Jorge (Bulbul) and middle-class white woman Cristina (Renée de Vielmond). The two are finally forced to separate due to the severe (even violent) aversion their relationship meets within society and in Cristina's family. This traumatic experience of rejection for the male character results in an ineluctable identification with the black condition and its general marginality in society, as comes out strongly toward the end of the film. After the screening, the debate became quite animated (though rather unidirectional), focusing on the problems of interracial relationships in modern times. The general comments within the audience can be summarized by the conclusion that black people should stop revering whites and look instead for partners within their same black racial group. Interracial relationships were discussed as dangerous by reinforcing the mystifying ideology of racial democracy and whitening.

At the end of the debate, I curiously looked for Flávia among the audience. However, she was no longer there. I felt disappointed until I received a text message from her. The message said that she had really enjoyed the screening and that she really needed to talk with me about the event. I had to control my impatience for a couple of days until we met again at university. The screening and the debate were discussed on several occasions, during which Flávia showed contrasting feelings. Somehow, these discussions encouraged new considerations by this student about blackness and Black politics, unveiling much of the symbolic and material contact that I mentioned in the introduction to this chapter. This process showed, at least in principle, a complicated intermixture of issues concerning race, class, space, and intellectual knowledge.

> *Flávia*: It was very interesting to see all those beautiful people . . . did you see all those girls with their hair freed into black-power styles and those alternative outfits? All those girls and boys were good-looking . . . they had an ethnic kind of African style (*estilo étnico* . . . *como Africano*) . . . there was a girl with a colorful skirt and another with braids and a band on her forehead . . . did you see her? . . . And what about that beautiful lady with a flower in her hair? . . . Who is she? She was really beautiful!
> *Me*: Those people are all from the UERJ, they are involved in the Black social movement. You never noticed them?
> *Flávia*: Really? No . . . maybe . . . but I have never actually seen so many people like them all together in a single place!

The conversation ended suddenly because Flávia had to go back to her studies in the library. It was eventually reopened spontaneously by her after about a week, when she came over to my flat for lunch. While I was preparing some food, Flávia was standing by my kitchen door, explaining why she saw racial quotas as a form of segregation. To make her point stronger she stated:

> [Racial quotas] are exactly the same kind of thing people were trying to defend in the after-film debate . . . they were criticizing interracial relationships, right? . . . What they say is highly discriminatory and absurd . . . it's true that there is discrimination in Brazil and that black people are the poorest of the poor . . . but look at that place, you were the only white person at the screening and I felt so uncomfortable for you! . . . It's like those beauty magazines that just picture black people . . . look, all this is really wrong. Racism cannot be fought with another kind of racism . . .

The screening event was eventually mentioned again in a trendy bookstore/café in Botafogo (Zona Sul), after Flávia and I had attended a Romanian film screening at Espaço do Cinema. We sat in a cozy wooden loft from where we could observe the rest of the store while sipping creamy mochaccinos accompanied by Swiss cake. Flávia concluded that our days out attending events and visiting places had been extremely nice, but that she had also felt somehow uncomfortable. She said that everything was quite different from her neighborhood.

I assumed that Flávia's feelings were due essentially to class matters and that she was referring to elegant places in the city, enhanced by the fact that she was often the only black person in such spaces. This might have been similar to the feelings of shyness and inferiority that many *cotistas* showed when comparing themselves to wealthier colleagues at the time of starting university. However, Flávia surprised me by stating that a moment when she had felt really "out of place" had been at the film screening of *Compasso de Espera*; the very event that had gathered a significant number of Black-politicized students, and which she had already stated to be extremely interesting on a different occasion.

> *Me*: Why out of place? You thought those people were so different from you?
> *Flávia*: They were.
> *Me*: You mean physically or socially?
> *Flávia*: Not physically, not the color (*não a cor*). The fact is that I don't see people like that in my neighborhood. I'm not used to it.
> *Me*: Do you think that they were wealthier than you?
> *Flávia*: I don't know, but for sure they were of a higher intellectual level (*de nível intelectual mais alto*) [than her] . . . or maybe the way they talked of certain things . . . they have read about lots of things, they could make comparisons, talk about slavery . . . could you see how confident they were? . . . I felt bad because I would not be able to do that . . .
> *Me*: Maybe you say this because most of those students are from the social sciences and they might have greater familiarity with discussing social topics . . . plus, most of them are also ahead of you in their studies.
> *Flávia*: . . . The way they were dressing was so different as well, their style . . . they were good-looking (*bonitos*), very confident . . . in my neighborhood people are not like that . . . nobody is involved in this Afro stuff (*nessa coisa afro*) . . .

This time, the difference that Flávia was highlighting did not relate much to the content of the activists' ideas but more clearly to the effectiveness of their verbal performances and outfits. However, the people Flávia was talking about were not very different from her in social terms; almost all of them were *cotistas*, lived in the suburbs, and were involved in (nonspecifically black) evangelical churches. One possible difference, as I said earlier, was that most of these students were from the social sciences and other departments, which are actually considered less prestigious than Flávia's. These students also wore outfits that Flávia considered to be nice and that she described as ethnic and African/Afro, although they looked to me like vague and cheaper reproductions of the casual urban outfits pictured in some Brazilian black beauty magazines or, more sporadically, in the mainstream media. A black informant described this style, for which I have no precise definition, as the model of the "young, urban, intellectual and globalized black" (*o tipo de negro que é novo, urbano, intellectual e globalizado*) or, as another student more simply called it, "*o negro fashion*" (the fashionable black person). This would be a type of black person who is well-informed, tries to convey political messages and identity through aesthetics (or wants people to believe they are doing so), or just wants to be cool. It can be observed simultaneously in various metropolises across the world, from New York to London, Paris to Cape Town. According to a number of informants, this is a black middle-class youth style, although this does not mean that those who adopt it are necessarily middle-class or involved in racial politics. It encompasses casual urban style such as All Stars trainers and jeans, in addition to more "tropicalized" accessories such as colorful shirts and skirts, linen trousers, sandals, and showy necklaces, as well as ethnic hairstyles: mainly black-power grooming, dreadlocks or shaved heads for boys, while braids or massive curly hair seemed more frequent among girls.[12] This style should be distinguished from other black styles (mainly male ones) such as the Rastafarian, the *funkeiro* (funk dancer), the rapper. and the beach goer, each one with their particular social subtleties and messages subject to people's readings in Brazil. In Rio de Janeiro, the black intellectualized "casual-tropical" image I have just described reached its highest visual concentration in Lapa[13] and, more specifically, in Black-politicized venues such as Cinema Afro-Carioca.

I could not believe that Flávia was being confronted with such styles for the first time. However, as she said, the more significant fact for her was seeing those people concentrated within a single small space, with the effect of a more striking visual impact in comparison to these styles being noticed on the street or even at the UERJ. All this gave some contrast to Flávia's less-defined style; in addition, her curly hair was not enhanced but softened and flattened with cream, making her fairly unnoticeable among thousands of other suburban girls. At the same time, the assertiveness and confidence with which activists' styles were promoted suddenly became something positive in Flávia's eyes. It represented a model she could easily achieve, apparently without much effort and with similar results to the Black activist girls she had found so pretty.

Another interesting fact is how the combination of affirmative black aesthetics and political articulation made activists appear higher status and good-looking to Flávia. This is something that goes beyond financial availability and relates more closely to the realms of information, knowledge, and power. In this sense, black, articulate and political speakers who try to dress more or less fashionably might be potentially perceived as relatively wealthy or middle-class, irrespective of their actual economic conditions. Consequently, activists' education, self-esteem, and the ability to claim rights are factors that potentially raise their status, in a similar way that money and a lighter skin color may also do in other contexts. Against a traditional pattern of race, money, and status in Brazil, student activists were seen as having higher status or being wealthier but not by appearing "whiter." They were instead seen as more educated but also able to use this education bravely to defend Black claims and express their arguments. This is an important point to make because one of the struggles of the Black movement is how to be wealthier without that somehow connoting whiteness.

What impressed Flávia was that the activists had clearly done a lot of reading, were able to speak in public, referred to relevant authors, and even established conceptual connections between national (slavery) history and present black conditions. In the end, even if Flávia strongly disagreed with the racist comments made about interracial romantic relationships, the activists made her feel that she had a narrow perspective and was somehow inadequate, pointing out the possibility of relating herself to something that was new not just in terms of aesthetics but particularly in terms of self-confidence.

A couple of weeks later, Flávia wanted to discuss these topics again, after our visit to the site of the slave mass graves (*Cemitério dos Pretos Novos*), the Jose Bonifácio Black Culture Centre, and other places reminiscent of slavery in the old port neighborhoods of Gamboa and Saúde.

> *Flávia*: At school we don't learn anything about black history and slavery . . . in my neighborhood people don't talk about this, they are not even interested in knowing . . .
> *Me*: Is it common for people to self-define as *negros* in your neighborhood?
> *Flávia*: Not really. The same black people discriminate against black people . . . for example it is very common that somebody tries to annoy you by saying things of the sort . . . "you'll end up getting married to a *pretinho* (mediocre black man)!," as if this was something horrible (*ruim*). My mom, she never defined herself as *negra* and never even mentioned the word . . . only lately (*ultimamente*)

she has started touching on the topic more often. The other day, for example, she said that in the hospital where she works none of the doctors are *negros*.

Me: And how come she has recently started touching on the topic more?

Flávia: Because when I was in high school I discussed these issues with some friends, after sociology classes. So I started arguing with my mom that we were *negras*.

Me: So now you're saying that you're *negra* very explicitly and that you have reflected deeply about this before . . . however, a couple of weeks ago you seemed more hesitant about this. You finally said you were *negra* but spent more time explaining to me why you were *parda* (brown).[14]

Flávia: Of course I'm *negra*! Look, what I was trying to say the other day is that my color is not very dark (*muito escuro*) . . . gosh, you question me a lot [with a shy laugh] . . . but I like it, OK? Please, go on . . .

Me: You're right. It's just that I find it interesting how people use these terms in different ways. For example, Eliane is about your complexion or has even fairer skin but she does not use the term *parda* for herself very much. She constantly says that she is *negra* or she even says *preta*.

Flávia: It's because *pardo* could be anything or nothing . . . Look, how can people ever say that they are *negros* when being *negro* is so negative (*ruim*)? The word itself implies something bad . . . you say black humor (*humor negro*), black market (*mercado negro*) . . . black (*o preto*) is a negative color. Look at the TV, how is the *negro* represented? What about black beauty? How many black models do you see? When I was a kid, my mom wanted to get me a black Barbie but she couldn't even find one!

Me: However, the 8pm soap opera [*Duas Caras*, at the time][15] shows a number of black people . . .

Flávia: Yes, but just because it is partially set in a *favela*. And who are these *negros* there? The cleaner in the wealthy households (*na casa do rico*), the helper of the boss of the *favela*, his family . . . the queen of the *bateria* (carnival parade) . . . so how can people say that they are *negros*? It's because of this that when the *pardo* category was introduced [presumably she means institutionally by IBGE] everybody preferred to say that they were *pardos* . . .

All these comments cascaded from Flávia's mouth. They made me realize that Flávia had reflected on these matters quite a lot in the past, in fact since high school, which she had completed about six years earlier.[16] The things Flávia said are very commonly heard and read about unequal race relations in Brazil. They sounded new and interesting to me only when considering the person who was saying them: a young woman who had until then felt rather uncomfortable touching on racial topics and had little questioned racial hierarchies in Brazil. I then realized that the gap between black student activists and Flávia was narrower than expected. This gap was less about content and more clearly about confidence in talking about these topics and taking a political (if not aesthetic) stance in this regard. However, these statements and the appreciation that Flávia showed for Black-conscious students did not convert her into an activist. She continued arguing that the strategies of the Black movement were wrong and somehow racist. She also insisted that if racial democracy was not real, people should try to create it without relying on racial affirmative action but using a class-based approach. However, I cannot deny that a conflict about content and strategies was emerging more clearly in Flávia, probably in a way that she had never experienced at the time of high school.

I would now like to return to the trendy bookstore/café in Botafogo and continue my account with further interesting remarks that Flávia raised in order to explain why she often felt "out of place" in certain urban spaces.

> I've never had the possibility to do cultural things, go to the theatre or the cinema . . . closer to my home they only screen horrible and commercial films . . . and people don't look interested in changing any part of the reality around them. So, when I come to places like these I feel out of place. I also never had much of this kind of life because I was working hard and did not have time . . . anyway, these places were not made for [people like] me. There are places for the rich and places for the poor, the segments of the society are quite neatly established . . . you're born in a specific place and for you it will be difficult to break out of this . . . moving up is something complicated . . . do you know what Plato said in this regard? He said that places in society are already assigned . . . When I decided to break this barrier, people in my neighborhood and my family told me that it was crazy on my part, that I should desist from applying to public university and, if anything, try a cheap private one . . . [Suburban] people don't even try because this is not part of their environment (*do entorno deles*) . . . I was sent to a technical school because the best I could aim for, in my *entorno*, was fixing printers [her previous job] . . . there was no better future for me . . . my future [I read this as social mobility] was constrained within certain parameters (*nível*) that one can't really transcend.

Flávia then pointed at the café itself, which was beautiful but unfamiliar. She explained herself while finishing off the last piece of cake, in the refined atmosphere of the place. "The way this place looks, the price of things . . . this place is not made for people like me (*a gente*)," she repeated. When I tried to understand what a place for people like her would look like, she reflected a while and finally stated: "really simple, chairs would be plastic, drinks cheaper . . . walls would not be painted as finely as these . . . However, please, don't take me the wrong way. I'm not saying I don't like it here. I'm loving it!"

There are two main aspects that I would like to highlight here. First, I was very impressed by Flávia's terminology and conceptual articulation. This was something she could not have demonstrated a couple of months earlier and was quite impressive for somebody who still felt like an academic failure. In her discourse, Flávia mentioned Plato, who had recently been a topic of study in the class of Direito do Pensamento Politico, whereas on other occasions she started drawing on a Foucaultian discussion of "truth," for example, to criticize some dogmatism in her evangelical church, the Igreja Batista Renovada (Baptist Renovated Church). These were certainly elements this student was drawing from university and that helped her to deal with her social reality in a more critical way. Second, Flávia shows how the discussion of blackness and class vulnerability has significantly developed as a process of personal and social discovery favored by higher education. It is also worth considering that the sense of displacement Flávia felt in certain urban spaces, including the Black movement, transcends color and racial identity. It is instead more directly related to Flávia's lack of familiarity with certain cultural/intellectual opportunities, or even the nice things that she missed in the suburbs. The unfamiliar, however, does not represent an insurmountable barrier; it may just require some time for adaptation and negotiation. This is even more the case if we consider that Flávia actually had more in common with activists that she had thought, in particular the desire to change things.[17] The prospects of possible new social alliances in her process of social ascension were opening up in front of her.

At a deeper level of analysis, what Flávia believed was not completely true. Many UERJ's Black people, in fact, developed some social consciousness in their poor neighborhoods, getting involved in local political and cultural groups. In Flávia's neighborhood (Fazenda Botafogo/Acarí), as I found out, there was a Carnival Samba School (GRANES Quilombo) that tried to rescue the original values of samba as an alternative to commercial, mainstream Carnival, placing particular emphasis on slavery issues and blackness, as well as organizing a number of cultural and social activities. In addition, the Educafro pre-vestibulares courses were spread across the suburbs, representing important gathering spaces for black students as well as a way to commit to their communities. It is likely that by virtue of being suburban (and, probably, black), these groups looked initially less attractive to Flávia, or not legitimately intellectual or respectable. It is interesting that to really appreciate similar spaces, Flávia had to "meet" them at university or, even more, in the geographically more central city location of Lapa, where they are consumed by people of any color and social class.

"But those haircuts are not cheap!": *Black* Girls and Being *Pretty* in a Process of Social Mobility

In Rio de Janeiro, I often heard that there are several ways to decide whether somebody is black or not. One of them is to ask the police, the doormen in Zona Sul's apartment buildings, or the security staff in shopping malls. Another one is to ask a hairdresser! As Yara said, "[W]hen the hair starts getting curly . . . this says it all (*o cabelo não nega*)." While socializing with female students throughout one academic year, I tried with imperfect results to recognize when hair is naturally straight and when it is straightened, something that my informants could always tell at a glance.

Hair is a very important matter when it comes to defining blackness in Brazil in a political sense (Cunha, 1991; Figueiredo, 1994; Teles, 2000; Caldwell, 2003; Gomes, 2006). Most militants, especially girls, referred to hair as a strategic field on which to build their black identity, as a number of female Black activists in their final years demonstrated.

> My process of building black identity was extremely painful. I started suffering when I stopped using the *tranças* (braids) that we wear when we were little girls. When I saw my hair grow normally for first time, I was traumatized.[18] I kept thinking that my hair was horrible (*ruim*) . . . Quite differently, now I see black aesthetics as a tool of self-affirmation for me; for instance, by thinking that my hair is not *ruim* and being proud of it. (Alicia, activist and final-year law student)

Tamara, a philosophy student, made explicit reference to university as the space where she affirmed her black identity through her hair. It is significant that this student, who initially identified primarily as *parda* (brown), reinforced her identity by leaving her hair curly and therefore less ambiguously black.[19]

> During my whole life I felt pressure to straighten my hair and be as white as possible . . . people always asked me "why don't you straighten? You can . . . your hair is not bad (*ruim*) . . . Why don't you dye it blonde? . . ." Initially, I paid attention to these comments and tried following white aesthetic models . . . I always said that I was *parda* because, in spite of having black features (*feições negras*), my skin is quite fair. When I joined university, however, all this suddenly changed. I started seeing lots of people like me, and many beautiful girls with their hair kinky . . . mostly people from the movement. I had not expected to see as many of them . . . I thought that was cool and I found the confidence to free my hair . . . whereas before I identified as *parda*, I gradually came to see myself primarily as *negra* . . . I started investigating more about the slave origins in my family . . . before I did not have any interest in it . . . (Tamara, philosophy student and Black-politicized)

Jurema, final-year law, adds to this picture not only by stating that those who straighten their hair deny their racial identity, but also by showing that not even all kinds of curly hair are natural.

> Those who straighten their hair do so because they deny their identity, their race (*a raça*). I always had some political consciousness and used *cacheado* hair [hair with broad curls] . . . you know, that *mulata* hairstyle[20] . . . everybody said it was nice. However, even that kind of hair, if you look at it, is industrialized. It's not our hair (*não é o cabelo nosso*). I didn't know my hair, actually, even though I never straightened it completely. Now it's different. I'm leaving my hair as it is . . . frizzy and nice (*crespo e belo*). I prefer to use braids because at least this is my hair . . . I'm aware that some people may not like it; however, for us [Black-politicized people] it's nice and we want to promote it . . . Look around you! With our hairstyles we have made this [university] space even nicer (*fizemos até o lugar mais belo*) . . . (Jurema, final-year law student and militant)

Although it is questionable whether braids really show hair as it naturally is, this activist finds ethnic affirmation through this particular hairstyle, in opposition to curly hairstyles that are achieved through complex transformation processes.[21] What really matters to this student is avoiding chemicals that would alter her hair structure and demean her "black" beauty. Jurema's view, anyway, is one among a very diversified set of strategies of how black women affirm blackness through their hair. As already stressed by Gomes (2006), who did extensive fieldwork at ethnic hairdressing salons in Belo Horizonte, several Black-politicized women in Brazil enhance their blackness through processed hairstyles that, in spite of being relaxed or extended, are still curly and never completely straightened.[22] This is something close to the idealized *mulata*'s hair, which—despite the negative connotation that this racial/phenotypic category faces in Black politics, is still considered both black and desirable by many Afro-Brazilian women with racial awareness (294).[23]

Activist discourses demonstrated some contrast with those I heard among first-year law female quota students (my main informants), who were detached from any Black-politicized discourse and for whom hair was not a matter of affirmation. Unlike activists with their fluffy manes, my main black female informants flattened their hair with a huge amount of softening cream (although usually without straightening it), or kept it stretched with hair-clips or in short ponytails. As already discussed in this book, these female students also considered themselves *negras* but, quite differently from what is seen among Black-politicized informants, this is an experience that shapes identification mostly through suffering and visible discontent.

> *Daisy*: ... I don't have any problem with being *negra*. However, what I don't really like is the [black] hair. The [black] hair is *ruim* (bad) ...
>
> *Eliane*: ... This is why I always say that I can't have kids with a black boy. I can get married to a black man but I will have my kids with a white one, with straight hair [in an ambiguously playful tone]. I won't let my kids pass through all this [she holds a lock of her hair, laughing]. Look, don't take me too seriously, OK? However, I think a lot about this ... I don't remember any single Saturday in my life that my mother hasn't spent at the hairdresser ... as for myself, I have to get up about one hour earlier every day in order to make my hair presentable, put lots of cream on ... [laughs] ... When I get up, it looks horrible, squashed on one side or the other, depending on which side I sleep [the other girls look at her with expressions of empathy and agreement].
>
> *Me*: Why don't you just leave it as it is?
>
> *Eliane*: What? Are you crazy? How do you think my hair would be? I need to use cream every day ... I also need to do chemical treatments (*fazer química*) once a month to relax my roots. I can only wash my hair two to three times per week ... shampoo and conditioner ...
>
> *Me*: But maybe you can avoid all this ...
>
> *Eliane*: No way! It's better for you if you don't see that [laughs] ...
>
> *Daisy*: This is why girls straighten (*fazem escova*) ... straightening is much easier ... your hair is always tidy and easier to keep; you get up and it's ready to go.

> *Eliane*: However, you can see that straightening is not the best for me . . . you can see it's not natural and doesn't even match my features. In addition, I cannot wash my hair as often as I would like . . . Not unless you do a good *escova*[24] (straightening) . . . but this is expensive . . . the good one is chemical . . . you can blow-dry it yourself but it won't be the same thing . . .
> *Me*: But, actually, I've seen many girls from the Black movement with beautiful and natural black curly hair . . . Flávia saw them in the Afro-Carioca cinema the other day and she was impressed . . .
> *Daisy*: I know the kind of haircuts you mean . . . they are nice but they need a lot of work. Who has the time for that in the morning if one has to be at university by 7 A.M.? This is why I always keep it like this [in a very short pony tail].
> *Eliane*: But it's not just a problem of work . . . Those [black] haircuts are not cheap!

A couple of weeks later, Eliane returned to the topic of fashionable black haircuts (*cabelo étnico*) at Flávia's flat in Fazenda Botafogo. To help me understand her point better she opened the website of *Raça*, the main black beauty magazine in Brazil. She started browsing beauty information and photos like a well-trained specialist on the subject.

> *Eliane*: Do you think I wouldn't like to have my hair as nice as this? Of course I'd like to . . . but let's now have a look at prices and we'll make an estimate . . . this plus this and that . . . here you need at least 300 *reais* to have your hair like this . . . these products are extremely expensive . . . they are all imported (*são produtos importados*). So, this is my dream . . . having enough money to buy these products. What do you think I'm studying law for? [laughs].
> *Me*: But some of the girls from the movement said that they don't put anything on their hair . . . they are low-income students and could not afford expensive haircuts . . .
> *Eliane*: In that case, it means that the hair of these girls is better (*então o cabelo delas é melhor*) . . . it's not like mine . . . Flávia's hair for example is better than mine . . . she doesn't need as much treatment as I do. You understand now?

In the end, what comes out from my ethnography is that female black students who are not Black-politicized are not obsessed with straightening (and whitening) at any cost in the same way that people and activists may think. What I perceive, instead, is that there are alternative models in which these students are more interested. These models are already championed in black fashion and are particularly visible in those magazines directed toward a black audience, such as *Raça* or *Afro*, which picture hairstyles more suitable to *cabelo crespo* (kinky hair). In very simplified versions, these hairstyles are visible among lower-class activists and in particular city locales such as Lapa, where mainstream Black artists and militants concentrated at the time of my research. The hairstyles I am talking about are seldom completely natural but they tend to be presented within the realm of black beauty as *cabelo étnico* (ethnic hair) even though they often require complex and expensive processing in order to become fully desirable. This might be true especially for nonpoliticized girls who do not have any political message to convey through aesthetics, who just want to look as nice as they can with their scarce economic resources, and who spend long hours every day on public transport. Paradoxically, it seems that there are economic constraints to the freedom these students would find by reinforcing their identity with styles that are seen as both black and nice. This economic factor, it is worth stressing, does not escape matters of color and *mestiçagem*; for instance, when students such as Eliane believe that being black and pretty is less expensive for black women whose hair is less hard and therefore are more visibly *mestiças*. The curls of these "luckier" girls are more easily moldable, without requiring, for example, the so-called Afro perms (*permanente afro*)[25] or too much of expensive products to relax the roots. Several of these processed ethnic hairstyles seem to negotiate between people's desire of setting out their blackness with culturally spread beauty models that appreciate long, floating manes (*o cabelão*) as expressions of sensuality and femininity (Gomes, 2006: 294, 296–298).[26] Something that should be noted is that the more black women's hair texture is naturally close to these wavy and softer manes, the higher they may rank on the racialized beauty scale.[27]

Social ascension would then presumably help first-year law quota girls to achieve these expensive haircuts that positively enhance their features much more than total straightening does. This fact is playfully but still significantly demonstrated when Eliane refers to law as an eventual channel to improve her (black) aesthetics. Waiting for wealthier times to come, these students use traditional straightening as a lesser evil on special occasions such as weddings, religious feasts, and other important events, whereas clips, creams, and oil help keep their hair "acceptable"-looking during normal academic life.

Other considerations are to be made. Some Black activist girls placed much emphasis on natural hair, which they often enhanced with accessories such as flowers and bands, even though some of them declared themselves not to be completely insensitive to tempting hairstyles, which implied chemicals or substantial usage of special shampoos and hair conditioners. On the other hand, within the process of aesthetic negotiation deployed by non-Black-politicized students, it is important to take into account that studying in the Law Department might imply some aesthetic requirements different from less prestigious departments. According to several students and teachers, law students should comply with more formal aesthetics as a way to match the dominant styles in the law sector.[28] This explains why first-year law informants might be, in principle, even more hesitant to display their hair as kinky and natural, or even curly, assuming that they might be penalized or considered to be less serious professionals. Eliane, for example, says "sometimes I can do braids, but please . . . I can't come here [to university] like that. I'm a law student!" In a similar vein, Juny, a brown quota student with wavy (albeit not kinky) hair, was teased about her hair by her English-language teacher at the UERJ: "My daughter (*minha filha*), are you really thinking to become a judge with that [curly] hair? Please, do something about it! (*você tem de dar um jeito nele!*)." The ethnic hairstyles that Black activist students use, on the other hand, is not very sophisticated but requires good doses of courage and political assertiveness; it is not, therefore, just a matter of money, as Eliane tried to suggest. This fact might also explain why final-year female activists in the Law Department, Alicia and Jurema, balanced their ethnic, courageous hairstyles with quite elegant clothing and accessories. In spite of their ethnic grooming, their outfits demonstrated a contrast with the more typical "casual-tropical" style of many students from social sciences, education, and social work. As students suggested, people in the social sciences are allowed to dress less formally, probably because they are already expected to have a more typically anticonformist role in society, a fact that can also be conveyed through outfit. Law students, quite differently, would be expected to fit into the more conservative aesthetics of the legal field.

Romantic Relationships and Marriage Issues in the Social Ascension of Black Female Students

> For black men things [in the relationship field] are easier because they are imagined as being good in bed and manly. There is also this idea of the black women being good in bed, especially the *mulatas* . . . but with the very different result of being seen as prostitutes . . . (Tamara, philosophy student)

At the screening of *Compasso de Espera*, Flávia had felt rather shocked by the declarations expressed against interracial romantic relationships by Black-politicized people. The difficulties that black people face in their relationships with whites, especially within the middle class, become reasons both for disappointment and ethnic affirmation for militants. Also in this area, we can identify some differences between Black-politicized and nonpoliticized students: the latter do not use intraracial relationships as an affirmative discourse. However, this does not mean that nonpoliticized black girls feel appreciated in the romantic field, especially if they are very dark-skinned. Another question is whether affirmative action might play any role in this field.

On several occasions when I walked across Rio's city center accompanied by Flávia, I noticed that a number of lower-class men, above all street vendors, looked at the shape of her bottom and hips with clear sexual interest. I remember that, when walking off Uruguaiana Street, male glances at Flávia became so numerous and insistent that I burst out laughing. Totally aware of the interest she had raised on the street, she gave me a naughty smile and said, "*é a bunda*" (it's my bottom). The *bunda* is an extremely black-racialized attribute in Brazil, as magnified by comedian Tom Zé. This artist, during one of his shows in Rio de Janeiro, problematically joked about the fact that "*a única coisa que os negros deram ao Brasil é a bunda*" (the only thing that black people gave to Brazil is the [pronounced] shape of the bottom).[29] Another day, a couple of hours after asking for street directions in the Gamboa area, a male informer recognized us again and addressed Flávia with enthusiasm: "hey *morena*[30] . . . did you find the place?" In that case, Flávia appeared more uncomfortable and observed that the man had been quite inappropriate by addressing her in that way. "He could have said 'hey *menina* (girl) . . .'" Flávia complained. Instead, the man had made a color reference: a polite, but still significantly racialized and sexualized one in that situation.[31] From Flávia's annoyed expression I understood that something was clashing with the respectability and status of a woman in a process of social ascension.

The *mulata*, the phenotypic category in which most people in Brazil would place Flávia, has become an export product and an integral part of national pride. "Is it not true that the *gringos* (male foreigners) come here for the *mulatas*?" Flávia asked me once. In fact, one of the inescapable questions I had the misfortune to have to answer when socializing with males of any class and color in Rio de Janeiro was whether I had already tried a *mulata*. In a few cases the term was replaced by *morena* or *brasileira*; however, that does not change much of the local and foreign image of the Brazilian woman as visibly Afro-derived *mestiça*, the fortunate but also—in common imagination—lascivious product of the national miscegenation praised by Gilberto Freyre. In response to my negative answer—"no, I haven't been with a *mulata*"—a male student seemed not to believe my words and responded, "why not? It's easy . . ." The stereotype of black (above all *mulata*) women as sexy but also (as a possible consequence) as easy has been pointed out by a number of authors and especially by Moutinho (2004), Pravaz (2003), and Giacomini (2006: 90). This idea was also reinforced by students who mentioned that the son of the *patrão* (boss) is usually sexually initiated by a black *empregada* (maid). It was further highlighted by the white middle-class male students who saw girls from Baixada Fluminense as both tasty and ugly, or not attractive in comparison to white middle-class girls. To complete this picture, a friend of mine mentioned that his male white middle-class friends "date white girls, but whenever they go with prostitutes they usually choose *negras* or *mulatas*."

According to a popular Brazilian saying, "white women are for marriage, *mulatas* for sex and *negras* for working [especially as maids]." It is therefore possible to see that the *mulata* and the *negra* often coincide but might sometimes emerge as two different products in the sex/love relationship market. Apparently, only the *mulata* (or the *morena*) is highly sexualized in this hierarchy by being seen as more actively sexy and tempting (Gomes, 2006: 290), whereas the *negra* is a less attractive, passive, and more Africanized version, sexualized mostly by sheer availability in the workplace. In the end, contextual distinctions between *negra* and *mulata* are not just a matter of color but also of social expectations about sexual properties and behavior. The *mulata*'s place in people's imagination is reflected in certain urban spaces such as the street and the brothel (Caulfield, 2000), the Carnival (da Matta, 1983), and the samba school (Giacomini, 2006).[32] The place of the *negra*, instead, is often more innocently sited in the white household,[33] a space that she shares with the "chaste"[34] white woman (Seigel, 2009). Being sexy or sexually available, however, does not automatically shape an important space for the black woman in the marriage market; it might in fact make this market even smaller.

Comparing Brazil to the United States, Telles (2004) shows that interracial marriage has always been much higher in Brazil than in the United States and South Africa, especially since the 1960s, and in Northern Brazilian regions in comparison to the South. However, the black Brazilian woman still faces particular problems in marriage and interracial romantic relationships (Moutinho, 2004; Telles, 2004; Schwartzman, 2007). Statistically, black[35] (*preta*) women marry white people less than black (*preto*) men do (15.9 percent versus 19.1 percent).[36] Telles observes that the substantial difficulties that black women face in the marriage market are increased by some preference that white women would have for black men, especially when such men have higher educational and class status than their lighter partner (see also Moutinho, 2004)[37]; this interest might be due to stereotypes of black men as sexually powerful and manly. Due to a demographic surplus of women over men of marrying age in Brazil, white (and brown) women absorb a good percentage of black men, making the shortage of potential partners even worse for darker-skinned women (Telles, 2004: 192–193). When intermarriage occurs for black women, they tend to have significantly higher education and status than their partner.[38] Telles also observes that interracial marriage is more widespread among the lower social classes, but relatively absent among the elite. As Schwartzman points out, people in the lower classes intermarry more not just because they are less racist, but also because lower-class blacks and lower-class whites have greater exposure to one another. This also explains why the few black middle-class people in Brazil are statistically more likely to intermarry than those in the United States, considering the more striking scarcity of middle-class black potential partners in Brazil (Schwartzman, 2007: 659).[39] Isolating the variable of geographical distribution (including the urban concentration of blacks and whites), Telles (2004: 182) states that "whites are 2.6 times as likely to marry whites as non-whites," which is admittedly a ratio much lower than that in the United States (where the value is 50.0) but is still clear evidence of the presence of skin prejudice in romantic relationships in Brazil.[40] This topic is debated politically within the Black movement. Militants highlight the function of black women in the creation of the Brazilian nation in a sort of collective rape by the white Portuguese man and as a way to whiten the country (Nascimento, 1979; Ferreira da Silva, 1998).

Even before the debate that followed the showing of *Compasso de Espera*, I already had some familiarity with the Black movement's stance on interracial relationships. In interviews with female students linked to the movement, it came out that some of them had been criticized by activists whenever they spent time with white men. I discussed this topic with Jurema, a female integrant of Denegrir. I asked her whether there was any formal rejection of interracial relationships within the Black movement.

> It's not that the movement has an official stance against interracial romantic relationships, but why do we always have to revere the things of the white people (*o que é do branco*)? We're all beautiful and there

> should be some harmony with this . . . however, there is not . . . In the field of love, the possibility of liking a white boy rather than a black one is much higher, due to the fact of us being a minority here [at UERJ]. But if you give things their right value . . . you know . . . Look at me for example, I don't make any distinctions . . . when I like somebody I like him, but what you need to understand is that interracial relationships imply several question marks (*poréns*). Obviously, dating and getting married [interracially] is not forbidden but it is difficult. It's like when you buy a top . . . you don't buy it unless you like it and unless you prefer it to the others available [meaning that white men will prefer the white women available] . . . But let's suppose that a white boy likes me. Is he going to stand up for me (*ele vai me assumir*)? Is he going to face his family or whatever his friends think? Let's now suppose that his family even likes me, noticing that I'm intelligent, I've graduated in two different subjects and I'm a polyglot . . . they might even like me but I would not be welcome in that family. They would probably dream of something better for their son. This is tragicomic but is the pure reality. Because of this we tend to prefer *o que é nosso* (what is ours) [boys and girls of our phenotype].

Coming to a crucial point for this book, activist Jurema mentioned that the unequal opportunities of black women in the love market are even more striking for black women in the process of social mobility.

> For me it's important to find somebody I choose because there is affinity (*tem afinidade*) . . . somebody with whom I can exchange ideas, who has the same intellectual level as me . . . who can discuss something and see a film with me. In the case of a black woman who is moving up socially [through university education] there are problems because she doesn't manage to stay (*ficar*) either with the white or with the black [men]. The *negro* man who is moving up socially will prefer white women to boost his social mobility, while the white man will never face society by standing up for (*assumir*) a black woman.

Constraints on finding a partner for university-educated black girls also take on particular shades in the racialized and class-divided cityscape. This fact is particularly clear when Jurema, as a student in the process of social mobility, describes the spaces in which she can more easily find a partner.

> I look for places where there are more *negros* . . . but it happens that I don't like *funk* music and not even *pagode*.[41] That's a problem because everybody knows that the majority of people involved in samba, in *funk* music and in the Carnival are *negros*. I always look for

places where there are more of my people (*dos meus*), because I find it easier to relate myself to them . . . but I need to do it in places where I can find other black university students. However, that's not easy. For example, if I went to the clubs in [wealthy] *Zona Sul*, I'd just find one or two like me! That wouldn't be interesting . . .

Gabriela, a social sciences student who moved from the suburbs to Copacabana, also highlighted the reference to social mobility, space, and romantic opportunities. "Even now that I have moved to Zona Sul," she said, "I never find anybody, and I always end up dating in Zona Norte."[42] Similar difficulties were made explicit, albeit not deeply articulated, by Flávia when she complained about her scarce romantic options at university. While she felt little considered by male students, all her suitors were from the social milieu of her neighborhood and family. She described these boys as "quite ignorant" and not able to have a good conversation (*o papo não é bom*). For example, about a *moreno* she met through her cousin, she commented: "He's quite good looking but he can only talk about *funk* and football . . . the worst was when he asked me whether UERJ was public or private . . . do you understand? Can I go out with somebody like that? Better I stay alone!" Lack of interest in black university-educated girls, however, does not only come from middle-class nonquota male students but also from male *cotistas*. Jamerson, for example, complained to me that the most beautiful girls in the class ignored him. These turned out to be white and middle-class girls from the *Barbárie*.

Questions relate to the effects that social mobility, and quotas as a vehicle for it, may exert on black students in terms of marriageability. There is a paradox here, where it seems that black female students actually count on fewer opportunities in the relationship market once they start moving up socially. Still not desired by white men, who are clearly the majority in the middle-class environments in which they dream of projecting themselves, these women often feel forced to fall back on less-educated men or to remain single. This fact is increased by the better opportunities in terms of interracial romantic relationships for socially ascending black men, as Telles and Moutinho discuss. The Black movement becomes more visibly a space where the inequality suffered by black girls is partially redressed, leaving some relationship options open for them. This is a space that militants somehow patrol and where black girls enter into contact with black boys in the process of social mobility, boys who might prefer them for political and ethnic reasons. On the other hand, the gap between Black-politicized and non-Black-politicized female students is reducing. Differences, like those mentioned with regard to hair and beauty, do not relate very much to an opposite view of gendered and racial inequality in the relationship field in Brazil, but to the strategies used to deal with it. While activists politically appreciate endogamy, for Flávia such a principle offends the ideal of racial democracy.

Considerations about some of the problematic effects of social mobility on the romantic options of black girls in the short term, I point out, do not aim to draw the simplistic conclusion that affirmative action could be paradoxically counterproductive for the lives of beneficiaries. In a way very similar to what I have shown for classroom geographies, contact initially displays more clearly historicized barriers that cannot be automatically solved by policies. However, in the long run, the exposure to horizontal socializing between white and black people with university degrees might raise the figures of middle-class marriages where at least one of the partners is a black person.

A rather different aspect relates to the difference between *pardo* and *preto* girls in terms of interracial relationships. Although, as shown in chapter four, the Black movement pursues a discourse of black unity, minimizing differences between *pardos* and *pretos*, some students stressed these differences not only with regard to beauty but also in the related field of romantic relationships. During interviews with self-defined black female students, I collected several complaints about the fact that the white girls are always the ones with whom boys flirt the most, although brown girls hold advantages over darker-skinned ones. Patrícia (social sciences), self-identified as *mulata* (and *negra*), has a very clear view of the racial hierarchies in the flirting scale (with white at the top). She shows how race might cast shadows even over other potentially relevant aspects of beauty. It is important to notice that Patrícia does not even use the word "*namorar*" (to go out with), which would imply a more serious relationship, but "*paquerar*" (to flirt, to hit on), which is immediately sexual and might easily result in one-night stands:

> This is something that seldom fails in my experience. Black women are constantly the less *paqueradas* and the more black you are, the more you experience that . . . For example, if I go out with Clarice and Cyntia, who are darker (*mais escuras*), I'll be the most *paquerada*. However, I remember that any time I went out with Vanessa, a white [female] friend of mine, nobody looked at me and all the men went for her! I don't consider myself to be beautiful, but ugly I'm not. While she . . . she is so fat! So, why did men prefer her, if not because she's white?!

The fact that white men prefer to romantically relate to light-brown women than to darker ones, especially when the white man is middle-class, was confirmed by another student. "Seeing a white middle-class man with a black woman is very uncommon in Rio. What you might see more often, instead, is a white middle-class man with a light-skinned *mulata* with well-straightened hair (*uma mulata clara de cabelo bem esticado*)." Brown girls are therefore more easily appealing on the market because they can better play with aesthetics that, according to need, may whiten them. Differences in this field between *pretas* and *pardas* are also pointed out by Telles. This author debates that, even though white people out-marry in Brazil more significantly than in the United States, and despite the clear salience of white endogamy, interracial relationships are mostly between white and brown (*pardos*) people. In fact, 20.4 percent of brown women and 26.0 percent of brown men are married to white partners, whereas the same is true for only 15.9 percent of *preta* women and 19.1 percent of *preto* men (2004:176). Furthermore, these data should not convince the reader that patterns for *mulatas* are the same as for brown-skinned women, generally speaking, of which *mulatas* represent a sort of visibly Africanized—and probably more discriminated against—subcategory, one that until now has not found yet any clear space in the IBGE racial/color classifications.

The distinctions made between *pardas* and *pretas* (and between *mulatas* and other brown-skinned women) might in any case have important consequences for the social ascension process promoted by quotas, due to the general aesthetic advantages of women who display mixture more visibly in phenotypic terms over darker-skinned and more typically "black"-looking ones. These advantages might result, for example, in easier marriageability for women who better approximate to the white ideal, if not in their easier access to the job market. This fact raises the issue that even though Black affirmation is improving the image of black people in general, this might happen more significantly and rapidly for black men than for black women, and for lighter-skinned black men and women more than for darker-skinned ones. Such a point integrates considerations already made in this book, setting out the impact of color shades for social mobility. It therefore partially problematizes certain approaches within the Black movement, the social sciences, and at some institutional levels where *pardos* and *pretos* are conflated into a single undifferentiated black reality.

Becoming "Black"?

In the final period of my fieldwork Flávia made the racial component more visible in her accounts of social identity. This does not mean that race started simplistically replacing class in her vision of experienced inequalities. The two variables were now made more explicit and enriched each other in the way Flávia understood her past, her present, and her possible future place in society. However, the fact that race was initially not made explicit in Flávia's social discourse does not mean that it really was invisible to her. What this suggests, instead, is that some people might downplay and disguise the racial variable because it is considered shameful. Race/color references, as Flávia notices, can be used to make girls feel uncomfortable, for example, by telling them that they will end up marrying a little (or mediocre) black boy (*um pretinho*). On the other hand, pretending they are irrelevant does not make these references disappear. In contrast, they are better defined by substantial invisibility or by the negative connotations they receive in the *novelas*, in fashion magazines, in the romantic field, and in the job market (there are no black doctors in the hospital where Flávia's mother works). The question at this point is: "Does the university experience enhance Flávia's 'blackness'?"

When asking this question I cannot simplistically overlook my own role in my fieldwork and the way that I interacted with my informants. I cannot deny that after the several months I spent with first-year law students, the ways that they dealt with and discussed racial issues had changed. This posed compelling questions of how much my research was influencing my informants. Quota students started sending me articles concerning race relations, making me aware of related events in their neighborhoods and introducing me to some students who, according to them, could provide interesting data for my study. Some students also asked me for more detail about affirmative action and how affirmative measures are seen abroad. What made me think was also the fact that, according to some students, the interview process was making them reflect better on their own identity. Flávia, for example, increasingly started using our chats as a way to understand herself, and she often said that she found my questions challenging and useful to her. However, even though this kind of interactions are never neutral, I came to the conclusion that I was probably overestimating my influencing power. For students, I was a foreign researcher; however, after months of intense socializing within and without university, my informants seemed to downplay this and often introduced me to others as the beneficiary of a program exchange (*bolsa sanduíche*) at the UERJ.[43] Our relationships, in fact, never looked like something particularly atypical within the framework of my informants' university lives, where contact with foreign students and researchers is, after all, quite common. In the end, the deeper interest in racial topics from my informants was part of a package of personal and academic growth that the university was opening up, and of which I was a component.

One day, after a visit to the Paço Imperial[44] with Flávia and Eliane, we were sitting in a *barzinho* (little bar) in Arco do Teles, off Praça XV, in the city center. Reflecting on her personal experience at university, Eliane said:

> Something we cannot deny is that, even after just a semester at university, we have all changed a lot . . . my mother, my sister and my friends say that I'm a different person . . . I don't know if you have noticed it but we even dress in a different way . . . we speak in a different way . . . and look at Flávia, I almost can't recognize her . . . she was always very shy at the beginning of the courses and now . . . look at her, she's always out, going to lots of events . . . have you seen her photos at the Carnival?[45] She was in the *blocos da rua* (street Carnival) in the *Centro* of Rio, really confident (*toda feliz*) and with lots of extravagant accessories in her hair!

Eliane's remark was part of a wider discourse about her enthusiasm for being at the UERJ, which I have already highlighted in chapter two when describing the value this student ascribed to the fact of studying at a high-standard public institution. Her words reminded me strongly of some student Black activists when they stated that being at the UERJ was crucial for black people because they were occupying an "*espaço de poder*" (space of power). Their reading was political in a Black sense but, in the end, went along with the fact that Flávia and Eliane, as both lower-class and black young women, were also occupying that "space of power" in the city (the city center or even wealthy Zona Sul). Moreover, these students gradually started to look more comfortable in these new spaces. Whether politically involved or not, there is therefore a metaphysical encounter between the politics of Black activists and the practical emancipation of black girls who look for high-standard education and social mobility.

As a further point, I highlight that Flávia had initially expressed particular discomfort about the social characterization of specific locales (her neighborhood, the university, the bookstore café). At another point, however, she also mentioned the Afro-Carioca cinema, with whose audience she could have identified herself somewhat, both in class and racial terms. The real distance she found from the other participants at the screening event was the confidence and knowledge that politically involved students showed by affirming racial issues. She had been used to seeing these things as negative, disturbing, and perhaps in contradiction with her dream of social mobility, whereas now the same issues became more of an interesting field in which to question herself and the reality around her. In the Afro-Carioca cinema, she might have noticed new strategies for personal and social understanding, as well as an additional potential space in which to build up social identification.

Toward the end of my fieldwork, I made my presence at the UERJ less regular than it had been, losing track of my informants' daily lives. When I went back to the university after some time, I was surprised to find that Flávia had become a rather assiduous frequenter of black music evening events in a city center that, only a few months earlier, was almost unknown to her and which she had considered quite dangerous. Several months after my return to Europe, I browsed some photos of my informants' university lives on the Orkut website. In some of these photos, Flávia was wearing braids in the classroom. In other photos both Eliane's and Flávia's hair looked more voluminous and less flattened than it had been before. This happened at the same time that the clothing style of female quota students gradually became more sophisticated, less typically "suburban," and more similar to that of nonquota girls. To conclude, in January 2009, during one of my telephone conversations with Flávia after leaving Brazil, she asked me if I could provide her with some contacts at the university Black movement. She was interested in becoming aware of the activities of the student Black movement. In July 2009, she told me that she had decided to avoid Denegrir, finding it still too radical "against whites"; she then established contact with another Black group with which she could identify herself more. At the time of writing, looking at the web communities to which Flávia is affiliated, some of these relate to blackness, and one of these is the Coletivo Sankofá I mentioned earlier in my list of Black organizations attended by UERJ students.

At this point, I restate my initial question: Does university make certain students identify as black? As I will show, the answer remains complex.

I believe that it was not coincidence that Flávia's interest in racial topics was sparked by certain experiences disclosed by university life. However, what Flávia came to discuss in a clearer and more articulated way was not something that she had previously ignored. As her testimony shows, she had already started reflecting on blackness in high school, when she became used to discussing her racial identity with schoolmates. On deeper examination, the process of racial identification and awareness for Flávia seems to be something generally and potentially provoked by education. Reflection, however, does not necessarily translate into taking on consistent political positions, which *might*, but not necessarily *will*, flourish at the UERJ. This is still an educational space of very good quality, where students are expected to develop their critical abilities, deal with theoretical frameworks, and engage in a number of activities that are not really available in their neighborhoods. In the end, the gap observed between activist and nonactivist students should be scaled down because it relies less on content and more on strategies or motivation to change things. In addition, this gap might be reduced as a consequence of contact between politicized and nonpoliticized people at university. This is not just a matter of whether students' identities have been manipulated by Black politics and by affirmative action. As Jurema says,

> This is a problem of self-esteem of my people. Imagine that you were born learning that you're ugly, that your hair and nose are horrible. Imagine that you are aware that finding a partner is difficult for you... not many people have the courage to recognize this politically and take a stance about it...

Jurema is talking of a self-esteem that is more specific than the broadly social self-esteem that Flávia mentioned during our chats. My impression is that Flávia was gradually articulating her identity as a black, lower-class, and socially ascending woman having entered the UERJ. Such articulation is also reflected by the new spaces in the city that this student had the opportunity to occupy, breaching the boundaries of the familiar, namely, her lower-class and intellectually depressing neighborhood. In this sense, her confidence as a black woman was probably growing along with her intellectual and social self-esteem. Separating one aspect from the other seems to me to be rather difficult even for analytical purposes. In any case, I should point out that the only main quota-informant who had become more politically involved by the second year of her undergraduate program was Daisy. Even though this student used black quotas and had always considered herself black, she did not join the Black movement. She became instead a leader of CALC, the student academic political organization that defends the interests of law students and does not have any racial connotations.

Turner (1985) shows that university has always been a key locale for the construction of black identity in Brazil, even from the 1970s, when the debate around affirmative action and quotas was probably unimaginable. Obviously, quotas enhance possibilities of contesting realities and truths, because they increase the number of black students at university, which multiplies chances for social identification and participation for students. Since quotas were introduced, several previously ignored topics came to be discussed at the UERJ. One of these topics is the substantial lack of academic disciplines that target black culture and African history, something that is slowly but surely changing, in part through the Black movement, and in part due to the higher number of potentially interested students. Students involved in Black politics, for example, claimed that the African History course in the History Department was basically a course on decolonization and did not address the subject from the diaspora perspective. In addition, the creation of the 10639 Law that established African and Afro-Brazilian History and Culture as an obligatory subject in schools created the need for the History and Education Departments to review their educational programs, as mentioned by some teachers. One of the main obstacles to the teaching of this subject in Brazilian school, in fact, is the substantial lack of trained professionals. Another important aspect is the higher number of students who decide to write their graduation dissertations on racial topics, especially among those students with some involvement in the Black social movement. This highlights a number of correlated problems to which the university will have to respond. For example, several students complained about the lack of supervisors specializing in the race-related research topics they would like to pursue.

It is still early to discuss how and whether Flávia is going to reinforce her blackness at the UERJ. If we look at it in terms of becoming a militant, according to Jurema, this happens only to a tiny minority of students. However, articulation of blackness is also closely related to the wider university experience and to general, potentially related, intellectual growth.

> I already had some [black] consciousness from before, but then you arrive at university, you meet people and study academic subjects . . . we read and comment on texts, we get to know very good black authors through the *grupo de estudo* [study group on racial issues] . . . so you start organizing scattered information that you already had, you start creating analogies, getting a deeper knowledge, even disagreeing with your other peers . . . (Jurema)

Another important aspect is that a high number of black people I interviewed and who had some Black political consciousness were not actually activists. Many of them participated in some of the Denegrir activities but declared themselves to have quite a flexible approach to political blackness (e.g., in terms of hairstyle and interracial romantic relationships). In many cases, students declared themselves to have a black identity independent of any link with the Black movement. "Look, the [Black] movement is not my cup of tea (*não é a minha praia*) because I'm not interested in politics in general," history student Janaina said. On the other hand, she continued, "although I'm not involved in the movement, my black identity has grown here and it will grow more. The opposite would be impossible, considering the huge amount of reading we have to cope with." Other students, even less politicized ones, look at the movement as an important point of reference. Michelle, for example, says: "[E]ven if you don't take part in the movement, you know that it is there if you need it . . . you can join specific activities and cultural events you are interested in at any time." Tamara, on the other hand, makes reference to the more extreme wings of the Black movement as an important stage (and space) for her construction of black identification. Even though her perspective has become less radical with time, she declared herself to now being more aware and critical of her actions and ways of thinking. Racial identification, indeed, may change in intensity and use, depending on personal experiences, achieved maturity, and context.

> When I started university I joined the movement, we went to Brasília with Denegrir, I met people from Bahia[46] . . . some of them were even lighter-skinned than me . . . I even competed as a candidate in the student "Black electoral list" (*a Chapa Negra*) at UERJ . . . all experiences which have been very relevant in my life . . . At one point I was getting to a stage where I was very against white things . . . but now I've overcome that feeling and I'm more relaxed about all this. I'm less confrontational. The other day, for example, I saw a straightened haircut (*um corte alisado*) on TV and I thought "I want it!" (Tamara)

André, history student and Educafro coordinator in Rio, also explains this fact quite well. According to him, the confrontational attitude of the Black movement can be a way of catching attention and making people reflect and talk about things, without aiming at real fractures in the social collective.

> At first, I was politically very belligerent and radical. I know that there are moments when we need to ask for all or nothing (*pedir tudo ou nada*) and make lots of noise in order to make people notice us. If we were completely soft in our approach, nobody would listen to us and consider what we say. However, now I've changed. I think that after the stage where you make noise, you also need to be able to negotiate

and be diplomatic. Otherwise you will achieve nothing. This is to me a more sensible approach that not everybody understands within the Black movement . . . For example, established anti-white attitudes become counterproductive after a certain point . . . If you're very much like that you won't go anywhere, politically speaking. (André, Educafro leader and history student at the UERJ)

Even though I sometimes faced obstacles to my research with the Black movement due to being a white researcher, I informally chatted with the most confrontational activists on a number of occasions in a very relaxed and cordial way. In addition, I noticed that, beyond the dogmatic façade of the Black movement, activist students related in a friendly manner to everybody else at university. Paradoxically, I noticed that some Black activists had clearly become appreciated and popular among their peers of all colors and status in their classrooms. These students were seen as confident and able to defend their ideas. Unexpectedly, their strong political stances enabled them to become much more easily integrated into the student collective than the shy first-year law *cotistas* I described in the first part of this book. Because of this fact, Black activists are often chosen by their classmates to discuss important issues with their departments and the university leadership. If seen from this perspective, becoming involved in Black politics might represent, for some young people, a way to connect more deeply with the social reality around them, to be appreciated and even to overcome racial boundaries without being blind to them. In this vein, I would like to return to the interest manifested by Tamara, a Black-politicized philosophy student, for a straightened haircut:

> We are girls and sometimes we love changing and transforming ourselves . . . In the end I can have a straightened haircut but now I constantly question myself . . . OK, why do I want it? In the end I can have it, but at least I question myself and my actions more than I would have done before starting university . . .

These are crucial points about the impact that university and the ideas of the Black movement may have on students like Flávia, not in terms of transforming them into radical militants in clear opposition to the "white" world, but in terms of reflecting more on their thoughts, the social system around them, and the history that has contributed to producing that system.

Another crucial aspect I call attention to is that the university potentially emerges as a bridge between central and peripheral locations in the city; this bridging phenomenon is deeply steeped in racial connotations but cannot simply be reduced to them either. Quite interestingly, the occupation of the space immediately beyond the university building seems a significant extension of the space of power represented by the university itself in a way that is not just about wealth but also knowledge and the power to question knowledge. These facts are positive and new, even though young women like Flávia still have to suffer sexualized and racialized comments when walking on the street.

Although the university process ended up scaling down Flávia's differences from activists and Black-conscious students, Flávia's dream of social mobility also points out another important aspect. It raises the question of what a bridge between center and periphery could represent for different people, as well as the impact that affirmative action might play in building such bridges. As I have often said, Flávia, at least initially, saw university as a way for her personal escape from a poor neighborhood to which she felt little attachment, even while she also started representing a successful and referential model for other people in her family and social milieu. In a rather different way, activists and other students from less prestigious courses seemed much more committed to bringing the center closer to their communities or to recreating a bit of that center in suburban locations. Several activists and other lower-class students, in this vein, helped in pre-vestibular courses in their neighborhoods in Baixada Fluminense or Zona Oeste, and involved themselves in a wide range of community projects. It is not clear if this deeper commitment was influenced by the fact that these less fortunate students had few chances for social mobility and would probably have to stay in their communities, or whether this fact related more to the social kind of studies that these students were forced to take due to the high competitiveness in the access to prestigious programs. Having said this, as a Denegrir activist noticed, the increased presence of black students in less competitive courses was crucial, even if this did not ensure a monetary social mobility. In such courses, people were encouraged to think critically about themselves and the reality around them, projecting this knowledge to their communities, and also potentially favoring their transition to active citizenship. It is still too early to foresee whether the university process will also make Flávia more committed to her community at the same time as she develops some social and racial consciousness at university. However, these considerations should be kept in mind in the planning of policies that aim to positively transform poor communities and not simply to dislocate individuals from poor urban areas to middle-class neighborhoods.[47]

Toward a Conclusion

This book was conceived as a journey that draws on my knowledge, impressions, and ethnographic experiences of Brazilian race relations in the framework of student quotas in public universities. The narrative has addressed race, class, gender, and space, presenting the latter as an effect, reflection, and metaphor but also as a structuring factor of these other variables. Having said this, I could not draw conclusions to my ethnographic study of affirmative action without commenting first on the actual performance of *cotistas*, and whether they are able to make any progress toward achieving their dreams. One of the main critiques of the quota system, in fact, has been that *cotistas* would not be able to keep up with their courses. Due to their low educational levels, these students have been largely expected to have low academic performance; this, accompanied by a lack of finances, would result in high dropout rates among the beneficiaries of the quota system, causing a waste of resources that could be used more efficiently by skilful others. Many final-year informants remember how prevalent these catastrophic predictions were, especially in the first years following the introduction of quotas. According to them, some teachers had made very overt comments about the fact that *cotistas* would affect the prestige of the university. These feelings were present across the university, but especially in the Law Department. UERJ law students had held until 2003 the highest pass rate of the OAB[1] (Association of Brazilian Lawyers) examination in the State of Rio de Janeiro compared to other state and federal public universities, and one of the highest in the country overall. Not only were there assumptions that quotas will affect the prestige of UERJ courses but also, somehow implicitly, that criteria of performance are in the end quite democratic in defining the sharing of public resources.

Struggling But Doing Well: Notes on the Academic Performance of Quota Students at UERJ

From October 2007 until July 2008, I followed the academic life of UERJ *cotistas* in the Law Department. I cannot forget the expressions of disappointment when these students, Flávia in particular, were given their assessments back and many of them had scored very low marks. These feelings were also amplified by unavoidable comparisons to non-*cotistas*, most of them middle- and upper-middle-class students who came from excellent private colleges and who, overall, scored extremely well in the assessments. Before the second evaluation of the first semester, however, I noticed a strong solidarity among first-year quota students who in some cases were helped by nonquota students from similar social backgrounds. Some quota students gathered in groups at university in the afternoon to discuss course topics and help each other. In general, I also noticed strong support from teachers whose constant encouragement became vital for students' motivation.

In the second round of assessments in each subject, quota students improved significantly, and in some cases scored very high marks, although differences to non-*cotistas* were still visible. These gaps tended to relate little to quota students' ability to understand topics but instead to writing skills and to the use of the Portuguese language. However, an interesting fact is that, according to students at all stages of their undergraduate program and several teachers I interviewed in the Law Department at the UERJ, the difference in performance between quota and nonquota students significantly decreases over time, becoming almost irrelevant in the final years. In fact, the year after I left Brazil, Flávia proudly informed me that she had done very well in civil law and that the teacher had praised her and other quota students' achievements publicly in front of the classroom. She and the other students, as Flávia incredulously observed, were positively presented as "examples of academic change." All the teachers I interviewed had a similar view; even those who did not support the idea of quotas in philosophical terms were very positive about their results.

> If I talk from a political point of view, I believe that quotas are not the best way to fight inequality in Brazil. The problem of these students is the fact that they studied in very low-standard schools and many of them have a difficult economic situation [meaning that the problem is the low standard of public schools in Brazil and that is not racial]. However, if I talk by looking at the results, my testimony has to be different. *Cotistas* are, overall, very motivated students from the beginning of the course. In comparison to the catastrophic predictions when the system was introduced, these students do quite well. But for the very start of the undergraduate programs, I don't see many differences between students and I believe that many *cotistas* will be excellent professionals. (Constitutional Law teacher)

Such a positive balance is confirmed by statistical evidence. According to first-hand data I processed in 2007 concerning the period 2003–2007, the difference in cumulative CRM[2] (Average Performance Coefficient) between quota and nonquota students was not striking in the Law Department. The CRM of public-school quota students and black-quota students, on a scale from 0 to 10, was in both cases 7.1, while that of nonquota students was 7.9 (DINFO, 2007). These figures, however, are affected by the more significant differences in marks between *cotistas* and non-*cotistas* during the first two years of the course. Unfortunately, DINFO data were not disaggregated by year, so it was impossible to assess statistically whether and when the CRM of quota students actually peaks positively or negatively during the undergraduate program. In any case, it is important to note that, even after the introduction of quotas (the first *cotistas* graduated in 2008), the UERJ Law Department maintained its leading position in the OAB among public and private universities in the State of Rio de Janeiro.[3] The percentage of successful UERJ candidates in 2008 was 79 percent, compared to 72 percent in the Federal University of Rio de Janeiro (UFRJ)—where quotas were not implemented at the time of writing—and 65 percent at the PUC, the elite private university of Rio de Janeiro. The UERJ kept its primacy in the OAB again in 2009 with 80 percent of candidates being successful.[4]

Interesting also are data about dropout rates in the Law Department. Only 3.7 percent of black-quota students had left their courses between 2003 and 2007, compared to 5.3 percent of public-school *cotistas* and 4.8 percent of nonquota students. This means that *cotistas*' hard work in order to survive academically and financially during their course was substantially successful. No data were available about the time of graduation, due in particular to the fact that the first *cotistas* had only recently started graduating, although it is reasonable to imagine that quota students might delay their graduation due to financial problems (Almeida, 2007). What cannot be said, however, is that these students drop out of courses more than others.

This account becomes even more important when considering the different social backgrounds of the students, especially their educational backgrounds, which were to some extent visible by their rank in the vestibular exam. In the first-year law course that started in 2007, nonquota law students passed the vestibular only if they ranked within the first 168 candidates, out of the almost 3,000 candidates who were admitted to the second phase of the examination. In contrast, the vast majority of quota students were ranked between the 1,000th and the 1,800th position out of these 3,000 candidates.[5] In this sense, quota students started from a very disadvantaged position but not for this were the weakest applicants on the market. Particularly in highly popular programs such as law and medicine, these students generally need to score at least "B" or "C" to qualify, on a scale between "A" (top) and "E" (failing). This fact also refutes the incorrect idea, spread even among teachers, about the fact that quota students would be able to enter university without any kind of examination. Most of these students, in fact, undertake the vestibular after attending community or private preparatory courses in which they invest most of their savings and time. They may attempt the examination a couple of times before succeeding.

I clarify that the situation presented relates exclusively to the Law Department, a very competitive and prestigious program, and consequently includes a significant number of upper-middle-class students. The scenario changes and is even more positive for quota students if looking at the average CRM and dropout rates calculated over a total of 49 graduation courses between 2003 and 2007 (processed from DINFO data, 2007). In this case, the average CRM is 6.56 for public-school quota students, 6.41 for black-quota students, and actually slightly lower, 6.37, for non-*cotistas*. Overall dropout rates at the UERJ are also surprisingly higher for nonquota students (17 percent), in contrast to black-quota students (13 percent) and public-school quota students (10 percent).[6]

The Ever-Contended Character of Quotas

The data about academic performance and dropout rates at the UERJ seem reassuring. In spite of this, while working on this book, racial quotas have remained a highly contested topic in Brazil. In May 2009, these measures, apparently solidly established at the UERJ, were suspended in the State of Rio de Janeiro due to claims of unconstitutionality. A state deputy, Flávio Bolsonaro, undertook this judicial action after hearing from some students that quotas generated constraining situations for users and increased racism at university.[7] Quotas were eventually reconfirmed by the Tribunal de Justiça do Rio de Janeiro in late 2009. More recently, in March 2010, an *audiência pública* (public hearing) was held at the Supremo Tribunal Federal (High Federal Court) to decide about the constitutionality of quotas at the federal level. The verdict of the High Federal Court, eventually released in April 2012, sanctioned the constitutionality of quotas with the unanimity of the voting members. The Estatuto da Igualdade Racial, on the other hand, was finally approved in 2010 rather emptied of its initial ambitions, without mentioning quotas and leaving the debate about the implementation of these measures through federal legislation still very open.

My work, overall, suggests that the implementation of a quota system at the UERJ has been positive. Far from generating the racial tensions and resentment that some people expected, these measures have produced a more diverse environment that favors urban encounters and that is gradually becoming part of the institution's identity. As a concrete effect, quotas have increased the number of black students in university with material and symbolic effects for the visibility of black people in certain public spaces. Although the university setting and its users represent limited segments of society, lower-class and black students have demonstrated that they can perform well, implicitly challenging stereotypes and social expectations somewhat related to color and class in Brazil. Diversity and social opportunities for marginal groups could be understood not just as an advantage for these groups but as advantages for universities or societies at large that want to implement more fully the principles of equality generally stated in democratic constitutions. Beyond the philosophical debates relating to racial quotas, there is something that the *cotistas*' good performance demonstrates clearly: Brazil has systematically wasted precious human capital. Therefore, quotas at the UERJ may give a taste of what Brazilian society might be if there was more equality.

The presence of black quotas, as I have often suggested, is not just a material output but also a symbolically charged one. The debate around this system has encouraged people to discuss issues traditionally hidden by the mystifying effects of "racial democracy" both in its lived and ideological representations. Affirmative action has the implicit power to contest cultural censorship about race, even though part of this censorship is still reproduced in academic settings that adopt quotas. Paradoxically, this happens because quotas allow a traditionally rather white and middle-class university space to reflect more faithfully the unequal social dynamics typical of the city. Although suddenly more visible, however, these differences are also reprocessed and renegotiated, favoring (potentially, at least) reciprocal knowledge and understanding between different groups of users.

The quota system also has multiple effects on black consciousness. First, several Black civil society organizations felt encouraged to take a political stance on this matter and converged to defend the system, fortifying the visibility of an otherwise extremely fragmented Black movement in Brazil. Second, access to good-quality higher education implies that many students will develop a different sensibility toward racial issues and might find it easier to articulate thoughts and employ strategies against racial inequality. I have shown that this process ends up involving less politicized students to some degree—even if they do not become militants and tend to use racial quotas only when really necessary to achieve an opening—due both to sharing spaces with activists and the growth of their critical thinking promoted by dealing with academic subjects. The strengthening of a Black social movement that deploys affirmative claims in favor of a black group, it is worth observing, should not be confused with forms of racialization that in the past have been enforced to oppress groups (apartheid, Jim Crow, slavery) without the consent of these same groups or of the people who claim to speak for them. Furthermore, it is important not to mistake the creation of black consciousness for something that necessarily contradicts traditional class-based approaches to inequality or national feelings of *mestiçagem*. In relation to the class-based approach, I have shown not only that black identity is something that develops together with class and other social identities and is promoted by academic study itself, but also that developing some racial consciousness can even be a reason for some students to join class-based politics. Racial identity, however, does not develop as something fixed, permanent in life, and secure from criticism. In relation to *mestiçagem*, I suggest that blackness and racial mixture are not to be considered as two irreconcilable and incommensurable concepts, for example, in the way that they are imagined and experienced by some non-Black-politicized black students at the UERJ. This consideration is crucial because it implies respecting the originality of the national system of race relations in Brazil without necessarily producing any clear biracialization. At the same time, this point suggests that systems of race relations are continuously in motion, also due to their interaction with external models; in addition, it suggests that official ways of classification might gradually need to adapt to social change.

As anticipated at the beginning of this book, the quota topic relates very closely to a discourse of recognition and/or transformation whose seminal exponents in the social sciences have been Charles Taylor and Nancy Fraser, respectively. If Taylor, in a liberal approach to multiculturalism, emphasizes the politics of difference as a way to grant equal rights and self-esteem to despised groups, for Fraser (1997), this politics is not transformative. Affirmative action, following Fraser, is a neoliberal measure or a palliative by which the state gives illusions of apparent equality in order to avoid more structural transformations in society.[8] Against this view, I could contend that university quotas are transformative in many ways, even if their more direct effects appear to benefit only a limited number of citizens (some higher education students) in limited settings (certain universities). These measures have reshaped the UERJ in a way that is now seen as more Brazilian, but are also gradually changing the lives of users.

It would be also tempting to conclude that quotas are not really redistributive since they tend to create new elites, for instance, a black elite, that become separate from the very poor and reproduce new inequalities. On the other hand, a question is whether creating a black elite does not in itself represent at least some form of redistribution and diversification among elites. In addition, change is not just material but also symbolic when considering, for instance, the motivational charge and hope that *cotistas* bring to depressed neighborhoods and socially vulnerable households. While studying on prestigious courses at a public university is often seen as out of reach and even pretentious for *cotistas*' extended families, the success of these students sometimes starts setting out opportunities and producing confidence in an entire social milieu. Some of my informants, for example, became points of reference and counselors for a number of relatives and neighbors during their studies. Some people in the students' social networks also developed ambitions to pursue university education, since the experience of *cotistas* made this goal somehow more achievable. Discourses of recognition (or affirmation) and redistribution (or transformation), therefore, cannot be sharply separated, and these processes do not need to happen one at the expense of the other (Honneth, 2003; Fraser, 2003 and 2010). Quite the opposite, the two approaches may actually strengthen and reflect each other. As an example, I have shown how reallocations of openings in a public university, by virtue of implementing differential rights, has contributed to the affirmation and recognition of blackness in the academic space. Whether this affirmation will exert a positive effect on future claims of social equality from black groups is difficult to foresee. However, it is arguable that a higher number of lower-class and black students with a university education will make this possibility more viable. Seen from this perspective, understandings that depict affirmative action as categorically nonredistributive have the limitation of reducing redistribution to something merely economic and material. In doing so, they downplay the value of raising a group's self-esteem, and overlook its possible impact on the future economic life of the same group, simply because the effects of this gained self-esteem cannot be automatically assessed in redistributive economic terms.

Similar considerations can be extended to the role of the Black social movement and how these organizations would be co-opted or, in general, become victims of a neoliberal process that fragments them, and of a state that controls them by inhibiting class mobilization. Although aspects of these criticisms are very pertinent, they also tend to minimize the power relations that certain social movements are able to manipulate by interacting with the state, and the new scenarios/opportunities that such interactions may open for redistribution. These organizations are not simply victims, as they need to be quite clever to negotiate the neoliberal framework available to them, deploying national and international alliances to achieve specific goals in realistic and tangible ways. In the end, even if their goals ultimately entail access to economic resources, why should these movements only rely on class-based mobilization strategies, when they spot alternative and effective forms of representation and action through identity politics?

My comments here might sound like an apologia for quotas. However, I clarify that my thoughts are not so linear, and were not even linear during the time of my fieldwork. I also admit that, beyond any attempts at objectivity, spending one academic year with *cotistas* made me feel closer to their struggle for life changes, even though most of these students did not even sympathize with racial quotas or quotas in general.

On the other hand, having a positive view of quota implementation at the UERJ does not mean unconditionally supporting the radical introduction of these measures into all sectors of Brazilian life. The fact that university racial quotas are not racializing Brazilian society might be mainly due to the fact that these measures are limited to higher education institutions and that they end up being quite flexible at the UERJ, for example, by including people of all colors.[9] It is instead quite different to say that race should become *the* structural criterion on which to base access to health, mass media, the workplace, and education through systematic quota systems. In that case, such measures might somehow rigidify race relations in Brazil, making antiquota fears more realistic. The most important fact, in any case, is that a strictly racial system might not be necessary. In fact, even though a debate about racial quotas tends to point out the presence of racial inequality and racism in Brazil, this does not mean denying that race relations also have positive peculiarities in Brazil in comparison to other national contexts. These positive peculiarities, according to Telles (2004: 224), can be described as "horizontal" race relations, referring to that interracial conviviality in certain spaces that gives the impression of Brazilian race relations as relaxed. Although "vertical" race relations (read also as constraints to social mobility for black people) seem to be more rigid in Brazil than in the United States, Brazil represents a crucial case study of how societies might not need to be strongly divided along racial lines as a precondition to define and implement policies of racial equality (see also Segato, 2007: 124).

Questions of structural transformation raised by Fraser should in any case be taken into serious account. It is a fact that affirmative action is flourishing at a time of progressive impoverishment of state investment, something also proven by the precarious physical conditions of the UERJ's infrastructure at the time of my research. During my research, the State of Rio de Janeiro massively cut funding for public universities, which had already been reduced in previous years. In this scenario of general decay, some informants expressed their feelings that the state is sending subliminal messages of privatization. Contradictions in this sense can also be seen by the fact that the State of Rio de Janeiro, aside from establishing quotas in public universities, is presently funding openings in low-standard private institutions for black and lower-class students through the PROUNI (University for Everybody) program.[10] A question is why these resources are not used to improve public universities and widen access to users, although a fairly obvious answer is that this would be highly expensive for the state.

Other doubts relate to the idea of the decreasing prestige of the UERJ in Rio de Janeiro as a consequence of quotas, even though statistics about performance suggest that such ideas are not well-founded. During my interviewing process, some teachers emphasized that the middle class seems progressively less interested in the UERJ and is diverting toward other universities. In this sense, it is not clear to what extent quotas are following a process of deterioration of the public sector and to what extent they are actually fostering such deterioration. To be more explicit, it is possible that social investment in a university *without* the middle class will be seen as less useful and compelling for the Brazilian elite, which is still very influential in defining policies and allocating state resources. If quotas are not accompanied by substantial investment to ensure high standards in the public sector, some of the traditional class/racial segregation that quotas aim to reduce will actually be reproduced, for example, by the fact that public universities might become places for the poor and for black people, as the mocking label "Congo" used for the UERJ at Interuniversity sport games suggests. In that case, quotas could paradoxically become even less useful and less necessary to increase the access of poor people to higher education. Similar issues relate to the program of expansion of federal universities, the REUNI.[11] This program aimed to double the number of openings by 2010 and increase the concluding courses ratio by 50 percent through a more rational use of human and (already precarious) physical resources, but without implying higher investment in these resources and subtending a reduction of quality. There is, therefore, some tendency to think that access to public universities can be widened only by decreasing its quality. It is possible that partnerships between the public and the private sectors will redress this imbalance; however, these kinds of partnerships will in any case need commitment and interest from the state to ensure minimum standards of quality in the provision of public services.

Another typical question around racial quotas relates to the way of identifying/selecting possible candidates and the risk of creating "racial tribunals," to use an expression coined by Maio and Santos (2005). Beyond technical and ethical problems, doubts also concern the real usefulness of the Black movement's discourse that merges *pretos* and all *pardos* into *negros*. From certain angles, this approach might even be counterproductive for the black struggle. For example, according to 2007 UERJ vestibular data (Law Department), 21 percent of 158 nonquota students self-classified as *pardos* and 4 percent as *negros*[12] (presumably meaning this term *pretos* or very dark-skinned and then contradicting the Black movement's idea of racial/color repartition) in the vestibular's socioeconomic questionnaire.[13] Translated into the Black movement's official jargon, this means that *at least* 25 percent of nonquota law students, broadly speaking 25 percent of the best candidates of the department's elite, would be *negros* (*pardos* + *pretos*) even without the implementation of quotas.[14] Conclusions of this sort could be made in relation to first-year public-school *cotistas* in the Law Department starting that same year, comprising 74 students distributed between different shifts and starting in different semesters. It was seen that 34 percent of this administrative category self-identified as *pardos* and 9 percent as *negros*, in theory suggesting that 43 percent of public-school quota law freshmen in 2007 were black, if using the black-unifying logic of the Black social movement. The same figure rises to 47 percent in education, albeit calculated over just 42 students. This fact might potentially play down the usefulness of *racial* quotas as an indispensable measure to provide black students with public higher education; at least, unless people agree that the importance of racial quotas is also very much symbolic and goes well beyond their actual implementation, usage, and the opinion of users. In the view of the Black movement, in fact, racial quotas are by and large a fact of *reparação histórica* (historical reparation) and a group project that transcends individual preference and use.

There is also a further problem with the logic that *pardos* + *pretos* = *negros*. Depending on the way this summatory process is realized in statistics and policies, it disguises differences between the two groups with a mystifying logic, which is not that different from that ascribed to the myths of racial democracy. In chapter four, I discussed the fact that some *pardos*, especially those with straight hair and "finer" features, are not clearly subject to racial stigmas in Brazil. This fact was directly or indirectly suggested not just by non-Black-politicized students but also by activists. In fact, as Wade (2004b: 358–359) argues, while Degler's theory of the mulatto escape-hatch has been largely (albeit not completely) refuted by socioeconomic statistics, it seems that Brazilians still ascribe certain values to different shades of blackness and whiteness. These differences, it is worth saying, are not only already systematically expressed by informants but might be enhanced even more in the presence of affirmative action in favor of a black group. Socioeconomic similarities between *pretos* and *pardos* observed by Hasenbalg and Silva, in fact, may be due to the fact that moving up socially is quite hard for anybody in Brazil, and that accumulation of capital has been traditionally and solidly kept within a white elite. If affirmative action became a structural component of Brazilian policies, on the other hand, it might highlight unequal social mobility chances between *pardos* and *pretos*, since light-/lighter-skinned people may enjoy a better economic and educational position to use certain policies. This point is not sufficient to invalidate the redistributive value of racial affirmative action, but at least stresses the importance of keeping the *pardo* and *preto* variables separate even within a statistically or politically created black group. This fact also calls for some care in the way that the *pardo* category is socially constructed and used.

As Renato Ferreira (PPCOR) points out, the Black movement might need to discuss further the idea of *mestiçagem* and what kind of mixture can be considered black. Referring more specifically to the quota system, I observed that, although self-declaration seems to be less ethically and politically correct as a method for candidate selection, it also obscures some information control over beneficiaries. Both the pro- and antiquota movements, in fact, have talked about the risks of racial fraud implicit in self-declaration.[15] Although the idea of racial fraud sounds at odds with personal freedom to self-identify, and with the view of race as a socially constructed concept, an overly inclusive approach to blackness might turn out to be little useful to Black political projects and its fight against prejudice due to the risk of "lightening" blackness. While self-identification hampers the potentially racializing character of these measures, a question is whether such a system may penalize dark-skinned students in favor of light-skinned ones. It is true that quotas are often based on income, and that lower-class students are seldom very light-skinned; however, the pool of users of racial quotas might be quite different from those that the Black movement ideally aims to empower. Friar David dos Santos, the Educafro's director, dealt with this point by saying that a sort of commission should be introduced for this reason and that the Black movement should have a say over the selection of quota candidates. From a less extreme position, Ferreira (PPCOR) argues that, without establishing any kind of "racial tribunal," the presence of photos and some interviewing for black-quota applicants would at least be a disincentive for fraud. A commission might, for example, ask students why they identify as black through some kind of in-person self-declaration.

> I don't think that a racial tribunal should be implemented to decide who is black and who is not . . . however it would be important to foresee the use of interviews in those dubious cases . . . to ask . . . to justify, as somebody said . . . "OK, [on the form] you said that you are *negro* . . . but why? Can you please explain this to me?" I believe that establishing these two points would be important: photos and a possible interview would deter many possible frauds, even if all candidates were finally accepted. (Renato Ferreira)

A further problem that should be considered in relation to racial quotas is the fact that most black and nonblack students do not seem to enjoy these measures, as clearly shown by a number of testimonies in this book. There are therefore crucial questions about the legitimacy of policies that the potential beneficiaries dislike. On the other hand, this point should be considered in its correct dimension. First, an aversion to quotas is partially influenced by candidates' fear of being stigmatized further in society; and this, in addition to influential ideals of racial democracy, is also due to prejudices in relation to the black phenotype that exist in Brazilian society independent of quotas. Second, the individual sympathy or antipathy students manifest for racial quotas loses some relevance at the moment that candidates actually use these measures. The fact that Eliane was unhappy about being a beneficiary of racial quotas, for example, is scaled down by her satisfaction about studying law at the UERJ, a fact that only black quotas have made possible for her. Other students, in fact, distinguished between the appealing character of black quotas and their necessity, suggesting that wanting racially affirmative action is secondary to the impact that this may produce in terms of social equality and diversity. In this sense, whether happy or not (and conscious or not), many black *cotistas* represent future resources potentially able to swell the ranks of the black intelligentsia and the middle class. In doing so, they will diversify spaces of power and offer important role models, independent of whether such intelligentsia and middle class are actually politicized in a Black sense. From this perspective, the effect of quotas might exceed the otherwise limited realm of people's individual lives and projects.

Color-Blind or Color-Aware Policies?

I have presented the quota system as a potentially useful process to redress some racial inequality. However, it is still not clear whether racial measures are really so indispensable. As discussed in this book, racial quotas imply problems that are both ethical and practical. I have shown, for example, that the social background of black *cotistas* and public-school *cotistas* is rather similar, while I have also suggested that dark- and light-skinned students may be present in both categories (also due to the fact that the blackness to be proven to apply for black quotas simply goes by self-declaration). These data suggest that racial measures might be rather unnecessary; class-based or other social approaches may instead have the impact of addressing race implicitly, without reinforcing the race concept in itself. To better discuss the necessity or lack of necessity of racial measures it is, however, important to consider factors that are not easily quantifiable or immediately direct. It is undeniable that universalistic policies will implicitly reduce some inequalities, but this might not be enough, for example, because, as a Black-activist student mentions:

> It is not a question of liking or not liking racial quotas. I don't even like these measures myself. You know, when I said this, one of my teachers thought I was joking . . . but it's true! However . . . racial quotas are necessary. Imagine, for example, that a white and a black lower-class student apply to the vestibular. White students, due to their ["good"] appearance, will have more options to find a better job

to pay for a good preparation course or study languages . . . in fact, all this provides them with better chances to pass the vestibular and survive at university. (Jurema, Denegrir)

In addition, some students claim that certain public high schools are not as color-blind as people might imagine. Because they are better quality, these institutions end up being frequented largely by white and other light-skinned students, who will then have some advantages in passing the vestibular as public-school quota applicants. On the other hand, racial quotas accept students from private schools who would be excluded from the public-school quota system but who are not competitive enough to avoid quotas entirely. The temptation, at this point, is to decide that income parameters should be the fairest and only way to select *cotistas*. However, not only can these parameters be manipulated, but they will presumably favor the wealthiest people from the lower class; these, as Telles (2004: 266) shows, might still be disproportionately lighter-skinned.

In their book *Colour Conscious*, Appiah and Gutmann (1998) explain that although racial policies imply some risks of reifying race, relying exclusively on a class-based approach would not be very useful in redressing racial inequalities. This is because class is not a monolithic concept that produces the same effects on everybody, and black people experience class in a very particular way. These authors discuss, for example, the fact that in a situation of economic crisis blacks are more likely to lose their jobs. Although Appiah and Gutmann refer specifically to the United States, the situation is not that different in Brazil, especially considering that—as I have widely discussed in this book—a number of authors have consistently scaled down the "money whitens" paradigm.[16] By comparing two Brazilian universities that adopt two different approaches to affirmative action, Guimarães, da Costa, and Kleinke (2009) show that the more universities embrace the mission to enhance the racial diversity of their users, the more black students have access to higher education. The Federal University of Bahia (UFBA) uses racial quotas, whereas the State University of Campinas (Unicamp) uses a system of bonuses, which grants 30 additional points in the vestibular to public-school students, and 10 to students self-declared as *pardos* and *pretos*. Guimarães, da Costa, and Kleinke (2009: 3–6) illustrate that while the presence of racial quotas at UFBA clearly accelerates the already historically positive trend of admission for black students to that university, the system at Unicamp substantially favors more white students from the public-school system but only marginally black students. Some important universalistic policies in Brazil are instead presently implemented under the Bolsa Familia Program, instituted by ex-president Lula (Neri, 2010).[17] This program provides small cash amounts to households whose monthly per-capita income is considered under the line of poverty (less than 70 *reais*), while further small money additions are granted per poor-family child who is vaccinated and attends school. Bolsa Familia is improving the life condition of millions of indigent people in Brazil, having a positive effect on child school desertion and child prostitution. The program has a color-blind approach, even though beneficiaries are mainly nonwhite and widely concentrated in the poor Brazilian northeast. However, despite these possible indirect achievements in terms of racial equality, it is questionable that Bolsa Familia is deeply challenging social gaps between blacks and whites, as well as inequalities that affect— even if differently—black people on the symbolic level in Brazil across all social classes.

A fact is that racial and social approaches to social inequality cannot be clearly divided. For example, I have already explained that in some cases race has represented the way through which students join politics and social involvement, which also signifies a way to becoming an active citizen. At the same time, quotas might favor the creation of a black intelligentsia that could positively represent role models and leadership for the black masses (Benedita da Silva, 1999a). Against possible claims that the black intelligentsia does not have much in common with the black masses—in the same way that the rich do not have much in common with the poor—it should be remembered that both poor and middle-class black people share similar stereotypes related to their phenotype. This is quite a common penalizing ground for the two groups that affects less directly the white rich and poor. It is clear that if the Black social movement has become stronger in the last decades it is partly due to the presence of a broader black intelligentsia that has the intellectual and economic resources to notice and react against racial inequality.

What I have said here does not intend to suggest that erasing quotas in a public university like UERJ will make the institution automatically "white," but that it will more likely stress segregation between courses that are usually achievable by lower-class and black people and those from which, traditionally, they have been largely excluded. Erasing racial quotas at this time in Brazil's history would also be ethically problematic. Hooks (1991: 28), for example, distrusts postmodern analysts who criticize the existence and coherence of the (collective) subject, because this occurs at a precise historical moment in which oppressed people realize for the first time that they can make their voices heard. Similarly, Gilroy (1988: 46) notes that "some of us [...] are just beginning to formulate our own big narratives, precisely as narratives of redemption and emancipation."[18] This criticism of postmodern analyses reminds anthropologists and other social scientists that their work may affect the process of empowerment of the subaltern, the same subaltern to whom they often offer their solidarity by contesting meta-narratives and hegemonic practices. It should be observed that the quota debate is itself quite racially structured and the position of certain speakers, unfortunately, cannot easily escape the racial structures that history has produced. The antiquota position, for example, would take on a completely different light if it were massively supported by the Black movement and did not so consistently come from a group of white (or nonblack) intellectuals as is the case in Brazil. This is not to say that antiquota claims simply are unfounded or wrong, but that, when discussing racial issues, it is never irrelevant to examine *who says what*.

As a further consideration, even if socially based and universalistic policies might help reduce racial inequality, experiences in other parts of the world prove that class is never totally able to defeat race. Looking at the Cuban case, Branche (2007: 182–184) notes that socialism did not manage to delete the racial structures of the national system and all its annexed baggage of stereotypes (see also De la Fuente, 2001). Along similar lines, Fernandes (2003) contends that the reappearance of free economy in recent decades in Cuba has boosted racial divides, especially in the tourism sector, where white people are tacitly rewarded as better-looking through employment dynamics. This suggests that racial structures have persisted under Cuban socialism in spite of being silenced and minimized by political propaganda and by the implementation of universalistic policies. The conclusion is that class and universalistic approaches might be less powerful in transforming society than Fraser (1997) suggests, although it should be agreed that mere recognition alone does not automatically imply a shift in power relations if this does not lead to effective redistribution and inclusion.[19]

The claim of the antiquota movement about the necessity of restructuring the public-school system is in any case a correct one because, in that situation, all candidates would be well-trained to pass the vestibular without quotas but through a color-blind system. In particular, it is clear that as long as public-school teachers are underpaid professionals, as is presently the case in Brazil, there will be a lack of high-standard teachers (or teachers in general) in the public-school market. However, hopes of massive investment in the public-school system sound fairly unrealistic within the neoliberal political framework in which Brazil is now a crucial international actor. A question is whether it is better to await an improbable strong inversion of liberal politics or to work, for now, with the concrete instruments that the neoliberal frameworks open. In addition, it is not so clear that improving the public-school system will provide equal chances to these students in achieving an opening in prestigious courses at public universities. In fact, it is rather unlikely that these people will ever be academically strong enough to compete with higher-class students coming from expensive private colleges. In the end, improving the public-school sector might help to increase the social mobility of the poor but will barely redress the distortions that are produced by certain income (and racial) inequalities in Brazil.[20]

A parallel reasoning is that improving the public-school system is crucial for quotas, and it is surprising that many intellectuals see these facts as incurable contradictions. One of the comments that I have often heard made by vestibular officials and in newspapers is that the number of quota beneficiaries (and applicants) has been drastically decreasing since 2003. Because of this, the economic cut-off parameter for quotas has been continually raised over the years in order to fill quotas. This paradox can be justified in several ways. Possible explanations include: the introduction of the PROUNI system, which favors access to lower-standard and thus less demanding private universities; the decreased interest in the UERJ among the middle class and the consequent reduced need for potential candidates to rely on quotas; and the fact that, in the first years immediately after the introduction of quotas, there was a pool of vestibular candidates who had massively piled up over decades of exclusion. However, this decrease at the UERJ—which reaches its lowest peaks in economics, statistics, and mathematics (all with 0 percent of enrolled black-quota students in the first semester of 2007)—is also explained by the fact that quota students are academically too weak in scientific subjects to pass the vestibular in certain undergraduate programs.[21] If this were true, improving public-school teaching is strategic to fill the quotas on these programs. Improving public schools will also automatically raise the percentage of applicants to the so-called prestigious courses that provide applicants with better chances of social mobility but also with higher expectations of passing the admission examination. What quotas clearly suggest, in the end, is that change cannot occur effectively through affirmative action in higher education unless it also happens more structurally in other spheres of society (Fraser, 2003), even while it should be observed that quotas might gradually and indirectly contribute to this structural change. On the other hand, it is important to bear in mind that a decrease in the demand for certain courses with less prestigious professional outcomes, such as education and social work, is something more closely related to the structure of the job market and the inability of the educational public service to adapt to it, and not only to the lack of preparation among candidates. I could not otherwise explain why quotas in competitive courses such as medicine, law, and journalism have been constantly filled to this day at the UERJ.

Toward a Multisided Approach?

I am somewhat convinced that color-blind policies would be the best and safest strategies to correct racial inequalities if they were really effective in tackling racial gaps.[22] Skeptical about this point, I wonder whether racially based policies could be used without reinforcing racial divisions and imageries that picture race as if it really existed and as an immutable concept with significance outside of the way people experience it (Hall, 1983). A question is how this may concretely happen. A similar strategy asks for a high degree of maturity from the state and from civil society actors. While I believe that universalistic and racial policies should not exclude but reinforce each other, I argue that solutions other than racial policies should be adopted whenever possible, addressing race in a way that does not reify it (see also Telles, 2004: 250). In other words, universalistic policies should still represent the first aim of the state; however, it is important to assess whether access to policies is racially equal and, if necessary, to devise noncolor-blind measures to correct these distortions. In this sense, preserving color/racial questions for surveys and for the processing of certain demographic outputs is crucial in assessing how different phenotypic groups perform in the access of certain resources and whether and how much racially based affirmative action is necessary in a country at a specific time.

I add that racially affirmative action does not necessarily mean quotas, and some kinds of affirmative measures imply lesser risks of reifying race than quotas may do. One possibility is to consider *un*constitutional those mass media that promote certain ideas of beauty and skill that foster (or reflect) racial inequalities. Similar actions could be deployed not just directly through formal sanctions and banning, but also through incentives.[23] Among other measures, I am thinking of tax allowances for those companies that commit to diversity in their employment processes and advertisement campaigns. The same could be said of a crucial cultural channel, Brazilian soap operas, which might start promoting, more consistently, black people in positive and wealthy roles that escape the stereotype of the *favelado*, the maid, and the drug-dealer.[24]

Affirmative measures that do not clearly racialize, after all, is already being implemented. Law 10639 is a concrete example. This law establishes the obligatory teaching of African and Afro-Brazilian culture and history in school and, if effectively implemented, this could be a way of increasing self-esteem as well as awareness about blackness and discrimination without relying on any divisive spirit. Although the logic of this law has been criticized (see Maggie, 2006a), in principle it aims to foster knowledge and awareness about Afro-Brazilian history and culture among all Brazilians.

A crucial need is to keep dialogue and confrontation constantly alive. In fact, it is widely recognized that the quota debate has somehow been even more important than the quota system itself. There are innumerable reasons for this. First, the presence of two different political positions that respect each other helps redress weaknesses that would otherwise be easily overlooked. Second, the debate encourages people to take a critical approach to the matter of quotas instead of simply being passive recipients of state decisions. Third, this debate has positively influenced the way that certain institutions averse to quotas deal with antiracism. It might not be random that the television channel Rede Globo, notoriously averse to racial quotas, has notably increased the presence of black people in its programs over the last decade. A possibility is that this television channel now has to actively demonstrate that racial quotas are not so necessary; in trying to do so, Globo would be contradicting itself by keeping Afro-Brazilians and dark-skinned people constantly invisible. Along the same lines, protests by the Black movement against certain banks and companies that tend not to employ black people might bring about serious reflection within these businesses, in addition to possibly disclosing new markets for their products.

As a concluding point, the Federal University of Rio de Janeiro, where antiquota sentiments have traditionally been quite intense, has recently decided to adopt quotas for public-school students.[25] This decision was made in 2010, after prolonged discussion, which I was able to follow in part at the time of my fieldwork in Rio. My point here is that, although the UFRJ has decided not to adopt racially affirmative action, the establishment of public-school quotas in that institution also functions as an indirect effect of, or as a reaction to, the racial quota debate. While the main argument of the antiquota movement at UFRJ was the fear of racialization, it might have been more difficult for this institution to justify categorical aversion to any other measures to de-eliticize its student collective. In this sense, public-school quotas are often described as a lesser evil that could help downplay the possible rise of racial claims. This fact adds to my impression that, albeit through intricate journeys, class- and racially-based strategies may end up working in similar directions or strengthening each other; much more, at least, than traditional oppositions between these approaches have taken for granted.

Notes

1 Toward an Ethnographic Study of Racial Quotas for "Black" Students in the University of the State of Rio De Janeiro

1. Other categories included in censuses are *amarelo* (yellow, mainly referring to Japanese and Chinese origin) and *indígena* (Native Indian or indigenous). However, these categories, according to IBGE Census data 2010 represent about 2 percent of the overall Brazilian population.
2. See also Holanda (1995 [1936]) and his concept of the "cordial man."
3. In the United States, unlike Brazil, race (rather than class) is commonly presented as the more powerful cause of social divisions.
4. Fernandes (1969), Hasenbalg (1979), Silva (1985), Nogueira (1985 [1954]), and Costa-Pinto (1998 [1953]).
5. At the time of my research, the racial quota matter was not yet regulated at the federal level in Brazil but only at the level of single Brazilian states. At that time, federal public universities could choose whether or not to implement quotas or other affirmative action systems. Very recently, in August 2012, such difference was erased. In fact, the Brazilian Senate has just approved a law that will make racial and social quotas obligatory also at the federal level. This law, already approved by the Chamber of Deputies, is now awaiting presidential signature.
6. Law 5074/2007 added to this 5 percent sons and daughters of firemen, policemen, and other state security workers whose death or disability was due to service activities.
7. Rosemberg (2000: 149) points out the exclusion of the poor and the black people in education in Brazil starts in the kindergarten. In institutions with scarce infrastructure, and with little-trained and underpaid teachers, lower-class kids are socialized with their subalternity.
8. In 2006, the literacy rate by race/color and gender in Brazil was as follows: white males, 93.7 percent; white females, 93.3 percent; black + brown males, 85.9 percent; black + brown females, 84.9 percent (Paixão and Carvano, 2008: 68). See also Jaccoud and Theodoro (2005: 105–106).
9. DataIBGE(2008).http://biblioteca.ibge.gov.br/visualizacao/monografias/GEBIS%20-%20RJ/sintese_indic/indic_sociais2008.pdf.
10. According to the Pesquisa Nacional por Amostra de Domicílios (National Research by Household Sample, PNAD 2008) by the Instituto Brasileiro de Geografia e Estatística (Brazilian Institute for Geography and Statistics,

IBGE), 48.8 percent of the Brazilian population self-identified as *branca*, 43.8 as *parda*, and 6.5 as *preta*, while the remaining categories *amarelo* and *indígena* together represented less than 1 percent of the Brazilian population. http://noticias.uol.com.br/especiais/pnad/ultnot/2009/09/18/ult6843u18.jhtm.
11. PNAD (2007); IBGE.
12. Htun (2004: 62).
13. Santos (2007). See also Amaral (2009).
14. Manifesto em Defesa da Justiça e Constitucionalidade das Cotas: 120 Anos de Luta pela Igualdade Racial no Brasil, available at http://www1.folha.uol.com.br/fsp/cotidian/ff1405200808.htm.
15. Maio and Santos (2005) and Maggie (2005).
16. http://siteprouni.mec.gov.br/.
17. Guimarães, Da Costa, and Kleinke (2009).
18. Arruti (1997) and Hoffman (2009).
19. Heringer (2001).
20. Among these, the Catholic organization Educafro and the organization Prevestibulares para Negros e Carentes (PVNC) were relevant.
21. An example is the NGO Palmares.
22. Lower social indexes, racial constraints to social mobility, and patterns of segregation for the Afro-Brazilian population have been widely documented in all sectors of social life, such as income and job market access (Lovell and Wood, 1998; Castro and Guimarães, 1999; Valle do Silva, 1999, Figueiredo, 2002; Paixão, 2003; Telles, 2004; Paixão and Carvano, 2008), housing and urban space (Telles, 2004: 194–214), education (Do Valle Silva and Hasenbalg, 1999; Teixeira, 2003; Telles, 2004; Paixão and Carvano, 2008), marriage (Telles, 2004: 173–193), criminality (Adorno, 1999), and mass media (Stam, 1997; Araújo, 2000). For a critique of Brazil as a racial democracy, see the so-called UNESCO project in the 1950s and in particular Bastide and Fernandes (1971 [1959]), Fernandes (1969), and Costa-Pinto (1998 [1953]) among others. Finally, see Andrews (2004) and Dávila (2003), who show how prejudice against black people in the job market and for social mobility even worsened at the beginning of the twentieth century, in comparison to the previous century, as an effect of the eugenic theories diffusing from Europe. Dávila particularly examines how the number of black teachers in public institutions started decreasing.
23. See Sérgio Costa (2006) and "113 cidadãos anti-racistas contra as leis raciais" in Folha online (2008a), http://www1.folha.uol.com.br/folha/educacao/ult305u401519.shtml. However, US influence on Brazilians black affirmative action found some critics well before the introduction of quotas. See, e.g., Bourdieu and Wacquant (1999) and Ferreira da Silva (1998).
24. "113 cidadãos anti-racistas contra as leis raciais." Folha online (2008a). http://www1.folha.uol.com.br/folha/educacao/ult305u401519.shtml.
25. The document became more commonly known as "Manifesto Contra as Cotas." Literature that critiques racial quotas will be deeply discussed in chapter four. Among this literature, see Fry et al. (2007), Kamel (2006), Maio

and Santos (2005), and Maggie (2005). In April 2012, the High Federal court eventually sanctioned the constitutionality of quotas with the unanimity of the voting members.
26. This document was finally approved by the Brazilian Parliament in 2010, although quite emptied of its original claims.
27. Winant (1999) and Hanchard (1994).
28. Examples of intellectuals who are more optimistic about racial quotas are Carvalho (2005), Sansone (2005), Guimarães (2005), and Medeiros (2004).
29. Folha online (2008b). http://www1.folha.uol.com.br/folha/brasil/ult96u470649.shtml.
30. It has been found that 49 percent of *brancos* and 44 percent of *negros* believe this, along with 52 percent of white men, 55 percent of people with high school education, and 63 percent of people with household incomes equal to 10 and 20 times the minimum Brazilian wage (the minimum legal wage was R$ 415 in 2008). Figures are basically reversed among people with low education levels and incomes, as well as among black people (Datafolha, 2008). http://datafolha.folha.uol.com.br/po/verpo.Php ?session=781.
31. From the time of my research, however, there has been an increasing number of studies that analyzed the implementation of quotas in specific universities with firsthand data. Among others, I mention the studies by Schwartzman (2009), which sociologically analyzes the reaction of the UERJ brown and black student in relation to racial quotas, and that by Francis and Tannuri-Pianto (2010), which quantitatively explores the influence of the use of black quotas on the racial identification of students in the University of Brasília. I also mention the study organized by Arruda (2007) and that by Cicalo (2008), which provided statistical information about the academic performance and dropouts of students at UERJ. In the last four years there has also been an increasing number of master and doctoral thesis about the implementation of quotas in certain universities and courses, some of them relying on a sociologic/ ethnographic perspective with use of participant observation. For student dissertations on this matter, see Santos (2009), Nery (2008), and Valentim (2005).
32. The physical and metaphysical distance of poor people from the city, in Rio de Janeiro, is discussed by Perlman (2010: 9).
33. "Carioca" is a noun and adjective used to mean "from Rio de Janeiro."
34. An important fact was that law, in spite of being an elite course, was still considered rather cheap and could be studied in evening shifts, allowing student workers to attend. Medicine and dentistry, quite differently, were full-day courses where students had to spend consistent amount of money to buy material for their practice. In addition, these courses asked for a good background in scientific discipline, the ones that are usually very poorly taught in the public school from where most quota student come. It is not random that the profile of medicine and dentistry quota students is usually wealthier and, along with this, fairer skinned.

35. "Denegrir" literally means "making something or somebody black."
36. Telles (2004) in particular compares the situation in Rio de Janeiro with that of São Paulo, whose urbanistic conformation is historically more segregating. See also Freeman (2002) about the imperfect exclusion of the poor in the carioca public space (e.g., the beach).
37. População total e respectiva distribuição percentual, por cor ou raça, segundo as Grandes Regiões, as Unidades da Federação e as Regiões Metropolitanas—Pesquisa Nacional por Amostra de Domicílios (National Research by Household Sample, PNAD) 2009, in IBGE (2010).
38. On this subject, see my ethnographic documentary *Memories on the Edge of Oblivion* (2010), available at https://vimeo.com/41609298.
39. Georges-Eugène Haussmann was a French architect associated with the urban reconfiguration of Paris in the nineteenth century according to parameters of urban rationality, prettiness, and sanitation.

2 Dreams and Hard Places

1. Zona Norte and Zona Oeste are generally considered poor and suburban areas within the Municipality of Rio de Janeiro, in spite of the presence of well-off neighborhoods in this area. Zona Oeste, in particular, is considered prevalently rural. Zona Sul, in contrast, is considered the wealthy area of the Municipality, including well-known areas such as Botafogo, Copacabana, Ipanema, and Leblon. The Baixada Fluminense is a ring of poor municipalities that remain part of the Greater Rio area.
2. Central do Brasil is the main rail connection in the heart of Rio de Janeiro, on Avenida Getúlio Vargas. It connects the center (*Centro*) with the suburbs.
3. According to Laura Segato (2007: 148–149), Brazilian anthropology has contributed to the representation of Brazilian society as highly stratified from an economic point of view but harmonious and cordial from a cultural one. According to Segato, e.g., Roberto da Matta has updated Freyre's language by adding football and Carnival, conferring the impression of the Brazilian lower classes as happy slaves, satisfied by [popular] culture.
4. For a further overview on the segregation of favelas in Rio de Janeiro, see also Perlman (1979) and Jaguaribe (2007).
5. Collection of Memory: commemorative exhibition of the UERJ's first 50 years.
6. "In July 1965 . . . when the Chancellor was about to travel to the US . . . he received a promise [from Governor Lacerda] that on his return he would not see the damned favela any more. And that happened!" (Cunha, 1988: 41). Cunha was himself the chancellor at that time. About the removal of favelas in Rio de Janeiro, see Perlman (1979: 195–223).

7. Low-income municipality on the opposite side of Guanabara Bay to Rio de Janeiro.
8. Lower-class neighborhood of Zona Norte in Rio de Janeiro.
9. I was told that it is common for siblings to build their houses in the courtyard of their parental house, adding to the preexisting household. See also Perlman (2010).
10. http://www1.folha.uol.com.br/folha/educacao/ult305u401519.shtml.
11. 1 Brazilian *real* = about 0.30 British pounds and 0.40 Euros at the time of my research.
12. In 2007, the maximum per capita family gross income in the household could not exceed 630 *reais* (about 250 Euros).
13. http://www.vestibular.uerj.br/portal_vestibular_uerj/index_portal.php.
14. Proving a lower income is apparently not so impossible, especially because data from the informal economy cannot be accounted for.
15. I refer to 2007 because this was the year when most of my informants started.
16. The scholarship was recently slightly increased and extended to the entire academic program (law 5230/2008). In spite of being an important contribution, however, this sum will hardly make any difference to *cotistas*' lives.
17. City in the State of Rio de Janeiro.
18. A subgenre of samba, which is very popular among lower-class people.
19. It is important to highlight that the term "*casada/o*" in Rio does not correspond exactly to "married" in English. It is in fact used to express cohabiting with a partner, something that often entails the presence of children.
20. The graduation photo boards hanging in the Law Department's corridors show that from the 1950s women started to become more frequent in the department, reaching a substantial parity with men around the 1980s. However, this increased gender equality did not necessarily correspond to a higher presence of lower-class women in the department, at least before quotas were introduced. This fact, according to some informants, can be visualized by realizing the very minimal presence of black women (and men) on the graduation photo boards until recent years.
21. Both Heilborn and Almeida use data from the GRAVAD research project entitled Teenage Pregnancy: A Multi-center Study on Youth, Sexuality, and Reproduction in Brazil (started in 1998). Goldani uses data PNAD 1984 (National Survey on Household Samples).
22. See also Perlman (2010: 222 and 233).
23. This consideration does not want to minimize the role that individual differences may also influence social mobility even among Pentecostal lower-class people (Perlman, 2010: 223).
24. This perception of *funk* offered by my main informants does not want to apply to anybody in Brazil. In fact, there is an increasing appropriation of *funk* among middle-class youngsters, where this music style with its

sensual movements and rude words is listened and danced to for fun, without implying any model for the dancers' lifestyle.
25. Alvito (2001) illustrates how the Evangelical Church also encourages a change in clothing style, which becomes more discreet both in women and men, contributing to conferring a better idea of respectability. He says, e.g., that some of his male interviewees in Acarí started wearing more formal clothes after conversion, avoiding the usual beach or *funk* Bermuda shorts/t-shirt/cap (I would include flip-flops or trainers) outfit.
26. Another aspect pointed out by the same student, and confirmed by others, is that black and lower-class students tend to prefer jobs in the public sector as they hope to receive fair treatment in the selection process, without being discriminated against because of phenotype, social background, and area of residence (favelas and suburbs). I avoid dealing with this point further in this chapter; however, an extensive discussion of how race and poor background may interfere with preference for the public job sector can be found in Morāes da Silva and Reis (2011).
27. Cheap private universities are those more typically attended by lower-class students who do not manage to achieve an opening in a public university or cannot afford good private universities.

3 Race Between the Class Rows

1. Perlman (2010: 233) points out that race relations affect darker-skinned people also in lower-class and favela environments.
2. See Valentim (2005).
3. The word *Cone/Cones* and its meaning coincides in the English and Portuguese language, while the word *Nerds* is used in Brazil as a language appropriation from English. For similar conclusions about student divisions in the classroom, see Holanda (2008).
4. In the evening shifts, according to informants, the *"frente-atrás"* pattern observed among the morning group was reversed. In the evening programs, quota and lower-class students tended to sit at the back because most of them had full-time jobs and arrived late at university, or needed to leave class earlier to catch the last train home. This is a further example of how patterns of urban social inequality may be reflected in the classroom.
5. Such public schools are somewhat closer to the concept of exclusive private high schools.
6. On a scale between A (top grade) and E (failing), quota students in the Law Department at UERJ usually have to score a B (more typical) or at least a C in the vestibular.
7. For differences between social patterns in law and those in the less elite courses such as education, see Holanda (2008).
8. See also Nery (2008).

9. Ibid.
10. About different students' lifestyles in the law course, see Holanda (2008: 136–37).
11. See Morães da Silva and Reis (2011: 72).
12. See Alvito (2001).
13. About the costliness of students' outfits as a factor of social division in the classroom, see Holanda (2008: 125–126).
14. Each semester, new groups of students start their undergraduate courses. When my main informants started their second semester, they were not considered freshmen anymore.
15. A popular online network similar to Facebook.
16. In this regard, see also Wade (2003), when he says that typically black people in Colombia are regarded as black no matter how wealthy they are. See also Hanchard's (1999: 75) point that "blackness taints."
17. It is significant that, just before my fieldwork, UERJ security guards (themselves presumably nonwhite) stopped and chased away a student with massive black-power grooming who was arguing animatedly with his girlfriend. This event had a big impact on the student Black movement, which brought the case to the Direction. The explanation that the security guards provided was that "that guy didn't match the profile of a student" (*não tinha perfil de estudante*).
18. By assumption or direct observation, it was explained to me that black and poor students tend to be employed during the day. Consequently, they would have no other choice but to study in the evening.
19. The teacher's decision to touch upon the quota topic in his class, although really unexpected to me, was very likely influenced by my presence. This is because, although classes are public and I had previous authorization by the university Direction for my study, I usually introduced myself to the teaching staff explaining the objectives of my research.
20. See also Valentim (2005: 121).
21. Gilliam (1998); Pravaz (2003); Moutinho (2004); Giacomini (2006).
22. This point already has been supported theoretically by Oracy Nogueira (1985 [1954]: xxix–li).
23. Holanda (2008: 136); Dayane Santos (2009). See also Morães da Silva and Reis (2011).
24. Holanda (2008).
25. To see how silence about race does not avoid racism in job advertisement, see Damasceno (2000) and her discussion of how expressions such as "*boa aparência*" (good appearance) act as indirect ways to address white applicants for job selections.
26. For a similar concept, see Telles (2004).
27. This term is highly demeaning in Brazil, especially when used by nonblack people. In fact it was used by Gabriel's grandmother in order to be harsher on Eliane, whom nobody in the class described as very dark-skinned.
28. I will deal extensively with Flávia's black identification in chapters four and five.

29. When the speaker after a while realizes the racial belonging of somebody who did something inappropriate (like banging the door in a shop or talking loudly on the bus).
30. Such carefulness might be also influenced by the fact that starting university encouraged lower-class students to behave more similarly to the middle class.
31. Sheriff (2001: 93) notes that black and brown people can often laugh at jokes, but that this creates "coercive constraint and rueful irony—as well as the delicate sense of danger—within the laughter" that that person hears.
32. See also Goldstein (2003).
33. Cited in Sales Dos Santos (2007: 519–520).
34. The most exclusive private university in Rio de Janeiro.
35. She refers to the fact that the UERJ is surrounded by a violent area, favelas, and general street criminality.
36. For an analysis of how quota students at the UERJ eventually manage to achieve an academic performance similar to that of nonquota students, see Valentim (2005), Arruda (2007), Sales Dos Santos (2007), Cicalo (2008), and Santos (2009).
37. See also Valentim (2005). However, most interviewees seemed very sceptical about the fact that any improvement of public education would be likely to happen in Brazil.
38. Gilberto Freyre (1961).
39. This kind of initiatives are spontaneously undertaken by some teachers while there are not specific official regulations at the UERJ promoting the social integration between the students as a goal for the academic staff.
40. Typically assumed name for maids in Brazil.
41. Edith Piza (2000: 119) states that the universal reference that white people have for black people is poverty, the impossibility of social ascension, associated to stereotypes of passivity and lack of [intellectual] abilities.
42. A similar point is expressed by Wade (2009). See parallels with the way Portuguese success in the tropics has been compared to the failure of the French and the British. This success was attributed to the ability of the Portuguese to strategically appropriate the wisdoms of Indigenous and African people, already used to inhospitable climates (Freyre, 1961).

4 From Race or Color to Race and Color?

1. See also Twine (1998).
2. http://www.ibge.gov.br/home/presidencia/noticias/noticia_visualiza.php?id_noticia=1602&id_pagina=1.
3. Substantially used for people of far eastern ancestry, especially Japanese. The "yellow" category has grown about 177 percent between 2000 and

2010, passing from 0.45 percent to 1.09 percent of the total Brazilian population. http://www.estadao.com.br/noticias/cidades,censo-2010-populacao-asiatica-no-brasil-cresceu-177-em-dez-anos,748616,0.htm.
4. http://www.bbc.co.uk/news/world-latin-america-15766840.
5. Datos Datafolha 1995 (in Telles, 2004: 82).
6. See Sheriff (2001: 40).
7. When used like this, *moreno* is both a more specific and a more complex term than *pardo*, which more typically refers to skin tone, especially as an adjective, and not to features and hair. As a consequence, *moreno* would be used more to indicate the overall phenotypic appearance of certain people. People, e.g., would say "ask that *moreno* in the queue!" not "ask that *pardo* in the queue!." Having said this, *pardo* is an adjective widely used for skin color in Rio de Janeiro, e.g., when speakers want to sound slightly more official by deploying the census terminology.
8. Some social scientists have used the term *mulato* as synonymous with *pardo*, e.g., Fry (2005: 194) and Alberti and Pereira (2007a: 640). This use, in my view, does not reflect the broader connotations of the term *pardo*, which relates more directly to color than to black and white racial mixture.
9. To be more precise, *preto* sounds quite offensive when used by nonblack people but is widely used in Black-activist circles in order to express black comradeship.
10. A phenotype often associated with Africanness and includes features, not only color.
11. See also Telles (2004) and Paixão (2003 and 2006).
12. This is an idea that finds precursors in Skidmore (1974) and in Nascimento (1982).
13. However, Peter Fry (2005) uses the same case study to show how public opinion had a very diversified understanding of the Black Cinderella's racial/color ascription, reacting to Hanchard.
14. Note that the word *negro* was presumably used here as synonymous to *preto* (or very dark-skinned and typically African-looking) and separate from *pardo*. This might create confusion because both groups are considered *negros* in the same law.
15. In 2003, the institutional language of the quota law was modified. Instead of addressing *pardos* and *negros* as in the 2001 law, the 2003 law simply started targeting students who self-identify as *negros* as candidates for racial quotas. Nothing explained the reasons for this change. On the one hand, the act of deleting the word *pardos* seemed to exclude this color category from policy benefits (Kamel, 2006: 49–51). On the other hand, the new terminology might be considered to be even more faithful to the philosophy of the Black movement, where *pardos* are automatically considered *negros* and do not need to be presented as a separate category. Alternatively, it is possible that the law aimed to address just the *pardos* who self-identify as *negros*, excluding those who do not. Seen

from this last perspective, the terminology might serve to draw a line between *negros* and non-*negros* within the *pardo* category, but there is no way to be sure about the real intentions behind this change. Despite the striking vagueness of the terminology and its development, what really matters is that quotas for *negros* have been largely understood as something that encourages racial bipolarization in Brazil.
16. http://www.planalto.gov.br/ccivil_03/_Ato2007-2010/2010/Lei/L12288.htm.
17. See also Fry et al. (2007).
18. See also Maio and Santos (2005); Baran (2007).
19. Bowker and Star (2000).
20. Klarman (2004).
21. Quotas for people identified as *negros* and as *indígenas* (20 percent of openings) have been finally introduced in public competitions (*concursos públicos*) in the State of Rio de Janeiro in June 2011 with the decreto nº 43.007. http://classificados.folha.com.br/empregos/926713-cotas-para-negros-e-indios-em-concursos-publicos-e-foco-de-polemica.shtml.
22. [As cotas raciais são] a face mais visível de uma racialização oficial das relações sociais que ameaça a coesão nacional . . . No Brasil, [o sistema de cotas] representaria uma revisão radical de nossa identidade nacional e a renúncia à utopia possível da universalização da cidadania efectiva. . . . Os julgamentos [do Tribunal Federal sobre as cotas] terão significado histórico, pois podem criar jurisprudência sobre a constitucionalidade de cotas raciais não só para o financiamento de cursos no ensino superior particular e para concursos de ingresso no ensino superior público como para concursos públicos em geral. Mais ainda: os julgamentos têm o potencial de enviar uma mensagem decisiva sobre a constitucionalidade da produção de leis raciais. The High Federal Court eventually sanctioned the constitutionality of quotas with the unanimity of the voting members in April 2012.
23. In chapter 11 of his book *A Persistência da Raça*, Peter Fry (2005: 331) debates in particular the introduction of quotas in the State of Rio de Janeiro and the case of the UERJ.
24. Gilberto Freyre (1956 and 1961) celebrated the constitution of Brazil as the democratic encounter of people of European, African, and Native Indian descent.
25. Of 381 freshmen who used black quotas in 2007 and provided information about their color, 12 students identified as white, 90 identified as brown, 1 as indigenous, and 1 as yellow (*amarelo*). The rest of the students (277) identified their color as black (socioeconomic questionnaire, vestibular UERJ 2007—question 25: *como você identificaria a sua cor?*) [data processed by the author from the electronic database vestibular UERJ 2007].
26. This recalls the concept of prejudice of "mark" (or color) in Nogueira (1985 [1954]), as different from prejudice of "origin" (or class).

27. This mixed approach to race that takes into account both social construction and biology differs from, but is not in contradiction with, the intersections between nature and culture analyzed in Wade (2004: 165–168). Wade discusses how cultural habits, or general lifestyles, affect people's phenotypes, which is something that can be observed more strikingly across different generations within the same group. In a similar vein, I have often heard that Italian women were curvier and had wider hips in the 1950s in comparison to the present. When I refer to culture in this section, however, I do not mean the way that nature might change over time but the different interpretations that a socially and culturally constructed vision might produce at different times. In this line, curvy women were considered quite attractive socially in Italy in the 1950s, in contrast to thinner models of female beauty that are dominant nowadays.
28. Sum obtained from data of *pretos* and *pardos* I found in Paixão and Carvano (2008: 23). Data IBGE-PNAD (*Pesquisa Nacional por Amostra de Domicílios*) 2006. According to data from the 2010 Census the sum of *pardos* and *pretos* is now more than 50 percent of the Brazilian population (http://globalvoicesonline.org/2011/11/29/brazil-census-black-mixed-population/). However, these data are still obtained by the sum of IBGE nonwhite color/race categories. Loveman, Muniz, and Bailey (2011: 11), in contrast, foresee a different scenario in case the Brazilian census became properly biracial since many *pardos* would self-identify as white. If people had to forcedly choose between white and black for self-identification in the census, according to these authors, whites would grow up to 68 percent, while people classified as black would be 32 percent of the Brazilian population.
29. It was extremely common, among informants, to use the word "*Africano/a*" to define people that they considered more typically black by the presence of certain physical characteristics that are widely racialized in a Brazilian context (i.e., hair texture, nose and mouth shape, and very dark skin). This is the way I make use of this term here. Such idea of "African" must refer to the idealized image of west-African people, who represented most of the slave population imported in Brazil.
30. Pesquisa Mensal de Emprego.
31. Schwartzman (2009) in her article about quotas at the UERJ mentions that a number of her informants never felt discriminated against in their lives for being *pardos* (and therefore not very dark-skinned).
32. In Alberti and Pereira (2006: 154).
33. In this sense, a *pardo* identification might be used to stress Brazilianness, e.g., by saying that nobody or almost nobody can be considered white in Brazil. I am therefore not completely sure about Telles's (1995: 1610) point that "Parda/o, on the other hand, clearly refers to a mixed-race individual throughout Brazil."
34. Famous television presenter, especially popular in past decades.

35. Internationally successful Brazilian model of German ancestry.
36. For this point, see also Guimarães, Da Costa, and Kleinke (2009: 4, 6). Comparing the UFBA (Federal University of Bahia) and the Unicamp (University of Campinas), these authors argue that students from federal public high schools have more chances to benefit from public-school quotas, due to the higher quality of these institutions. He also shows that public-school quotas favor white students.
37. "There are plenty of very cheap private schools in the Baixada where you pay 60 *reais* per month [about 25 Euros per month in 2008] . . . many private schools in the Baixada are really worse than many public ones . . . private schools in the suburbs are not like those in Zona Sul, where there are exclusive private secondary institutions that may cost between 1,000 and 2,000 *reais* per month [400–800 Euros] . . ." (Daisy).
38. The fact that most users of racial quotas are from private schools is recognized by activists. See Friar David dos Santos (Educafro leader) in Alberti and Pereira (2007b: 419).
39. The question in the questionnaire is *"como você definiria a sua cor?"* (How would you define your color?). UERJ students can choose between the following categories: *branco/pardo/negro/amarelo/indígena*. It is clear that in this case *pardos* and *negros* are considered as two separate categories by the university administration. It is also clear that *negro*, in the administrative language of the university, means *preto* (very dark-skinned), and this language contradicts the discourse of the Black movement, according to which *pardos* and *pretos* are *negros*. Additional inconsistency of this language is represented by the fact that *negro* is usually understood as broadly referring to race and not as black color, which is more typically represented by the term *preto* and can be considered as a specific phenotypic aspect of a person in Brazil (see Sansone, 2003: 47).
40. As shown in chapter two, these non-*cotistas* have a similar socioeconomic profile to *cotistas* in programs such as law and medicine. In this sense, the reason for their self-exclusion from quotas might relate more to proving their merit than to their wealthier socioeconomic conditions.
41. http://www.vestibular.uerj.br/portal_vestibular_uerj/2008/dados_socioculturais/dados_socioculturais.html.
42. This is an example of how it is not enough to observe how students answer specific questions in race/color surveys to have an idea of their phenotypic identification. It is instead quite important to explore the context where these questions are placed (a vestibular questionnaire, for example) and also reflect over the alternative labels available to students and their general meanings in Rio de Janeiro.
43. In these sense, interviewees presumably tried to scale down possible incoherences between the use of black quotas and not identifying as blacks.
44. How certain students self-identify as *negros* based on opportunism at the time of applying for a quota is an issue widely discussed by Schwartzman (2009).

45. Presumably, people in the community prevestibular course she attended at the UENF (Universidade Estatal do Norte Fluminense) in Caxias.
46. I suggest that students found it constraining to admit that they chose black quotas merely due to their school of origin and not because of more objective factors relating to phenotype and identity.
47. Unlike at the UERJ, where color and racial labels are mixed up in the socio-economic questionnaire, UnB students have to answer survey questions about skin color and then, in addition, also say if they identify as *negros*.
48. It remains that data about the shift of racial identification among *pardo* students at UnB are hardly comparable with the UERJ for innumerable reasons. In addition to the lack of as detailed a statistical study about this matter at UERJ as Francis and Tannuri-Pianto carried out in Brasília, the racial quotas and their selection criteria vary a lot between these two universities. Not only has the UERJ a public-school quota system that excludes those poor students who come from private schools, but the application process for racial quotas is completely based on self-declaration. The UnB, instead, uses also photo examination and interviews of candidates about racial matters. It is therefore the case that the number of students who adapt their racial identification contextually to achieve a quota at the UERJ might be far higher than at the UnB, even though this identification has no reason to become permanent in everyday life.
49. Telles (2004) mentions that, despite a wider usage of this term by people with different skin tones, the term *negro* is still more commonly used by (and presumably for) people around the darkest end of the color scale. See also Francis and Tannuri-Pianto (2010).
50. In a previous chapter I described how this student had been unhappy about using racial quotas.
51. The fact that *pardo* is often associated with mixture does not mean that it is always perceived this way in Brazil. People with a Southern European phenotype, e.g., are not easily associated with ideas of *mestiçagem* (see Telles, 2004; Petruccelli, 2007) but they can often be considered of *pardo* skin color.
52. I remind the reader that Eliane had been insultingly defined as a *"pretinha de cabelo duro, duro, duro"* (a little *preta* girl with very hard hair) by a classmate's grandmother (chapter three). In the next chapter, the same student will complain about her "hard" hair and the expensive treatments required to look good.
53. "Mixture pedagogy" is used here with some contrast to the concept of "racial pedagogy," coined by Maio and Santos (2005) and used by Maggie (2006a).
54. Gomes makes a point similar to mine by discussing the image of a whitened mestiço described by Oliveira Vianna (1933: 161–163), Bastide and Fernandes (1959: 188), and Nogueira (1998 [1955]: 199). Vianna presented this kind of *mestiço* as superior.

55. The expression *raça ou cor* in any case leaves some doubts as to whether the two terms are really understood as synonymous or as two vague but different concepts that people can use for identification. The reason might be that people should at least be able to identify one of these concepts in relation to their person.
56. For some conceptual separation between race and color in Brazil, see Sansone (2003: 47). However, what is missing in Sansone is an attempt to untangle the relations between race and color in a process of personal identification. Also, for some ethnographic division between race and color in relation to Afro-Peruvian communities, see Golash-Boza (2010).
57. It should be observed that Sheriff's informants were from a favela and that identification with blackness might have been influenced also by status and social stigmas for this population in the city.
58. For this point, see Sansone (2003: 47) and also Santos et al. (2009: 794).
59. I realize that my account has overly simplified the variability by which certain color and racial terms might have been used by my informants. Some informants, e.g., self-identified as *pretos* (dark black) even after describing their skin as *parda*. In this way, students would reinforce their identification with a black group through an extreme (and more crucially stereotypical) phenotypic term. This mechanism might be especially important when brown- or light-skinned students want to stress their difference from other *pardos* or *morenos* whose features would not be significantly—or at least not automatically—racialized in Brazil. In this sense, the term *preto* can also take on racial—in addition to color—connotations depending on context. I also note that the term *preto* was preferred to *negro* as a racial label by some Denegrir activists. They argued that this word would be more appropriate in politics because the term *negro* had been introduced by the white colonizer and its etymology comes from the Greek *nekrós* (death). The use of *preto* as a racial term might also be preferred because it is more strikingly phenotypic than *negro*, which in some cases might instead be used by very light-skinned people in order to highlight black ancestry. On the other hand, the term *preto* as a racial term has not reached the same popularity as *negro* within and outside the Black social movement.
60. Telles (2004: 87) observes that the term *negro* is still mainly used by people at the *preto* end of the Brazilian color scale.
61. The point discussed in this section is barely reflected in the way the vestibular administration at the UERJ uses classification language. UERJ administration mixes color and racial terms, taking into little account semantic trends in the use of certain words and concepts within the Black movement and in folk understandings among students. In support of my argument, a clear distinction between race and color is made by the administration at the University of Brasília (UnB). As mentioned in Francis and Tannuri-Pianto (2010), the UnB submits a sociocultural

questionnaire to students in which they are asked to define their color as *branco, pardo, preto, amarelo* (typically color labels in Brazil); the same questionnaire then asks the students separately if they consider themselves *negros*, thus enriching the previous color information with a typically racial term. At the UERJ, quite differently, the same questionnaire asks students whether their color is *branco, pardo, negro, amarelo*. UERJ quota applicants are then requested to fill a separate *negro* self-declaration but are not told whether this blackness should, for instance, have color, racial, or cultural connotations.

62. See also Fernández (1992), Wade (2004b), and Warren and Sue (2011). About a discussion of the Latinamericanization Theory of race relations in the United States, see Bonilla-Silva (2004) and Sue (2009). On the long-term dialogue/exchange between Brazil and the United States in terms of race relations, see Landes (1994 [1947]), Nobles (2000:177), and Seigel (2009).
63. However, racial quotas are not the system of racially affirmative action used in the United States, where a bonus system is preferred, e.g., to draw the final ranking of university access exams.
64. Class obviously plays an important role in this sense.
65. These, of course, are general and not exhaustive contexts; racial and color perceptions, in fact, may also vary depending on whether people of a specific class and color cross a lower-class or middle-class space. Having said this, most Brazilians are able to generalize about how their phenotype is generally perceived in the urban or rural context where they live.
66. It is not clear to me why *negros* should have to be as numerous as over 40 percent of the population—as presently proposed—and not, e.g., just 12 percent in order to have racially based affirmative action in favor of this group.
67. I observe also that the (ex) Brazilian president Cardoso, whose discourse aimed to encourage the change of IBGE terminology in 1986, distinguished between *pardos* and *mulatos* (in Telles, 2004: 86).

5 Narrowing Political Gaps

1. In his book *Orpheus and Power*, Hanchard (1994) criticizes the excessive African culturalism of the Black social movement (mainly MNU) as a factor that weakens Black collective action and the dialogue of activists with black lower classes.
2. Quota students informed me that some rigor about aesthetics exists only in certain evangelical churches "where women are even asked not to shave their armpits" (Eliane). These kinds of morally more rigorous churches, as already pointed out, are not those most popular among my informants.

3. It is interesting that even activists linked to Educafro (a Catholic organization) turned out to be mostly evangelical.
4. This tendency is also pointed out by Burdick (2005 and 2008), although this author mentions that evangelical self-identified blacks living in the suburbs and in poor conditions in São Paulo are in general more interested in defending class issues than racial ones. He also mentions that racial stances are taken more easily by black people who have already moved up socially and moved from the suburbs to nicer neighborhoods (Burdick, 2008). I am not sure how to place my informants in Burdick's account. In fact, although they are lower-class and live in the suburbs, informants were at a first stage of a social mobility process initiated by higher education. To be frank, in Rio de Janeiro I also met lower-class black evangelical people who were not in a clear process of social mobility but were strongly involved in Black political and cultural activities. In this sense, the relevance of place and class on certain black religious attitudes might be less influential than Burdick (2008) suggests. On the other hand, further ethnography would be useful to clarify whether militant quota students just represent a special and intermediate category in relation to Burdick's data. I have already mentioned, for example, that they are already rather more flexible about issues that are officially problematic for their churches (e.g., homosexuality and Afro-Brazilian cults).
5. This fact is demonstrated by the fact that the MNU had not even a website but a blog at the time of my research.
6. However, a very minor sector of Black activism rejects quotas. An example is the Black Socialist Movement.
7. This one works specifically to conduct research about racially based affirmative action at the national level and publish PPCOR collections on this matter.
8. http://www.gazetadopovo.com.br/mundo/conteudo.phtml?id=765893. This was initially foreseen by the UERJ only for the first year at the amount of 210 *reais* per month. The change was justified by the new Law 5230/2008 but also as a result of negotiations between the university and the State of Rio de Janeiro.
9. This somehow recalls how the Bolivian MAS political movement (*Movimiento al Socialismo*) is a combination of indigenous and class politics.
10. It was a common idea among lower-class suburban students that the city center of Rio de Janeiro was a dangerous space at night, especially due to the fact that most of this area is a site of business and thus largely nonresidential, becoming dark and empty at night, but for the concentration of homeless people and beggars.
11. The meaning of which is "pause" or "stand-by."
12. Gomes (2006) gives an extensive account of how these hairstyles are appropriated and used for aesthetic and political affirmation by black people of different social classes.

13. Note that this style more clearly distinguishes intellectual black students. There are other styles like the *funk* and rapper ones, which might be more frequent among other black groups, especially lower-status ones.
14. I refer here to the ethnography about Flávia's racial/color identification seen in chapter four.
15. The 8 P.M. soap opera on the Globo TV Channel is considered by most people to be the main television event on a weekday in Brazil.
16. This point reinforces ideas already expressed in chapter four about the fact that the black identities that affirmative action is assumed to create are also influenced by many factors external to the quota institution itself. These aspects are obviously acknowledged by antiquota thinkers (Fry, 2005), whose real problem with racially based affirmative action is that the state is feeding such a divisive process by policy intervention.
17. In the ethnographic documentary Memories on the Edge of Oblivion (2010), I offer further examples of how the black affirmative ideas of a young male character have much in common with the less politicized "black" experience of an elder woman in Rio de Janeiro; both characters share, in fact, suffering and different forms of reaction to historic marginalization of the black people in Brazilian society. The film is freely available online at: https://vimeo.com/41609298
18. For a similar point, see Gomes (2006).
19. This is a process that can be considered opposite to the one of black and *mestiça* women who, at least in theory, whiten themselves by practicing straightening and hair extensions (Gomes, 2006: 294).
20. Jurema does not refer to natural kinky hair, but to its conversion to wide and soft curls, one of the stereotypical traits of the samba *mulatas*. This hairstyle is also known as *permanente afro* (Afro perm).
21. For a detailed account of how black women relate to ethnic hairstyles, see Gomes (2006).
22. Cunha (1991) and Figueiredo (1994) note that natural hair is not intended to be hair without "interference." Figueiredo in particular describes some kinds of hair as "more" natural. This means that there is a hierarchy of naturalness that can also be enhanced by the use of fewer chemical products. However, the *Raça* magazine promotes a wide range of black ethnic hairstyles that might be natural or not, but are seldom completely straightened (www.racabrasil.uol.com.br). These considerations match Gomes's point about the possibility of negotiating Black politics with chemically processed or extended hairstyles (which are anyway rather expensive and out of the reach of lower-class students).
23. It is in this sense that Gomes (2006: 375) describes hairdresser salons as "spaces full of the ambiguities and tensions typical of the Brazilian racial reality," where efforts of black affirmation and myths of racial democracy deeply combine.
24. She refers to a definitive straightening (*escova definitiva*), which relaxes the hair by using a powerful, but also dangerous, chemical, formaldehyde

(*formalina*). This kind of straightening lasts longer and allows girls to wash their hair by avoiding it curling up.
25. Which makes very kinky uncurled hair curly.
26. This vertical, downward growth of the hair is something that is less typical of black natural hair, which grows more slowly and does not really fall vertically over the shoulders (Gomes, 2006: 293). Gomes shows that also white women with vaporous and curly hair rely on hair manipulation in order to fit these beauty models more fully.
27. See when Flávia, in chapter four, proudly points out that her hair is "better" (naturally softer) than that of most black girls in her classroom.
28. For a similar point, see, again, Gomes (2006: 204–205) when she describes hairstyles' whitening as a must for black people who pursue some highly regarded jobs and professions.
29. Show in the Caixa Cultural Rio (Centro Cultural da Caixa Econômica), September 4, 2007.
30. It is clear to me why the man did not call Flávia "*mulata*," this term being offensive when directly used to address a woman, whereas the term "*morena*" is more often used to conceal blackness in a polite sense (Sheriff, 2001).
31. See Wade (2009).
32. Giacomini (2006) describes the *mulata* as a cultural product that can be of any color as long as they can dance, although darker women are always assumed to embody this ideal better.
33. This role of the "mami" entirely dedicated to the white household has also found a place in cinema (Stam, 1997; Araújo, 2000).
34. This is the way that, according to Seigel (2009), the place of the white woman in the middle-class household was represented in public imagery throughout the twentieth century. Seigel explores gender and racial representations within middle-class households by analyzing the visual language of the advertisement of certain Brazilian products diffused in North America in the last century.
35. Brown is considered as a separate category (*pardo*), which is why black in this case means *preto* (very dark-skinned).
36. Data 1991 Brazilian Census, in Telles (2004).
37. Coherently with this, the only (very few) interracial love affairs I was acquainted with in the Law Department were between white girls and black boys.
38. Similar patterns are observed by Lovell and Wood (1998) in the job market. In order to receive the same salary as whites in the same job positions, black managers need higher educational titles.
39. Schwartzman contrasts this situation with the US context, where middle-class black people are more likely to marry lower-class blacks than middle-class whites.
40. Unfortunately, Telles's data do not say whether intermarriage shows a random distribution within the lower classes, where the white/black

distribution is more even; also, Telles does not say how easy it is for black women, in comparison to white ones, to find a partner within the lower class.
41. Popular version of samba, usually associated with the lower class.
42. About the fact that socially ascending black professionals in Rio de Janeiro prefer to live in Zona Norte see, Morães da Silva and Reis (2011). The authors stress that some of their black informants felt out of place in wealthy Zona Sul even after their socioeconomic life had improved.
43. I interpret this fact also as a possible expression of Brazilian cordiality, as a way to minimize difference.
44. The old Imperial Palace.
45. This point is especially relevant when considering that most female quota students seemed to have some aversion to Carnival. Many of them referred that they were used to traveling outside Rio to avoid the *bagunça* (confusion) at that time of the year (usually January–February). This might be partially related to the involvement of most student Pentecostal churches, where Carnival is seen as a worldly thing, or perhaps they associated Carnival with confusion, crime, and sexual harassment.
46. Salvador da Bahia, a city that is typically associated with blackness and Black politics in Brazil.
47. A study realized by Morães da Silva and Reis (2011) among black professionals in Rio de Janeiro shows that, contrary to the dreams expressed by my informants about living in wealthier neighborhoods, socially ascending black professionals eventually preferred to live in socially relatively deprived Zona Norte. The reason provided by the authors was that these professionals felt out of place in wealthier areas, even after achieving a professional job.

Toward a Conclusion

1. Ordem dos Advogados do Brasil. Students need to pass this examination in order to work as lawyers.
2. *Coeficiente de Rendimento Médio.*
3. http://www.sejabixo.com.br/vestibular/mural2.asp?id=13077
4. http://www.oab-rj.org.br/index.jsp?conteudo=12226. Flávia passed the OAB exam brilliantly in 2012.
5. It is worth stating that applying through quotas is indispensable for most quota students. By analyzing the classification for the UERJ Law Program in the 2007 vestibular, I noticed that only 2 public-school quota students (out of 64-positions available in this category) and only 2 black-quota students (out of 64 positions available) would have passed without applying through the quota system. An additional public-school quota student and 3 black-quota students would have been admitted if the quota system was not implemented, because in that case the pool of total posts available would have been wider (312 posts). In total, just

8 students who applied through quotas ("public school" and "black") out of 312 candidates admitted to the Law Program would have been approved without the implementation of a quota system. A similar situation was observable in 2008.
6. In relation to good performance of quota students at the UERJ and in other Brazilian universities, see also: Valentim (2005); Arruda (2007); Sales dos Santos (2007); Cicalo (2008); Dayane Santos (2009).
7. http://www.colegioqi.com.br/blog/fim-das-cotas-nas-universidades-do-rio/
8. In this regard, see also Hale (2004) and Gros (1997). Fraser, in any case, makes this stance much less radical in her dialogue with Honneth (2003).
9. As I clarified in chapter four, neither the quota law nor the university specify what being "black" means and whether this kind of identification should rely on color.
10. http://siteprouni.mec.gov.br/.
11. The Decree 6096/2007 established the *Programa de Apoio a Planos de Reestruturação e Expansão das Universidades Federais*. http://movebr.wikidot.com/reuni:artigos:para-onde-caminha.
12. It is curious that although for the Black movement *pardos* (brown skinned) and *pretos* (black skinned) are *negros*, it seems that the UERJ administration sees *negros* as *pretos* (black- or very dark-skinned). This is at least the way I interpret this terminological shift from IBGE classification.
13. Note that the terminology used in the UERJ socioeconomic questionnaire is different from that of the Black movement because in the questionnaire "*negro*" (presumably interpreted here as "*preto*") is not inclusive but terminologically and conceptually separate from "*pardo*."
14. In less prestigious courses like education, the total of self-identified brown and black nonquota students is even higher: 42 percent of this student category (30 percent *pardo* + 12 percent "*negro*").
15. For a discussion, see Schwartzman (2009).
16. In a similar vein, Figueiredo (2000) adds that black people in the process of social mobility count on less network support and lower capital accumulation than whites, while they usually also have a broader social network to support.
17. Souza (2010).
18. See also Spivak (2003).
19. This is a point on which Fraser and Honneth finally seem to agree in their dialogue in *Redistribution or Recognition?* (2003), and is also retaken in Fraser (2010).
20. The hypothesis of raising the salaries of public-school teachers hardly vanishes doubts of whether some training can convert these teachers into competitive ones.
21. Students pointed out the fact that mathematics and sciences are badly taught in the public school and this is why they tend to become less confident about undertaking scientific programs and careers.

22. This is the position of Black activists such as Jurema Batista (in Alberti and Pereira, 2007b: 407).
23. This, after all, seems the approach followed in the Estatuto da Igualdade Racial approved in 2010.
24. These points, which were strongly expressed in the project of the Estatuto da Igualdade Racial presented in 2006, became less explicit in the law finally approved in 2010, and whose aim is setting the framework for further laws and actions that will favor racial equality. http://www.planalto.gov.br/ccivil_03/_Ato2007–2010/2010/Lei/L12288.htm.
25. I remind the reader that, as a federal university, the UFRJ did not have the obligation to implement quotas at the time of my research, since this kind of university was only subject to federal law. Only very recently, in August 2012, the Brazilian Senate has approved a law that will make racial and social quotas obligatory also at the federal level. At the time of writing, this law, already approved by the Chamber of Deputies, is awaiting presidential signature.

References

Abreu, Mauricio. 1988. *A evolução urbana do Rio de Janeiro*. Rio de Janeiro: Iplanrio.
Adorno, Sérgio. 1999. "Racial discrimination and criminal justice in Sao Paulo," in *Race in Contemporary Brazil: From Indifference to Inequality*, edited by Rebecca Reichmann, pp. 123–137. University Park: Pennsylvania State University Press.
Alberti, Verena, and Amilcar Araújo Pereira. 2006. A defesa das cotas como estratégia política do movimento negro contemporâneo. *Estudos Históricos* (37): 143–166.
———. 2007a. "O movimento negro contemporâneo," in *Revolução e remocracia (1964–)*, edited by Jorge Ferreira and Daniel Aarão Reis, pp. 637–669. Rio de Janeiro: Civilização Brasileira.
———, eds. 2007b. *Histórias do movimento negro no Brasil: depoimento ao CPDDC*. Rio de Janeiro: Pallas.
Almeida, Maria da Conceição C., Estela M. L. Aquino, and Antoniel Pinheiro de Barros. 2006. School trajectory and teenage pregnancy in three Brazilian state capitals. *Cad. Saúde Pública* 22 (7): 1397–1409.
Almeida, Nival Nunes de. 2007. "Introdução: a política de ações afirmativas na UERJ," in *Políticas de ações afirmativas na universidade do estado do Rio de Janeiro*, edited by J. R. Campelo Arruda et al., pp. 10–12. Rio de Janeiro: UERJ, Rede Sirius.
Alvarez, Sonia, Evelina Dagnino, and Arturo Escobar, eds. 1998. "Introduction: the cultural and the political in Latin American social movements," in *Culture of Politics, Politics of Culture*, pp. 1–29. Oxford: Westview.
Alves-Silva, Juliana, Magda da Silva Santos, Pedro E. M. Guimarães, Alessandro C. S. Ferreira, Hans-Jürgen Bandelt, Sérgio D. J. Pena, and Vania Ferreira Prado. 2000. The ancestry of Brazilian mtDNA lineages. *American Journal of Human Genetics* 67: 444–461.
Alvito, Marcos. 2001. *As cores de Acari: uma favela carioca*. Rio de Janeiro: Editora FGV.
Amaral, Shirlena. 2009. A política de cotas e o acesso do negro a universidade pública. *Confluenze* 1 (2): 227–243.
Andrews, George Reid. 2004. *Afro-Latin America, 1800–2000*. Oxford and New York: Oxford University Press.

Appiah, Anthony, and Amy Gutmann. 1998. *Color Conscious: The Political Morality of Race*. Princeton, NJ: Princeton University Press.

Araújo, Joel Zito. 2000. *A negação do Brasil: o negro na telenovela brasileira*. São Paulo: Senac.

Arruda, José Ricardo (org.). 2007. *Políticas de ações afirmativas na universidade do estado do Rio de Janeiro*. Rio de Janeiro: Rede Sirius UERJ.

Arruti, José M. 1997. A emergência dos remanescentes: notas para o diálogo entre indígenas e quilombolas. *Mana* 3 (2): 7–38.

Baran, Michael. 2007. Girl, you are not morena. We are negras!: questioning the concept of "race" in southern Bahia, Brazil. *ETHOS* 35 (3): 383–409.

Bastide, Roger, and Florestan Fernandes, eds. 1971 [1959]. Edited. *Brancos e negros em São Paulo*. São Paulo: Companhia Editora Nacional.

Bastos, Paulo, and Fernando Cavallieri. 2002. *Como andam as taxas de homicídios no Rio e em outros lugares*. No 20020602, June 2002. Rio de Janeiro: IPP/Prefeitura da Cidade do Rio de Janeiro.

Bonilla-Silva, Eduardo. 2004. From bi-racial to tri-racial: Towards a new system of racial stratification in the USA. *Ethnic and Racial Studies* 27 (6): 931–950.

Bourdieu, Pierre, and Loïc Wacquant. 1999. On the cunning of imperialist reason. *Theory, Culture and Society* 16 (1): 41–58.

Bowker, Geoffrey, and Susan Leigh Star. 2000. *Sorting Things Out: Classification and its Consequences*. London, UK: MIT Press.

Branche, Jerome. 2007. "Soul for sale? Cuban counterpoint in Madrid," in *Erasing Public Memory: Race, Aesthetics and Cultural Amnesia in the Americas*, ed. Joseph A. Young and Jana Evans Braziel, pp. 157–186. Macon, Georgia: Mercer University Press.

Burdick, John. 1998. *Blessed Anastácia: Women, Race, and Popular Christianity in Brazil*. London: Routledge.

———. 2004. *Legacies of Liberation: The Progressive Catholic Church in Brazil and the Start of a New Millennium*. Aldershot, UK: Ashgate.

———. 2005. Why is the black evangelical movement growing in Brazil? *Journal of Latin American Studies* 37 (2): 311–332.

———. 2008. Class, place and blackness in São Paulo's gospel music scene. *Latin American and Caribbean Ethnic Studies* 3 (2): 149–169.

Caldeira, Teresa. 2000. *City of Walls: Crime, Segregation, and Citizenship in São Paulo*. Berkeley and Los Angeles: University of California Press.

Caldwell, Kia Lily. 2003. "Look at Her Hair": The Body Politics of Black Womanhood in Brazil. *Transforming Anthropology* 11 (2): 18–29.

Campos, Andrelino Oliveira de. 2006. O planejamento urbano e a "invisibilidade" dos afrodescendentes: discriminação étnico-racial, intervenção estatal e segregação sócio-espacial na cidade do Rio de Janeiro. Tese apresentada ao programa de pós-Graduação em Geografia (PPGG) da Universidade Federal do Rio de Janeiro.

Carvalho, Jose Jorge. 2005. *Inclusão étnica e racial no Brasil: a questão das cotas no ensino superior*. São Paulo: Attar.

Castro, Nadya, and Antonio Sérgio Alfredo Guimarães. 1999. "Racial inequalities in the labor market and the workplace," in *Race in Contemporary Brazil: From Indifference to Inequality*, ed. Rebecca Reichmann, pp. 83–108. University Park: Pennsylvania State University Press.

Caulfield, Sueann. 2000. *Em defesa da honra: moralidade, modernidade e nação no Rio de Janeiro (1918–1940)*. Sao Paulo: Editora da UNICAMP.

Cavalli-Sforza, Luigi. 2003. *Genes, povos e línguas*. São Paulo: Companhia das Letras.

Cicalo, André. 2008. What do we know about quotas? *Vibrant* 5 (1): 65–82.

Clark, David Anthony Tyeeme, and Joane Nagel. 2000. "White men, red masks: appropriations of 'Indian' manhood in imagined Wests, 1876–1934," in *Across the Great Divide: Cultures of Manhood in the American West*, ed. Matthew Basso, Laura McCall, and Dee Garceau. New York: Routledge.

Conde, Maite. 2007. "Early film and the reproduction of Rio," in *Visualizing the City*, ed. Alan Marcus and Dietrich Neumann, pp. 31–49. London and New York: Routledge.

Costa, Sérgio. 2006. *Entre dois atlânticos: teoria social, anti-racismo, cosmopolitismo*. Belo Horizonte: Editora da UFMG.

Costa-Pinto, Luiz. 1998 [1953]. *O Negro no Rio de Janeiro: Relações de raça numa sociedade em mudança*. Rio de Janeiro: UFRJ.

Cunha, Haroldo Lisboa da. 1988. *Contribuição à memória histórica da Universidade do Estado do Rio de Janeiro*. Rio de Janeiro: UERJ.

Cunha, Olívia M. Santos dos. 1991. *Corações rastafari: lazer, política e religião em Salvador*. Dissertação de mestrado. Universidade Federal do Rio de Janeiro.

Da Matta, Roberto. 1983. *Carnavais, malandros e heróis: para uma sociologia do dilema brasileiro*. Rio de Janeiro: Zahar Editores.

Damasceno, Caetana M. 2000. "'Em casa de enforcado não se fala em corda': Notas sobre a construção social da 'boa' aparência no Brasil," in *Tirando a Máscara: ensaios sobre o racismo no Brasil*, ed. Antônio S. Guimaraes and Lynn Huntley, pp. 165–199. São Paulo: Paz e Terra.

Daniel, G. Reginald. 2006. *Race and Multiraciality in Brazil and the United States: Converging Paths?* University Park, PA: Pennsylvania State University Press.

Dávila, Jerry. 2003. *Diploma of Whiteness: Race and Social Policy in Brazil, 1917–1945*. Durham, NC: Duke University Press.

De la Cadena, Marisol. 2000. *Indigenous Mestizos: The Politics of Race and Culture in Cuzco, 1919–1991*. Durham: Duke University Press.

De la Fuente, Alejandro. 2001. *A Nation for All: Race, Inequality, and Politics in Twentieth Century Cuba*. Chapel Hill: University of North Carolina Press.

DINFO—Diretoria de Informatica. 2007. *Relatórios com informação de alunos ingressantes pela reserva de vagas*. Rio de Janeiro: DINFO Diretoria de Informática da UERJ.

Escobar, Arturo, and Sonia Alvarez, eds. 1992. *The Making of Social Movements in Latin America: Identity, Strategy and Democracy*. Oxford: Westview.

Fernandes, Florestan. 1969. *The Negro in Brazilian Society*. New York: Columbia University Press.
Fernandes, Sujatha. 2003. Fear of a black nation: local rappers, transnational crossings, and state power in contemporary Cuba. *Anthropological Quarterly* 76 (4): 575–608.
Fernández, Carlos A. 1992. "La raza and the melting pot: a comparative look at multiethnicity," in *Racially Mixed People in America*, ed. Maria P. P. Root, pp. 126–143. London: Sage.
Ferreira, Denise Silva da. 1998. Facts of blackness: Brazil is not (quite) the United States . . . and racial politics in Brazil? *Social Identities* 4 (2): 201–234.
Figueiredo, Angela. 1994. *Beleza pura: símbolos e economia ao redor do cabelo negro. Monografia para conclusão do curso de Ciências Sociais.* Universidade Federal da Bahia.
———. 2000. São quase todos brancos de tão ricos? Trajetórias e percepção das diferenças entre os empresários negros. XXIV Reunião da ANPOCS Associação Nacional de Pós-Graduação em Ciências Sociais. Petrópolis, 23–27 de Outubro de 2000 GT 15- Relações Raciais e Etnicidade. Unpublished paper.
———. 2002. *Novas elites de cor: estudo sobre os profissionais liberais negros de Salvador*. São Paulo: Annablume.
Folha Online. 2008a. 113 Cidadãos anti-Racistas contra as leis raciais. http://www1.folha.uol.com.br/folha/educacao/ult305u401519.shtml.
———. 2008b. Brasileiros vêem cota como essencial e humilhante, revela Datafolha. http://www1.folha.uol.com.br/folha/brasil/ult96u470649.shtml.
Francis, Andrew, and Maria Tannuri-Pianto. 2010. "Endogenous race in Brazil: affirmative action and the construction of racial identity among young adults." Working paper. http://userwww.service.emory.edu/~afranc5/Endogenous%20Race%20in%20Brazil.pdf.
Fraser, Nancy. 1997. *Justice Interruptus: Critical Reflections on the "Postsocialist" Condition*. London: Routledge.
———. 2003. "Social justice in the age of identity politics: redistribution, recognition and participation," in *Redistribution or Recognition? A Political-Philosophical Exchange*, ed. Nancy Fraser and Axel Honneth, pp. 9–109. London and New York: Verso.
———. 2010. Injustice at intersecting scales: on "social exclusion" and the "global poor." *European Journal of Social Theory* 13: 363–371.
Fraser, Nancy, and Axel Honneth, eds. 2003. *Redistribution or Recognition? A Political-Philosophical Exchange*. London and New York: Verso.
Freeman, James. 2002. Democracy and danger on the beach: class relations in the public space of Rio de Janeiro. *Space and Culture* 5 (1): 9–28.
French, Jan Hoffman. 2002. Dancing for land: law making and cultural performance in northeastern Brazil. *Political and Legal Anthropology Review* (1): 19–36.

---. 2009. *Legalizing Identities: Becoming Black or Indian in Brazil's Northeast.* Chapel Hill, NC: University of North Carolina Press.
Freyre, Gilberto. 1956. *The Masters and the Slaves (Casa-Grande & Senzala): A Study in the Development of Brazilian Civilization.* London: Weidenfeld and Nicolson.
---. 1961. *O Luso e o Trópico; sugestões em torno dos métodos portugueses de integração de povos autóctones e de culturas diferentes da européia num complexo novo de civilização: o Luso-tropical.* Lisboa: Comissão Executiva das Comemorações do V Centenário da Morte do Infante D. Henrique.
Fry, Peter. 2000. Politics, nationality, and the meanings of "race" in Brazil. *Daedalus* 129 (2): 83–118.
---. 2005. *A persistência da raça: ensaios antropológicos sobre o Brasil e a África Austral.* Rio de Janeiro: Civilização Brasileira.
Fry, Peter, Yvonne Maggie, Marcos Chor Maio, Simone Monteiro, and Ricardo Ventura Santos, eds. 2007. *Divisões perigosas: políticas raciais no Brasil contemporâneo.* Rio de Janeiro: Civilização Brasileira.
Giacomini, Sonia Maria. 2006. Mulatas profissionais: raça, gênero e ocupação. *Revista Estudos Feministas* 14 (1): 85–101.
Gilliam, Angela. 1998. The Brazilian mulata: images in the global economy. *Race and Class* 40 (1): 57–69.
Gilroy, Paul. 1988. "Nothing but sweat beside my hand: diaspora aesthetics and Black arts in Britain," in *Black Film, British Cinema*, ed. Kobena Mercer, ICA Document 7.3, pp. 207–222. London: ICA.
---. 1993. *The Black Atlantic: Modernity and Double Consciousness.* London: Verso.
Golash-Boza, Tanya. 2010. Does whitening happen? Distinguishing between race and color labels in an African-descended community in Peru. *Social Problems* 57 (1): 138–156.
Goldani, Ana Maria. 1999. "Racial inequality in the lives of Brazilian women," in *Race in Contemporary Brazil: From Indifference to Inequality*, ed. Rebecca Reichmann, pp. 179–194. University Park: Pennsylvania State University Press.
Goldberg, David Theo. 1993. "Polluting the body politic: racist discourse and urban location," in *Racism, the City and the State*, ed. Malcolm Cross and Michael Keith, pp. 45–60. London and New York: Routledge.
Goldstein, Donna. 2003. *Laughter Out of Place: Race, Class, Violence and Sexuality in a Rio Shantytown.* Berkeley: University of California Press.
Gomes, Nilma Lino. 2006. *Sem perder a raiz: corpo e cabelo como símbolos da identidade negra.* São Paulo: Autêntica.
Gotham, Kevin Fox. 2002. *Race, Real Estate, and Uneven Development: The Kansas City Experience, 1900–2000.* Albany, NY: State University of New York.
Gros, Christian. 1997. "Indigenismo y etnicidad, el desafío neoliberal," in *Antropología en la modernidad*, ed. M. V. Uribe and E. Restrepo, pp. 15–59. Bogotá: Instituto Colombiano de Antropología e Historia.

Guimarães, Antonio Sérgio. 2005. Entre o medo de fraudes e o fantasma das raças. *Horizontes Antropológicos* 11 (23): 215–217.
Guimarães, Antonio Sérgio, Lilia Carolina da Costa, and Mauricio S. Kleinke. 2009. *Bônus e cotas, comparando políticas de inclusão racial: Unicamp e UFBA*. Unpublished paper presented at the 2009 LASA Congress in Rio de Janeiro.
Hale, Charles. 2004. Rethinking indigenous politics in the era of the "indio permitido." *NACLA Report on the Americas* 38 (2): 16–22.
Hall, Stuart. 1983. "The problem of ideology: Marxism without guarantees," in *Marx 100 Years On*, ed. B. Mattews, pp. 57–86. London: Lawrence&Wishart.
———. 1996. "What is this 'black' in black popular culture," in *Stuart Hall, Critical Dialogues in Cultural Studies*, ed. Morley D. and K. Chen, pp. 465–475. London: Routledge.
Hanchard, Michael G. 1994. *Orpheus and Power: The Movimento Negro of Rio de Janeiro and Sao Paulo, Brazil, 1945–1988*. Princeton, NJ: Princeton University Press.
———, ed. 1999. "Black Cinderella? Race and the public sphere in Brazil," in *Racial Politics in Contemporary Brazil*, pp. 59–81. Durham: Duke University Press.
Harris, Marvin. 1952. "Race relations in Minas Velhas, a community in the mountain region of central Brazil," in *Race and Class in Rural Brazil*, edited by Charles Wagley, pp. 47–81. Paris: UNESCO.
———. 1963. Racial identity in Brazil. *Luso-Brazilian Review* (1): 21–28.
———. 1970. Referential ambiguity in the calculus of Brazilian racial identity. *Southwestern Journal of Anthropology* 26 (1): 1–14.
Harris, Marvin, Josildeth Gomes Consorte, Joseph Long, and Bryan Byrne. 1993. Who are the whites?: imposed census categories and the racial demography of Brazil. *Social Forces* (72): 451–462.
Hasenbalg, Carlos. 1979. *Discriminação e desigualdades raciais no Brasil*. Rio de Janeiro: Graal.
———. 1985. "Race and socio-economic inequalities in Brazil," in *Race, Class and Power in Brazil*, ed. P.-M. Fontaine, pp. 25–41. Los Angeles: UCLA, Centre of Afro-American Studies.
Heilborn Maria Luiza, Tania Salem, Fabíola Rohden, and Elaine Brandão. 2002. Aproximações socioantropológicas sobre a gravidez na adolescência. *Horizontes Antropológicos* 8 (17): 13–45.
Heringer, Rosana. 2001. Mapeamento de Ações e Discursos de Combate às Desigualdades Raciais no Brasil. *Estudos Afro-Asiáticos* 23 (2): 1–43.
Holanda Maria A. 2008. Trajetórias de vida de jovens negras da UnB no contexto das ações afirmativas. Unpubl. MA diss., University of Brasília.
Holanda, Sergio Buarque de. 1995 [1936]. *Raízes do Brasil*. São Paulo: Companhia das Letras.
Holston, James. 1989. *The Modernist City: An Anthropological Critique of Brasília*. Chicago: University of Chicago Press.
Honneth, Axel. 2003. "Redistribution as recognition: a response to Nancy Fraser," in *Redistribution or Recognition? A Political-Philosophical*

Exchange, ed. Nancy Fraser and Axel Honneth, pp. 110–197. London and New York: Verso.
hooks, bell. 1991. *Yearning: Race, Gender, and Cultural Politics.* London: Turnaround.
Htun, Mala. 2004. From "racial democracy" to affirmative action: changing state policy on race in Brazil. *Latin American Research Review* 39 (1): 60–89.
IBGE. 2007. *Síntese de indicadores sociais: uma análise das condições de vida da população Brasileira.* Rio de Janeiro: IBGE.
———. 2008. *Síntese de indicadores sociais: uma análise das condições de vida da população Brasileira.* Rio de Janeiro: IBGE.
———. 2010. *Síntese de indicadores sociais: uma análise das condições de vida da população Brasileira.* Rio de Janeiro: IBGE.
IPEA. 2010. http://www.ipea.gov.br/sites/000/2/boletim_mercado_de_trabalho/mt37/mt37a/08_Diferenciais_de_rendimento.pdf.
Ireland, Rowan. 1991. *Kingdoms Come: Religion and Politics in Brazil.* Pittsburgh: University of Pittsburgh Press.
Irwin, Robert Mckee. 2003. *Mexican Masculinities.* Minneapolis: University of Minnesota Press.
Jaccoud, Luciana, and Mário Theodoro. 2005. "Raça e educação: os limites das políticas universalistas," in *Ações afirmativas de combate ao racismo nas Américas*, ed. Sales Augusto dos Santos, pp. 103–119. Brasília: Ministério da Educação, Secretaria.
Jaguaribe, Beatriz. 2007. "Cities without maps: favelas and the aesthetics of realism," in *Urban Imaginaries: Locating the Modern City*, ed. Alev Çinar and Thomas Bender, pp. 100–119. Minneapolis and London: University of Minnesota Press.
Kamel, Ali. 2006. *Não somos racistas: uma reação aos que querem nos transformar numa nação bicolor.* Rio de Janeiro: Nova Fronteira.
Klarman, Michael. 2004. *From Jim Crow to Civil Rights: The Supreme Court and the Struggle for Racial Equality.* Oxford: Oxford University Press.
Kottak, Conrad Phillip. 1995. *Assault on Paradise: Social Change in a Brazilian Village.* New York: Basic Books.
Kymlicka, Will, and Wayne Norman, eds. 2000. "Citizenship in culturally diverse societies: issues, contexts, concepts," in *Citizenship in Diverse Societies*, pp. 1–41. Oxford: Oxford University Press.
Laclau, Ernesto, and Chantal Mouffe. 1985. *Hegemony and Socialist Strategy: Towards a Radical Democratic Politics.* London: Verso.
Landes, Ruth. 1994 [1947]. *City of Women.* Albuquerque: University of New Mexico Press.
Latour, Bruno. 2005. *Reassembling the Social: An Introduction to Actor-Network Theory.* New York, Oxford: Oxford University Press.
Lehmann, David. 1996. *Struggle for the Spirit: Religious Transformation and Popular Culture in Brazil and Latin America.* Cambridge, UK: Polity Press.
Lovell, Peggy. 1999. "Women and racial inequality at work in Brazil," in *Racial Politics in Contemporary Brazil*, ed. M. G. Hanchard, pp. 138–153. Durham: Duke University Press.

Lovell, Peggy, and Charles Wood. 1998. Skin color, racial identity, and life chances in Brazil. *Latin American Perspectives* 25 (3): 90–109.
Loveman, Mara, Jeronimo O. Muniz, and Stanley R. Bailey. 2011. Brazil in black and white? Race categories, the census, and the study of inequality, *Ethnic and Racial Studies* DOI:10.1080/01419870.2011.607503.
Maggie, Yvonne. 1991. *A ilusão do concreto: análise do sistema de classificação racial no Brasil.* Instituto de de Filosofia e Ciências Sociais. Rio de Janeiro: Universidade Federal do Rio de Janeiro.
———. 2005. Políticas de cotas e o vestibular da UnB ou a marca que cria sociedades divididas. *Horizontes Antropológicos* 11 (23): 286–291.
———. 2006a. Uma nova pedagogia racial? *Revista da USP—Dossiê Racismo* 1 (68): 112–29.
———. 2006b. Racismo e anti-racismo: preconceito, discriminação e os jovens estudantes nas escolas cariocas. *Educação e Sociedade—Especial* 96 (27): 739–751.
Maio, Marcos, and Ricardo Santos. 2005. Política de Cotas Raciais, os "Olhos da Sociedade" e os Usos da Antropologia: o Caso do Vestibular da Universidade de Brasília (UnB). *Horizontes Antropológicos* 11 (23): 181–214.
Mariz, Cecília Loreto. 1994. *Coping with Poverty: Pentecostal Churches and Christian Base Communities in Brazil.* Philadelphia: Temple University Press.
———. 2000. "Religion as culture strategy of the urban poor in Latin America," in *Rethinking Poverty: Comparative Perspective from Below*, ed. Will Pansters et al., pp. 121–135. Amsterdam: Van Goruim & Assen.
Medeiros, Carlos A. 2004. *Na lei e na raça: legislação e relações raciais, Brasil-Estados Unidos.* Rio de Janeiro: DP&A Editora.
Mesquita, Wania Amélia Belchior. 2007. Um pé no reino e outro no mundo: consumo e lazer entre Pentecostais. *Horizontes Antropológicos* 13 (28): 117–144.
Morães da Silva, Graciela, and Elisa Reis. 2011. Perceptions of racial discrimination among black professionals in Rio de Janeiro. *Latin American Research Review* 2 (46): 55–78.
Moutinho, Laura. 2004. *Razão, "cor" e desejo: uma análise comparativa sobre relacionamentos afetivo-sexuais "inter-raciais" no Brasil e na África do Sul.* São Paulo: Unesp.
Nagel, Joane. 2003. *Race, Ethnicity, and Sexuality: Intimate Intersections, Forbidden Frontiers.* Oxford: Oxford University Press.
Nascimento, Abdias do. 1979. *O genocídio do negro brasileiro.* Rio de Janeiro: Editora Paz e Terra.
———. 1982. *O Negro revoltado.* Rio de Janeiro: Nova Fronteira.
Neri, Marcelo. 2010. *The New Middle Class in Brazil: The Bright Side of the Poor.* Rio de Janeiro: Fundacao Gerulio Vargas Press.
Nery, Maria P. 2008. Afetividade intergrupal, política afirmativa e sistema de cotas para negros. Unpubl. MA diss., University of Brasília.

REFERENCES

Nobles, Melissa. 2000. *Shades of Citizenship: Race and the Census in Modern Politics.* Stanford, CA: Stanford University Press.

Nogueira, Oracy. 1985 [1954]. *Tanto preto quanto branco: estudos de relações raciais.* São Paulo: T.A. Queiroz.

———. 1998 [1955]. *Preconceito de marca: as relações raciais em Itapetininga.* São Paulo: Edusp.

Oliveira, Ney Santos dos. 2000. Segregação em favelas e mobilização política: um estudo comparativo de raça e classe. *Colóquio Arquitetura Brasileira: Redescobertas.* XVI Congresso Brasileiro de Arquitetos, Cuiabá, September 26 and 29.

———. 2001. The Location of the Poor in Rio de Janeiro: The Influence of Race on Favela. Unpublished paper. http://sitemason.vanderbilt.edu/files/erZAKA/Oliveira%20Ney%20dos%20Santos.pdf.

Osorio, Rafael G. 2004. "O sistema classificatório de "cor ou raça" do IBGE," in *Levando a raça a sério: ação afirmativa e universidade,* ed. Joaze Bernardino and Daniela Galdino, pp. 85–135. Rio de Janeiro: DP&A.

Paixão, Marcelo. 2003. *Desenvolvimento humano y relações raciais.* Rio de Janeiro: DP&A.

———. 2006. *Manifesto anti-racista: ideias em prol de uma utopia chamada Brasil.* Rio de Janeiro: DP&A.

Paixão Marcelo, and Luiz M. Carvano. 2008. *Relatório anual das desigualdades raciais no Brasil 2007–2008.* Rio de Janeiro: Garamond.

Pena, Sérgio, Denise Carvalho-Silva, Juliana Alves-Silva, Vânia Prado, and Fabrício Santos. 2000. "Retrato molecular do Brasil." *Ciência Hoje* 27 (159): 16–25.

Perlman, Janice. 1979. *The Myth of Marginality: Urban Poverty and Politics in Rio de Janeiro.* Berkeley, LA, and London: University of California Press.

———. 2010. *Favela: Four Decades of Living on the Edge in Rio de Janeiro.* New York: Oxford University Press.

Petruccelli, José Luis. 2007. *A cor denominada: estudos sobre a classificão étnico-racial.* Rio de Janeiro: DP&A.

Piza, Edith. 2000. "Brancos no Brasil? Ningúem sabe, ninguém viu," in *Tirando a Máscara: ensaios sobre o racismo no Brasil,* ed. Antônio S. Guimaraes and Lynn Huntley, pp. 97–126. São Paulo: Paz e Terra.

Pravaz, Natasha. 2003. Brazilian *mulatice*: performing race, gender, and the nation. *Journal of Latin American Anthropology* 8 (1): 116–146.

Rawls, John. 2001. *Justice as Fairness: A Restatement.* Cambridge, MA: Belknap Press.

Rede Sirius. 2001. *Acervo de memorias: exposição comemorativa do cinqüentenário da UERJ.* Rio de Janeiro: UERJ.

Restrepo, Eduardo. 2004. "Esencialismo étnico y movilización política: tensiones en las relaciones entre saber y poder," in *Gente negra en Colombia,* ed. O. Barbary and F. Urrea, pp. 227–244. Medellín: Lealon.

Rodrigues, Luiz Augusto F. 2001. *Universidade e a fantasia moderna: a falácia de um modelo espacial único.* Niterói: Editora da Universidade Federal Fluminense.

Rosemberg, Fulvia. 2000. "Educação infantil, gênero e raça," in *Tirando a Máscara: ensaios sobre o racismo no Brasil*, ed. Antônio S. Guimaraes and Lynn Huntley, pp. 127–164. São Paulo: Paz e Terra.

———. 2004. Acción afirmativa para negros en la enseñanza superior en Brasil. *Alteridade* 14 (28): 65–74.

Sanjek, Roger. 1971. Brazilian racial terms: some aspects of meaning and learning. *American Anthropologist* (73): 1126–1143.

Sansone, Livio. 2003. *Blackness without Ethnicity: Constructing Race in Brazil.* New York: Palgrave Macmillan.

———. 2005. O bebê e a água do banho—a ação afirmativa continua importante, não obstante os erros da UnB! *Horizontes Antropológicos* 11 (23): 251–254.

Santos, Dayane. 2009. Para além das cotas: a permanência de estudantes negros no ensino superior como política de ação afirmativa. Unpubl. PhD diss., Federal University of Bahia.

Santos, Marcio André dos. 2007. Transformações político-institucionais dos movimentos negros brasileiros. *Jornada conjunta de alunos do PPGSA/IFCS, PPGAS/Museu Nacional e IUPERJ/UCAM.* Unpublished paper.

Santos, Ricardo Ventura, Peter H. Fry, Simone Monteiro, Marcos Chor Maio, José Carlos Rodrigues, Luciana Bastos-Rodrigues, and Sérgio D. J. Pena. 2009. Color, race and genomic ancestry in Brazil: dialogues between anthropology and genetics. *Current Anthropology* 50 (6): 787–819.

Santos, Ricardo Ventura, and Marcos Chor Maio. 2004. Qual "Retrato do Brasil"? Raça, biologia, identidades e política na era da genômica. *MANA* 10 (1): 61–95.

Santos, Sales Augusto dos. 2007. Movimentos negros, educação e ações afirmativas. Unpubl. PhD diss., University of Brasília.

Schwartzman, Luisa Farah. 2007. Does money whiten? Intergenerational changes in racial classification in Brazil. *American Sociological Review* 72: 940–963.

———. 2009. Seeing like citizens: unofficial understandings of official racial categories in a Brazilian university. *Journal of Latin American Studies* 41 (2): 221–250.

Scott, James. 1985. *Weapons of the Weak: Everyday Forms of Peasant Resistance.* New Haven and London: Yale University Press.

Segato, Rita Laura. 2007. *La nación y sus otros: raza, etnicidad y diversidad religiosa en tiempos de políticas de la identidad.* Buenos Aires: Prometeo.

Seigel, Micol. 2009. *Uneven Encounters: Making Race and Nation in Brazil and the United States.* Durham and London: Duke University Press.

Sesardic, Neven. 2010. Race: a social destruction of a biological concept. *Biology and Philosophy* 25 (2): 143–162.

Sheriff, Robin. 2000. Exposing silence as cultural censorship: a Brazilian case. *American Anthropologist* 102 (1): 114–132.

———. 2001. *Dreaming Equality: Color, Race, and Racism in Urban Brazil.* New Brunswick: Rutgers University Press.
Silva, Benedita da. 1999a. "The black movement and political parties: a challenging alliance," in *Racial Politics in Contemporary Brazil*, ed. M. G. Hanchard, pp. 179–187. Durham: Duke University Press.
———. 1999b. "Race and politics in Brazil," in *Black Brazil: Culture, Identity, and Social Mobilization*, ed. Larry Crook and Randal Johnson, pp. 17–21. Los Angeles: UCLA Latin American Center Publications.
Silva, Nelson Valle do. 1985. "Updating the cost of not being white in Brazil," in *Race, Class and Power in Brazil*, ed. Pierre Michel Fontaine, pp. 42–55. Los Angeles: UCLA Centre for Afro-American Studies.
———. 1999. "Racial differences in income: Brazil, 1988," in *Race in Contemporary Brazil: From Indifference to Inequality*, ed. Rebecca Reichmann, pp. 67–82. University Park: Pennsylvania State University Press.
Silva, Nelson do Valle, and Carlos Hasenbalg. 1999. "Race and educational opportunity in Brazil," in *Race in Contemporary Brazil: From Indifference to Inequality*, ed. Rebecca Reichmann, pp. 53–65. University Park: Pennsylvania State University Press.
Skidmore, Thomas. 1974. *Black into White: Race and Nationality in Brazilian Thought.* New York: Oxford University Press.
———. 1993. Bi-racial USA vs multi-racial Brazil: is the contrast still valid? *Journal of Latin American Studies* 25: 373–386.
Somosur, ed. 1994. *Luiz Paulo Conde: um arquitecto carioca.* Bogotá: Somosur.
Souza, Jessé. 2010. *Os Batalhadores brasileiros: nova classe media ou nova classe trabalhadora?* Belo Horizonte: UFMG.
Spivak, Gayatri Chakravorty. 2003. "Can the subaltern speak?," in *Marxism and the Interpretation of Culture*, ed. Cary Nelson and Lawrence Grossberg, pp. 271–313. Urbana, IL: University of Illinois Press.
Stam, Robert. 1997. *Tropical Multiculturalism: A Comparative History of Race in Brazilian Cinema & Culture.* Durham and London: Duke University Press.
Sue, Christina. 2009. An assessment of the Latin Americanization thesis. *Ethnic and Racial Studies* 32 (6): 1058–1070.
Taylor, Charles. 1994. "The politics of recognition," in *Multiculturalism: Examining the Politics of Recognition*, ed. Amy Gutmann and Charles Taylor, pp. 25–73. Princeton, NJ: Princeton University Press.
Teixeira, Moema Poli de. 2003. "Negros egressos de uma universidade pública no Rio de Janeiro," in *Relações raciais: novos desafios*, ed. Iolanda de Oliveira, pp. 193–208. Rio de Janeiro: DP&A.
Teles, Jocelio Santos dos. 2000. O negro no espelho: imagens e discursos nos salões de beleza étnicos. *Estudos Afro-Asiáticos* 38: 49–65.
Telles, Edward. 1995. Who are the morenas? *Social Forces* 73 (4): 1609–1611.
———. 2004. *Race in Another America: The Significance of Skin Color in Brazil.* Oxford: Princeton University Press.

Telles, Edward, and Christina A. Sue. 2009. Race mixture: boundary crossing in comparative perspective. *The Annual Review of Sociology* 35: 129–146.
Turner, Michael. 1985. "Brown into black: changing racial attitudes of Afro-Brazilian university students," in *Race, Class and Power in Brazil*, ed. Pierre Michel Fontaine. Los Angeles: University of California.
Twine, France W. 1998. *Racism in a Racial Democracy: The Maintenance of White Supremacy in Brazil*. New Brunswick: Rutgers University Press.
Valentim, Daniela F. 2005. *Políticas de ação afirmativa e ensino superior*. Unplubl. MA diss., PUC-RIO.
Vargas, João Costa. 2006. When a favela dared to become a gated condominium: the politics of race and urban space in Rio de Janeiro. *Latin American Perspectives* 33 (4): 49–81.
Vianna, Francisco José Oliveira de. 1933. *Evolução do povo brasileiro*. São Paulo: Cia Editora.
Wade, Peter. 1999. "The guardians of power, biodiversity and multiculturality in Colombia," in *The anthropology of Power*, ed. Angela Cheater, pp. 74–87. London: Routledge.
———. 2002. *Race, Nature and Culture: An Anthropological Perspective*. London: Pluto Press.
———. 2003. *Blackness and Race Mixture: The Dynamics of Racial Identity in Colombia*. Baltimore: John Hopkins University Press.
———. 2004a. Human nature and race. *Anthropological Theory* 4 (2): 157–168.
———. 2004b. Images of Latin American *mestizaje* and the politics of comparison. *Bulletin of Latin American Research* 23 (3): 335–366.
———. 2005. Rethinking *mestizaje*: ideology and lived experience. *Journal of Latin American Studies* (37): 239–257.
———. 2009. *Race and Sex in Latin América*. New York: Pluto Press.
Warren, Jonathan, and Christina Sue. 2011. What anti-racists can learn from Latin America. *Ethnicities* 11 (1): 32–58.
Winant, Howard. 1999. "Racial democracy and racial identity: comparing the United States and Brazil," in *Racial Politics in Contemporary Brazil*, ed. M. G. Hanchard, pp. 98–115. Durham: Duke University Press.

Index

abertura democrática (democratic
  opening), 4, 97
Abreu, Mauricio, 18, 30
academic
  life, 15, 21, 82, 149, 167
  performance, 8, 35, 38, 58,
    68, 167–171, 175, 189n.31,
    194n.36, 206n.6
activism
  activist, 128, 153, 156, 161,
    164–165, 172
  black, 12, 15, 17, 75, 85, 94,
    98, 102–104, 116, 127–133,
    134–136, 139–145, 159, 164,
    202n.6
  black female, 145, 146, 149
  class-based, 135
  discourse, 118–119, 147
  nonactivist, 128–129, 132, 161,
    162
  See also Black social movement
affinities, 62, 67, 85
  See also socializing
affirmative action, 11, 13
  approaches, 180
  black, 7, 102, 177, 188n.23
  definition, 3–5
  impact of, 10, 165, 171–175,
    177–179
  inclusive potential of, 12
  programs, 9, 187n.5
Afro-Brazilian, 7
  faiths, 130, 134, 202n.4
  invisibility of, 185
  marginality of, 4
  segregation of, 188n.22

women, 42, 147, 151
  See also candomblé
Afro-Brazilian culture
  cultural practices, 129, 136
  teaching of, 5, 162, 185
Afro-descendants, 5, 30, 99, 110
Alberti, Verena and Amiclar
  A. Pereira, 104, 195n.8,
    197n.32, 198n.38, 207n.22
Almeida, Nival Nunes de., 35, 169
Alvarez, Sonia, Evelina Dagnino,
  Arturo Escobar, 4, 132
Alvito, Marcos, 8, 46, 192n.25,
  193n.13
amarelo (yellow), 92, 95, 103,
  187n.1, 188n.10, 196n.25,
  198n.39, 201n.61
antiquota, 91, 99, 100, 128, 174,
  177, 182, 185, 186, 203n.16
antiracism
  debate around, 4
  discourse, 89
  promotion of, 9
apadrinhamento (sponsorship), 39
appearance, 66, 100–101, 110, 179,
  193n.25
Arruda, José Ricardo, 189n.31,
  206n.6
Arruti, José M., 3, 188n.18
ascriptions
  racial, 59, 96, 121–124, 195n.13
  social, 68, 74

Barbárie (Barbarians), 57–62,
  67–68, 73, 79–82, 86
  See also Cones

batalhadores (class fighters), 39–40, 48
believers (religious) 46, 47, 48, 49
black identity, 7, 10, 110, 114, 129, 145, 161, 163, 172
blackness, 4, 18, 72, 94, 95, 102, 104, 109–116, 118–123, 128–129, 135–136, 138, 144–146, 149, 160, 162–163, 172, 173, 178, 179, 185, 193n.16, 200n.57, 201n.61, 204n.30, 205n.45
Black politics, 111, 127, 131, 203n.22, 205n.46
   effects, 92, 120
   involvement in, 128, 132, 162, 164
black-skinned, 1, 3, 6, 7, 70, 108, 118, 129, 137
Black social movement, 12, 18, 132, 134, 162, 172, 174, 176, 181, 200n.59, 201n.1
"black" spaces, 33
biracializing
   logic, 7
   negative power of, 91
   tendencies in Brazilian society, 121
biracial model, 10, 96, 97
Bolsa Família Program, 181
boundaries
   breaching of, 161
   delimitation of, 66
   racial/color, 116
   social, 83
   space, 32, 81
Bourdieu, Pierre and Loïc Wacquant, 96, 188n.23
branco (white-skinned), 1, 6, 92–105, 115, 124, 189n.30, 198n.39, 201n.61
Brazilian Constitution (of 1998), 5
Brazilian population
   demographic data, 3, 7, 101, 187n.1, 188n.10, 194–195n.3, 197n.28
   division, 6, 92, 95

brown-skinned, 1–7, 17, 43, 44, 59, 61, 70, 79, 93–94, 98, 103, 109–124, 150, 156–157, 187n.8, 189n.31, 194n.31, 196n.25, 200n.59, 204n.35, 206n.14
   See also mixed-race; *pardo*
Burdick, John, 8, 12, 30, 46, 55, 128, 129, 130, 202n.4

cabelo, 77, 103, 114, 145–149, 157, 199n.52
   See also hair; hairstyle, haircut
Campos, Andrelino Oliveira de., 18, 30, 55
candomblé, 48, 129, 130
categorization
   logics of, 6
   process of, 59, 61, 68
censorship (social and cultural), 72, 74, 75, 84, 117, 171
class/space, 76
   deployment of, 118
   middle/upper-class, 76
   racial, 89, 171
   state-sponsored, 72
   See also silence
census, 1, 7, 92, 95, 187n.1, 195n.7, n.28, 204n.36
church
   Catholic, 46, 49, 131
   evangelical, 46, 50, 79, 130, 139, 144, 192n.25, 201n.2
   neo-Pentecostal, 45, 47–48
   Pentecostal, 45, 50, 51, 129, 205n.4
   Protestant, 45
   support from, 45, 49
citizenship
   acquisition of, 54
   active, 165
   effective, 96
   impact of quotas on, 8
city
   center, 18, 24, 30, 52
   center/periphery, 8

cityscapes, 57, 154
landscape, 24, 25, 30, 117
space, 30, 55, 135
university in the, 23, 26
class, 1, 4, 8–11, 13, 16–19, 35–36, 43, 56, 63, 68, 71, 75, 79, 81–82, 86, 100, 128, 138, 159, 180, 182
  aesthetics, 117
  approach, 143, 172, 180
  classroom division, 58, 60
  discourses, 10
  measures, 3, 4–5
  mobilization, inhibition of, 174
  movements, 132
  politics, 172
  and racial strategies, 186
  segregation in terms of, 17, 60, 175
  status, 153
  vulnerability, 144
classification (racial)
  models (or systems) of, 91, 95, 97, 122, 123, 125
  United States system, 6, 96, 121
classroom
  division, 57, 58, 60, 61, 81
  geographies, 10, 57, 131, 156
  socializing process in, 57, 84, 86
  student distribution in, 60, 62, 81
  See also *Barbárie*; *Cones*
clothes, 65–66, 69, 192n.25
  See also outfit
color *See* race and color
Cones, 57–68, 81, 85–86
  non-black, 61, 76
  white, 77, 79
  See also *Barbárie*
Congo, 88, 175
conjuntos, 32
consciousness
  black, 7, 121, 130, 162, 172
  Black Consciousness Day, 134
  quota system effects on, 171
cotistas (quota students)

black, 19, 61, 70, 155, 179
  description in terms of class, 35
  impact of, 82–83, 87, 133, 167, 171, 173
  profile, 32, 34–37, 40–45, 139, 168, 198n.40
  white, 61, 71, 78, 81
  See also *Cones*
courses
  community pre-vestibulars, 128–129
  and socio-economic profile, 36–37
  See also Educafro
cursos de elite (elite undergraduate courses), 11, 13, 27, 35, 36, 107, 127, 189n.34
  less prestigious, 12, 35, 54, 58, 108, 128, 150, 165, 192n.7
  pre-vestibulares (pre-exam courses), 12, 33, 127, 135

Da Silva, Benedita, 94, 181
Datafolha surveys, 92, 189n.30, 195n.5
Denegrir, 12, 128, 132, 133–134, 136, 137, 160, 165, 190n.35
DINFO, 14, 169, 170
discrimination
  "black Cinderella," 95
  class, 63, 77, 192n.26
  racialist/racial, 6, 78, 97, 103–104, 117, 119, 124–125, 157, 185
  social, 61, 72, 117
  suffered by *pardos*, *pretos* and *negros*, 94, 102–103, 105, 113, 115, 138
dízimo, 46, 47
Durban Conference (World Conference against Racism), 4

Educafro, 12, 33, 127–135, 144, 188n.20, 202n.3
education
  higher, 2, 4, 144, 153, 159
  public, 106, 194n.37

educational
  background, 34, 57, 58, 169
  level, 42, 43, 167
  Education Department, 36, 37, 54, 63, 127
empregadas (housemaids), 30, 52, 56
ensino fundamental (schooling of aged between 7 and 14), 3
equality
  gender, 191n.20
  production of, 9, 179
  racial, 95, 175, 181
  through difference, theories of, 3
  universalistic approaches of, 107
Escobar, Arturo, 132
Escobar, Arturo and Alvarez, Sonia, 4, 46, 132
escuro (dark-skinned), 66, 93, 99, 112, 142
Esqueleto (favela), 29–30
essentialization (risk of), 62
Estatuto da igualdade racial, 7, 95, 103, 170, 207n.23
ethnic
  aesthetics, style, 104, 130, 133, 138–140
  affinities, 155
  affirmation, 146, 151
  ethnicity, 124, 132
  ethnocentrism, 96
  See also clothes; hairstyle; outfit
exclusion
  through color, 100
  discourses of, 30
  and mixture, 117
  patterns of, racial, 56
  of the poor, 187n.7, 190n.36
  process of, 68
  through quotas, 91
  school as a reason for, 53

family
  income, 36, 37, 38, 43
  networks, 41, 45
  patterns, 40
  structure, 42
  support, 45
favelas
  favelado, 32, 62, 185
  as a place, 8, 17, 19, 25–26, 29, 30, 32, 33, 51, 55, 93, 142, 190n.4, 192n.1, 194n.35, 200n.57
  music *See funk*
  features (physical), 110, 119- 121, 148–149, 195n.7
  black, 74, 104, 111–115, 117, 146, 195n.10
  "finer", 66, 93, 101–102, 111, 124, 177
  negroid, 102–103
financial
  scarcity, 34, 39, 41, 169
  support, 35, 42, 45, 129
Fraser, Nancy, 172, 173, 175, 182, 183, 206n.8,n.19
freshmen (*calouros*), 11, 12, 14, 16, 44, 81, 86, 107, 127–131, 136, 176
Freyre, Gilberto, 1, 87, 97, 152, 190n.3, 194n.38,n.42, 196n.24
Fry, Peter, 1, 69, 93, 95–97, 121, 195n.8,n.13, 196n.23, 203n.16
Funk music, 17, 50–51, 154–155, 191n.24, 192n.25, 203n.13
funkeiro (funk dancer), 140

geography of Rio de Janeiro
  Baixada Fluminense, 15, 19, 24–25, 29–32, 58, 73–75, 85, 102, 152, 165, 190n.1, 198n.37
  Botafogo, 25, 31–33, 38, 41, 46, 47, 52, 58, 138, 143, 144, 148
  Maracanã, 17, 21, 25–27, 38, 39, 41, 135
  Tijuca, 19, 27, 29, 41, 58
  Zona Norte, 15, 19, 24–25, 30–32, 58, 155, 190n.1, 191n.7, 205n.42
  Zona Oeste, 15, 19, 24, 30, 32, 58, 61, 77, 113, 165, 190n.1

Index

Zona Sul, 17, 19, 24–25, 27–33, 46, 52, 55–69, 73, 75, 81–85, 103, 135, 138, 145, 155, 159, 190n.1, 198n.37
Goldani, Ana Maria, 42, 43, 44, 191n.21
Goldstein, Donna, 8, 16, 30, 39, 64, 65

hair (and race and color), 77, 93, 94, 99, 102, 103, 105, 111, 112, 114, 140, 145–148, 150, 157, 163–164, 177, 199n.52
hairstyle, haircut (ethnic), 85, 140, 146–147, 148–150, 202n.12, 203n.21,n.22
Hall, Stuart, 132, 184
Hanchard, Michael G., 94–95, 96, 189n.27, 193n.16, 195n.13, 201n.1
Harris, Marvin, 92, 93
hetero-based classification, 124
hierarchies
  in constitution of social collective, 88
  construction of, 30, 97
  racial, 117, 143, 156
  reproduction of, 8
History Department, 12, 35, 69, 127, 134, 162
household, 39, 41, 43–45, 47, 49, 181, 187n.10
  female headed, 42
  middle-class, 30, 39
  students', 32, 35–37, 86, 173
  white, 152, 204n.33
Htun, Mala, 4, 188n.12

identification
  construction of,160, 163
  racial/color, 6, 15, 69, 92, 93, 97, 116, 122, 160, 189n.31, 199n.48, 200n.55, 203n.14
identity
  national,1, 10, 83, 96
  politics, 4, 132, 174

racial/color, 92, 111, 144, 160
income, 2, 30, 35–43, 47, 61, 107, 178,180–181, 183, 188n.22, 189n.30, 191n.12
See also salary
indígena (indigenous), 92, 95, 103, 109, 187n.1, 196n.21, 198n.39
inequality
  class based approaches to, 1, 6, 158, 172
  historical, 7, 91, 129
  racial, 125, 183, 184
  reproduction of, 123, 173, 179
Instituto Brasileiro de Geografia e Estatística (IBGE), 3, 41, 92–95, 98, 101, 103, 115–116, 117, 121–123, 125, 157
interracial
  marriage, 152–153
  relationships, 137–138, 141, 150, 153, 156, 157, 163, 204n.37
  socializing, 77, 89, 174

jobs
  institutional positions, 53
  market, access to, 157–158
  underpaid, 52, 129

law
  10639 law, 2, 5, 162, 185
  Estatuto da igualdade racial, 7, 95, 103, 170, 207n.23
  law of quotas (3.708/2001), 95
Law Department, 11, 12, 70, 72, 106, 107, 127, 129, 169
Lovell, Peggy, 42
Lovell, Peggy and Charles Wood, 188n.22, 204n.38
lower-class
  areas, 15, 24, 27, 30–31, 33, 52, 58, 191n.8
  people, 2, 17, 37, 39–40, 43, 56,77, 82–83, 93, 129, 134, 151, 181, 191n.17,n.23

lower-class—*Continued*
  students, 2, 38, 45, 52–53, 57–58, 66–67, 70, 72, 75–85, 130–131, 165, 171–178, 192n.26,n.4, 194n.30, 203n.22
  women, 43, 73, 159, 161, 191n.20

Maggie, Yvonne, 94, 95, 185, 188n.15, 189n.25, 199n.53
Manifesto Contra as Cotas, 7, 35, 96, 128
marginality, 4, 39, 137
marriage, 86, 150, 152–153, 155, 156, 188n.22
  See also interracial marriage; interracial relationships
masculinity, 87–88
Medicine Department, 12, 27, 34, 35, 69, 107–108, 170, 184, 189n.34
mass media, 6, 17, 48, 72, 82, 92, 100, 105, 120, 131, 133, 140, 174, 184, 188n.22
merit, 6, 72, 80, 106, 198n.40
Mesquita, Wania, 46–47, 49
mestiçagem (miscegenation), 1, 9, 15, 88, 95–105, 111, 113–123, 149–151, 172, 177, 199n.51
mestiço, 33, 87, 88, 93, 97–98, 109, 111–114, 116, 117, 119, 123, 149, 151, 199n.54
  See also race and color
methodology, 10, 11–16
metropolises, 9, 17, 28, 33, 140
metropolitan
  area, 33, 35, 46, 52, 131, 133
  space, segregation of, 31, 55
middle class (*classe média*)
  area, spaces, 24, 27, 29, 32, 52, 56, 58, 61, 62, 68, 79, 84, 88, 165, 201n.65
  black people, 153, 181
  courses, 34, 81
  different kinds of, 19, 82, 168, 170
  marriages, 156–157
  students, 48, 53, 58, 67, 68, 72–76, 80, 81, 83–87, 131
  representation of, 54, 77, 81, 87, 140–141, 179
mixed-race, 1, 5, 6, 92, 95, 110, 197n.33
moreno, 93, 102–103, 109–111, 114, 118, 123, 155, 195n.7, 200n.59
  See also race and color
morro (hill), 17, 25, 31, 32, 55, 80
motherhood, 43, 44
Movimento Negro Unificado (MNU), 129, 131
mulata, mulato, 17, 74, 93, 95, 104, 124, 146, 150–152, 156–157, 195n.8, 201n.67, 203n.20, 204n.32
multiculturalism, 3, 172
multisided approach, 184–186
municipalities, 24, 35, 40, 190n.1

nation, 8, 91, 96, 97, 153
national
  communion, 130
  ideology, 89
  imagery, 7, 17
  pride, 6, 93, 117, 151
needy (*carentes*), 2, 4, 5, 12, 33, 37–38, 135
negroid, 94, 102, 103
negro
  in Black movement discourse, 99–106, 115, 124, 176
  IBGE classification, 94–95, 103, 115, 121, 206n.12
  in legislation, 95, 99, 195–196n.15, 196n.21
  self-identification as, definition of, 2, 15, 98, 108–116, 121, 124, 141–143, 176–178, 198n.39,n.44, 199n.47
  use of term, 15, 18, 94, 98, 112, 118–119, 195n.14, 199n.49, 200n.59,n.60
  See also race and color

Index

neo-Pentecostal churches *See* church networks
family, 41, 62, 129
social, 45, 51, 61, 86, 173, 206n.16
Nobles, Melissa, 92–94, 97, 124, 201n.62
nongovernmental organizations (NGO), 5, 131–132, 136, 188n.20
nonquota students, 13–15, 35, 37, 40, 42, 44, 48, 53, 60–61, 64–65, 70–73, 82–85, 105, 108, 113, 155, 160, 168–170, 176, 194n.36, 206n.14
nonwhite, 3, 94, 181, 193n.17, 197n.28
nordestinos, 33

Oliveira, Ney Santos dos., 8, 30, 55
outfit, 51, 55, 61, 65–66, 68, 72, 83, 104, 133, 138–140, 150, 192n.25, 193n.13
See also clothes

pagode, 41, 154
pardo (brown-skinned/mixed), 1, 92, 114, 157
distinction from other categories, 103, 119, 156, 195n.14, 198n.39, 199n.51
and *preto* as *negro*, 3, 6, 7, 94–96, 98–102, 112, 115–118, 121–122, 157, 176–177, 197n.28
self-identification,98, 105, 109–111, 123, 176, 180
use of term, 94, 98, 108–109, 118, 142, 195n.7,n.8, 195–196n.15
See also race and color
Petruccelli, José Luis, 1, 82, 92, 93, 103, 117, 122, 199n.51
phenotype, 11, 18, 56, 59, 66–68, 80, 85
identification by, 71, 94, 104, 109, 113, 124, 125, 178, 192n.26, 199n.46, 201n.65
reference to, 66, 98, 100, 181, 195n.10
social construction of, 100
physically challenged people (*deficientes físicos*), 2, 3, 5
politicization (non-black students), 9, 10,15, 117, 125, 128, 130, 150, 155, 172, 177
preto (black-skinned), 1, 67, 79, 92, 99,101, 103
and *negro*, interchangeable use of, 94, 119, 195n.14, 198n.39
self-identification, 102, 109, 110, 116, 180
use of, 113, 118, 195n.9, 200n.59
See also race and color
pre-vestibular *See* courses
private sector, 4, 53, 176
prosperidade, 46, 49, 65
Protestantism, 46, 47, 130
PROUNI, *Universidade para Todos*, 4, 175, 183, 188n.16
public opinion, 6, 7, 91, 95, 195n.13

quota
black, 106–110, 114, 120,161, 171, 179, 189n.31, 196n.25, 198n.43, 199n.46
debate on, 8, 97,182, 185, 186
impact of, 8, 11, 83, 84, 89, 95, 96, 98, 100, 109, 171–173, 179, 185
other kinds of, 6, 8
public school quotas, 70, 106–107, 110, 185–186, 198n.36
racial, 6–20, 72, 91, 95–113, 120–121, 129–133, 138, 170–181, 185, 188n.25, 189n.28, 195–196n.15, 198n.37, 199n.48,n.50, 201n.63

race and color
  articulation of, 99, 116–121
  categories, 91–93, 95, 98, 118–124, 129
  classification, 69, 91, 92, 97–98, 124–125
  interchangeable use of, 9, 102, 112, 119
  race relations, 12, 15, 16, 57, 73, 78, 82, 96, 120, 142, 158, 167, 174–175, 192n.1, 201n.62
  bipolarization of, polarization of, 91, 94–95, 120
  model, system, 9, 10, 93, 94, 101, 121–123, 128, 172
racial
  democracy, 5, 10, 17, 83, 88–91, 129–130, 137, 143, 156, 171, 177–178, 188n.22, 203n.23
  groups, 6, 7, 98, 118, 124, 137
  mixture, 1–2, 11, 87, 93, 96, 120, 172, 195n.8
  racialization, 96, 98, 108, 111, 121, 172, 186
  racially based (affirmative action), 1, 4–7, 12, 91, 123, 143, 184, 201n.66
  tribunal, 176, 178
racism, 1, 4–9, 75–80, 89, 91, 97, 134, 138, 170, 174, 185, 193n.25
ralé, 39–40, 45, 48
rampa/escada (ramp/staircases), 21, 22, 52
recognition, 172, 173, 182
redistribution (economic and social), 3, 39, 107, 173–174, 182
religion, 10, 46–51, 129, 132
REUNI, 176
rights
  differential, 3, 4, 7, 173
  ethnic, 3
  land, 3, 5

Rio de Janeiro
  city, 8, 10–24, 28–33, 41, 46, 52, 55–56, 62–63, 69–77, 84, 102–103, 124, 129–140, 145, 151, 189n.32, 190n.35,n.2,n.6, 191n.7, 202n.10, 205n.42
  state, 2, 17, 95, 135, 167, 169, 170, 175, 191n.17, 196n.21,n.23
salary, 43, 127, 204n.38
samba, 17, 51, 52, 144, 152, 154, 191n.17, 203n.20, 205n.41
Sanjek, Roger, 93, 94
Sansone, Livio, 92–94, 114, 120, 121, 123, 189n.28, 198n.39, 200n.56, 200n.58
Schwartzman, Luisa, 97, 123, 152–153, 189n.31, 197n.31, 198n.44, 204n.39, 206n.15
scholarship, 4, 38, 80, 134, 191n.16
school
  private, 61, 107, 180, 198n.37, 199n.48
  public, 2, 34, 48, 53, 58, 71, 83, 106–108, 131, 168, 180, 182–183, 189n.34, 192n.5
schooling, 40, 41, 43
Segato, Rita Laura, 100, 121, 175, 190n.3
self-declaration, 4, 61, 106–109, 177–179, 199n.48
self-esteem, 50, 141, 161, 172–173
self-identification, 19, 59, 105, 110, 178, 197n.28
Sheriff, Robin, 1, 8, 69,72, 74, 78, 80, 92–93, 114, 118, 194n.31, 195n.6, 200n.57, 204n.30
silence, 7, 18, 66, 72–78, 85, 182, 193n.25
  See also censorship
Skidmore, Thomas, 94, 128, 195n.12
slavery, 1, 5, 30, 100, 119, 139,141, 144,146, 172, 190n.3

socializing, 10, 50, 62–64, 67–69, 85, 86, 156
social mobility, 10–11, 13, 39–40, 42–47, 49, 51, 54, 62, 84, 143–144, 149–151, 154–159, 165, 175, 177, 183, 188n.22, 191n.23, 194n.41, 202n.4, 206n.16
social status, 44, 45, 54,55, 61, 71, 81, 87, 128, 141, 151, 153, 200n.57
Social Work Department, 11, 12, 54, 127, 150, 184
socio-economic questionnaire, 36, 42, 47, 59, 98, 108, 116, 176, 199n.47
Souza, Jessé, 39–40, 45–46, 48–50, 66, 206n.17
stigma, 53, 62, 65, 66, 70, 102, 106, 177, 200n.57
subalternity, 8, 68, 187n.7
suburbs, 8, 10, 12, 15, 18, 19, 24, 26, 28–31, 33, 46, 50, 55, 61, 63, 64, 75–76, 129, 136, 139, 144, 155, 190n.2, 198n.37, 202n.4
Supremo Tribunal Federal (Federal High Court), 7, 96, 170, 196n.22
resolution about constitutionality of quotas' (April 2012), 170

Telles, Edward, 55, 67, 80, 92–95, 99, 101, 117, 120, 121, 124, 152–153, 155, 157, 174, 180, 184, 188n.22, 190n.36, 193n.25, 195n.11, 197n.33, 199n.49,n.51, 200n.60, 201n.67, 204–205n.40
transport, 24–26, 31, 38, 62–64, 75, 136, 149

UERJ (University of the State of Rio de Janeiro)
description of, 21–24
location of, 24–31
umbanda, 130
university
Pontifícia Universidade Católica (PUC), 73, 82, 87, 169
university administrative autonomy, *autonomia administrativa*, 2, 6
University of Brasília (UnB), 4, 199n.47,n.48, 200–201n.61

Vargas, João Costa, 8, 30, 55
vestibular, 2, 5, 13, 34, 36–37, 42, 44–49, 59, 80, 87, 98, 106–110, 115, 116, 131, 169, 170, 176, 180, 182, 183, 191n.13

Wade, Peter, 3, 87–88, 97, 100, 116, 117, 177, 193n.16, 194n.42, 197n.27, 201n.62
white-skinned
access to education, 3
aesthetics 114, 146
area, space, 24, 30, 88, 164, 171
identification,5, 122–123
middle-class, 16, 34, 56,67, 81, 89, 152
people, population, 6, 12,17, 55, 76–77, 101, 152, 182, 194n.40
relationships, 151–154, 157
self-identification, 61, 79, 93, 98, 101, 110, 115, 196n.25
student, 70–72, 77, 79, 80, 104–105, 134, 180
women, 44, 137, 152–156
See also Barbárie; *branco*; *cotistas*; nonquota students; race and color
whiteness, 135, 141, 177
Winant, Howard, 94, 120, 121, 189n.27